"AND GOD SAID WHAT?"

"AND GOD SAID WHAT?"

An Introduction to Biblical Literary Forms for Bible Lovers

MARGARET NUTTING RALPH

PAULIST PRESS
New York/Mahwah

Excerpts from THE JERUSALEM BIBLE, copyright © 1966 by Darton, Longman & Todd, Ltd and Doubleday & Company, Inc. are reprinted by permission of the publisher.

Copyright © 1986 by
Dr. Margaret Ralph

All rights reserved. No part of this book may be reproduced or transmitted in any form or by any means, electronic or mechanical, including photocopying, recording, or by any information storage and retrieval system without permission in writing from the Publisher.

Library of Congress
Catalog Card Number: 85-62931

ISBN: 0-8091-2780-6

Published by Paulist Press
997 Macarthur Boulevard
Mahwah, New Jersey 07430

Printed and bound in the
United States of America

Contents

Acknowledgments

To name the numerous students whose thoughtful questions have contributed to this book is impossible. However, I would like to name my family and friends who have helped me in the final "writing the book" stage. Thanks to:

My husband, Don, who by his constant love, support, and willingness to share all the responsibilities at home has made it possible for me to write.

My friend of 26 years, Arline Hagan Whelan, who first encouraged me to write a book and who paved the way to Paulist Press.

My critics: My husband, Don; my son, Dan; Rev. Joseph Rueter, Dr. Joseph Engelberg, and Rev. Thomas Heath, O.P., all of whom read an early draft of the manuscript and offered many valuable suggestions.

My typist, Sandy Casey, who was always reliable and prompt.

My co-workers at the Department of Catholic Education, especially Rev. Leonard Callahan, and my co-workers at the University of Kentucky who have helped me develop the personal confidence and have given me the professional opportunities which have contributed to my ability to write this book.

Those at Paulist Press, especially Rev. Lawrence Boadt, who read the manuscript as it was being written and gave encouragement as well as helpful and prompt criticism.

To each of you I say, "I thank my God whenever I think of you; and every time I pray for all of you I pray with joy, remembering how you have helped to spread the good news" (Phil 1:3–4).

This book is dedicated to my students who have asked questions over the years. You taught me what I needed to know in order to write this book

Foreword

When John begins the Book of Revelation, the last book in the New Testament, he immediately tells his audience, "This is the revelation given by God to Jesus Christ . . ." A "revelation," also called an "apocalypse," was a familiar kind of writing to John's audience. An "apocalypse" is a literary form that purports to be about the future but is actually about the present. John's readers knew this. By telling them that his book was a "revelation" John was telling them exactly what to expect so that they would not misunderstand his intention as they read this book full of visions and symbols. Unfortunately, this form is not familiar to us, and so people of our time may misunderstand what they read in the Book of Revelation.

When Luke wrote his Gospel he also helped his readers correctly understand the intent of various sayings by identifying their literary form. In Luke 14:7–11 we read:

> He (Jesus) then told the guests a parable because he had noticed how they picked the places of honor. He said this, "When someone invites you to a wedding feast, do not take your seat in the place of honor. A more distinguished person than you may have been invited, and the person who invited you both may come and say, 'Give up your place to this man'; and then to your embarrassment, you would have to go and take the lowest place. No, when you are a guest, make your way to the lowest place and sit there, so that, when your host comes, he may say, 'My friend, move up higher.' In that way everyone with you at the table will see you honored."

Why does Luke introduce Jesus' "advice" as a parable? It seems a straightforward enough direction, not a parable at all. However, if one responds to Luke's helpful advice, and thinks about the words as a parable, a whole new meaning comes to light. The function of a parable is to criticize and thus correct the audience to whom it is addressed. Luke, by telling his readers that this is a parable, is helping them see the ironic humor, and the critical teaching, behind Jesus' words. Jesus' statement to the guests is not straightforward advice at all. Jesus is not interested in etiquette. When one understands that this is an ironic parable, one is able to see that Jesus is criticizing his audience's open or hidden attempts to gain worldly honor. Neither of the people in the parable is humble. The man who chooses the lower seat adds cunning to his pride. Luke pictures Jesus criticizing the whole group for their concern about having their dignity recognized. Luke also helps his readers recognize the tone and intent of Jesus' words by alerting them to the literary form.

My intent in writing this book is to aid the adult reader of Scripture in exactly the same way that John and Luke helped their readers. "Apocalypse" and "parable" are only two kinds of writing found in the Bible. The Bible is a collection of books written in many different literary forms. One must understand the various kinds of writing in the Bible in order to understand the meaning of each book.

Anyone who reads a newspaper is familiar with the idea of various kinds of writing, various literary forms or genres. "Genre" is a French word meaning "kind" or "type." In a newspaper we read a variety of kinds of writing—we read straight news reporting, editorials, comics, and advice columns, to name a few. There are not little explanations of the kinds of writing with each column because the reader is supposed to be able to recognize the differences. The form, or genre, tells the reader something about the intent of the writer. If the reader misunderstands the genre, the reader may think that the author has said something which the author hasn't said at all. For instance, Erma Bombeck, the humorist, claims that dryers eat socks. Everyone who uses a dryer knows what she means. If a person from another culture were unacquainted with a "dryer" and did not know the literary form in which Erma Bombeck was writing, he or she might miss the intent of the writer and misunderstand entirely.

One who does not understand the literary form of an editorial might also draw erroneous conclusions about political affairs. If a person reads an editorial as though it were a balanced, objective report rather than one person's point of view, that person would be misinformed after reading the article. It is not the author's fault that the reader has misunderstood. The form "editorial" does not claim to be objective. The author presumes that the reader understands this. Those who misunderstand the various kinds of writing misinform themselves, whether they are reading the newspaper or the Bible.

Genre divisions are not always as neat as we might like them to be. Not everyone agrees on the exact definition of various genres or even on the rationale for a definition. Should kinds of writing be divided on the basis of form? The difference between prose and poetry is one of form. Or should such considerations as the attitude, tone or purpose of the author be considered as well? The word "satire" says something about the attitude, tone and purpose of the author. In satire the attitude is critical, the tone is humorous and the purpose is usually to egg others on to change or improvement.

Because both external characteristics—form—and internal characteristics—attitude, tone and purpose—are important considerations in determining genre, it is sometimes difficult to determine which of two genres best describes a particular work. The comic strip "Doonesbury" illustrates this difficulty. Newspaper editors differ on whether they place Doonesbury on the editorial page or with the comics. Doonesbury bears the characteristics of both a political cartoon and a comic strip.

One might ask, "If clear genre distinctions are not always possible, why make them at all?" It is extremely useful when reading or when speaking about literature to be able to group works in regard to their genres. This is true not merely to classify, but to clarify similarities and differences in both tone and intent. A knowledge of form is essential for an understanding of content.

Many adults have never realized that the Bible includes a variety of kinds of writing. Such a lack of understanding about

LITERARY FORM

Answers the question:	—"What kind of writing is this?"	
When we say a work is one particular form we are describing such things as	—External Characteristics Poetry? Prose? Number of Lines? Rhyme scheme? —Internal Characteristics Attitude? Tone? Purpose?	
Some possible forms are	—Riddle	Epic
	Poem	Mock Epic
	Fiction	Sonnet
	Myth	Elegy
	Legend	Epigram
	Parable	Blessing
	Biography	Curse
	Autobiography	Fable
	Parody	Fairy Tale
	Editorial	Romance
	History	Satire
	Letter	Proverb
	Revelation	Midrash
	Allegory	Oracle
	Debate	Novel

If we misunderstand the form we misunderstand the meaning!

form leads to a misunderstanding about what a particular book in the Bible is actually saying, reflected in such questions as:

"Why did God create a forbidden tree in the first place?"

"Why would a loving God make the whole human race suffer just because Adam took one bite of that apple?"

"Why did God tell Abraham to practice child sacrifice? Isn't that cruel?"

"Why did God tell the Israelites to slaughter women and children in the countries they conquered?"

"Was Samson's strength really in his hair?"

"Did Jonah really spend three days inside a fish and come out perfectly healthy?"

"How did Luke know what Jesus prayed when he was alone on the Mount of Olives?"

These questions are some of many which I have been asked over the years by intelligent and thoughtful students. Each of these questions has its root in a misunderstanding about the literary form of what has been read. Unless a person reads each passage in the Bible in the context of the form in which it is written, that person will misunderstand what he or she reads.

"Literary form" is not the only context which people sometimes ignore when reading Scripture. In addition to understanding the form of a passage, the reader must also be aware of the historic context—"What were the beliefs of the people at the time this was written?"—and of the context within the process of revelation—"Why is the religious insight revealed in this passage a growth in understanding as compared to the ideas which preceded it?" When all three of these contexts are considered, the way is open to understanding the meaning, the revelation, in Scripture.

Most of us who read the Bible read it as part of our prayer lives. Our intent is not to grow in knowledge but to grow in holiness. For some it seems simply off the point to stop and study the Bible as literature. Some say, "God can speak to me through Scripture without my knowing all that business about literary form. Talk about genres and authors detracts from Scripture for me. It makes Scripture seem less holy." I have a word of caution for those who have such an attitude.

Those of us who use the Bible as a prayer book are basically interested in having a conversation with God. We may use passages in the Bible to express our own feelings of love, praise, or perhaps distress. Or we may use the Bible to help us listen, hoping to hear an answer, perhaps a very direct answer, to a personal dilemma. Saints and sinners alike have had the experience of opening Scripture and seeing a passage which seems to fill them with knowledge, peace, and power, and literally enables them to make difficult decisions and act on those decisions.

Nothing in this book denies the reality of such an experience. However, those of us who do use the Bible to find answers to particular questions do so at some peril if we do not have any knowledge about the overall message and meaning in Scripture. Such a method of prayer may result in misunderstanding and sin as well as in wisdom and grace. History bears witness to this fact. People have used Scripture to support their own misunderstanding about slavery and the subjugation of women. ("Didn't God order society with slaves and women inferior?")

If one truly wants to listen to God's word, and as part of this listening he or she wants to take passages out of their biblical context and apply them as answers to personal questions, that person would be well advised to learn something about the Bible. If study does not accompany prayer, prayer may turn out to be self-delusion.

The conversation between one prayerful person and God is not the only conversation taking place through Scripture. Actually, there are other levels of conversation upon which the prayer level should be built.

The earliest conversation which is reflected in Scripture is on the level of events. Jesus lived and spoke to his contemporaries. What he said derived some of its meaning from the historical context in which he said it. An obvious example is, "Do not turn your steps to pagan territory, and do not enter any Samaritan town; go rather to the lost sheep of the house of Israel" (Mt 10:5). While the meaning of these words is clear in their historical context, the words cannot be interpreted as a statement addressed by God to successive generations. Not too many years after Jesus gave these instructions to his disciples the Holy Spirit directed Peter to include Gentiles in the covenant.

A second level of conversation is that going on between an author and his contemporary audience. The Church did not repeat what Jesus said to teach history but to make his teachings applicable to the lives of a contemporary audience. By the time the Gospels were written this application had been going on for a generation. The Gospels were written to say particular things to particular audiences. Why did the authors choose and arrange their materials as they did? What are they trying to say? An example: Why does Matthew specifically picture Jesus as standing on a mountain when he says the Beatitudes, while Luke has him standing on a plain? You may respond, "Who cares?" But the answer to this question leads to the core of Matthew's message to his audience. Matthew did care.

Another level of conversation is the level that one hears in sermons. For the last two thousand years the Christian churches have used the Bible to teach contemporary audiences. Sometimes such teaching is grace filled and sometimes it is erroneous, depending on whether or not the person speaking has understood what he or she has read. The newspaper recently reported a decision taught by one church body which is based on a misunderstanding of the literary form of the first chapters of Genesis. According to this decision, women should not be admitted to the clergy because "They are second in the order of creation and first in the Edenic fall."

We have defined four levels of conversation, the level of the event, the level of the written Scripture, the level of the teaching, preaching Church, and the level of personal prayer. Anyone who wants to engage in the third level as a clergy person or on the fourth level as a prayerful person would be well advised to learn something about levels one and two.

This book deals primarily with the second level. To understand what an author is saying to an audience, we must understand the literary form in which the author is writing.

LEVELS OF CONVERSATION

	Speaker or writer		Audience
1.	Jesus spoke	to	his contemporaries—apostles, Pharisees, crowds, etc.
2.	Mark wrote	to	persecuted Christians
	Matthew wrote	to	settled Jewish Christians
	Luke wrote	to	Gentiles
	Paul wrote	to	various local churches
3.	Preaching, teaching Church through history spoke and wrote, speaks and writes	to	contemporary audiences through history
4.	God speaks	to	prayerful people

Levels three and four need to be rooted in levels one and two!

Only then will we understand the revelation which the writing contains.

Review Questions

1. What does "literary form" or "genre" mean?
2. Why is it important to know the literary form you are reading?
3. What two contexts, in addition to literary form, must one take into consideration when reading the Bible?

4. What four levels of conversation might one see taking place in Scripture? Give an example of each.

5. When the Church repeated Jesus' teaching to later generations, what was the reason for doing so? Would this motive affect the content of what was passed on? Why?

Discussion Questions

1. Have you ever misunderstood something you read because you misunderstood the form? What was the result?
2. Have you ever experienced the fact that Scripture can speak directly to a deeply personal problem? How did you feel before and after this experience? How did you respond?
3. What would you say to a person who was planning revenge if the person justified his or her conduct by saying, "God wants me to get back at this person. An eye for an eye and a tooth for a tooth"?
4. Think of instructions which a parent gives a child over the years. Are some time-bound? Are some just for this one child? Are some universal truths? How does this relate to instructions which Jesus gave his contemporaries?
5. Think of sermons you have heard in which a clergy person applied Scripture to contemporary problems such as nuclear war, capital punishment, abortion, etc. Was the sermon giver using or abusing the text? Explain.

1

What Is the Bible?

The Bible is not one book but many books. This fact is all important. When you hold a Bible you are not holding one book with many chapters. You are holding a library, a collection of many books of diverse forms.

In a library you find a large variety of kinds of literature: biography, poetry, science fiction, autobiography, reference books, and many more. You know that what you can expect from one kind of writing is not what you can expect from another. No one supposes that an autobiography will be objective. Nor are we surprised when science fiction fails to reflect the world as we know it from experience. The very fact that a book is placed in a particular category in the library tells us something about the intent of the author.

Just as all the books in a library were not written by one person, neither was the Bible written by a single author. In addition, the individual books in the Bible are the work of many people. The Bible, and the many books in the Bible, in the forms in which we have them, are the last step of a growth process which involved many people over a period of centuries. Understanding the growth process is essential to understanding the Bible

Stages of Growth

Events

The written Bible grew out of historic events. Some of these events are familiar to nearly everyone: the call of Abraham and his move to Canaan, the years of the other patriarchs, Isaac, Jacob and Joseph, four hundred years of slavery in Egypt, the exodus when Moses led his people out of slavery, the time of the judges and the settlement of the holy land, the period when Israel was a nation with kings such as Saul, David and Solomon, the splitting of the nation into two as the prophets called the people to be faithful to their God, the exile in Babylon, the return to the holy land, the period of Hellenization, sometimes accompanied by terrible persecution, and finally the Pax Romana during which Jesus was born. Events which preceded the New Testament were the birth, ministry, death, and resurrection of Jesus, and the effect of these events on his followers which led to the birth and growth of the early Church.

Oral Tradition

God revealed himself to his people through these events, and people talked about their experiences. As accounts of these experiences were handed on from generation to generation by word of mouth, a body of oral traditions about the events grew. The oral traditions themselves contained different forms—blessings, curses, songs of battle, and laws, as well as accounts of the events, stories which today we would call legends.

As you think about this period of oral tradition it might be helpful to think about your own experience. Our lives, even in a time of ready access to all kinds of written and recorded materials, still contain some elements of what might be called oral tradition. Most of us hear and tell jokes rather than read and write them. Our families have stories which are told and retold, particularly at holidays or family reunions. When I was a child I used to jump rope to a number of rhymes which I had never read. When my family went to church, I heard, absorbed and recited prayers and a creed which I could not yet read. Through life in a family and a community, I was exposed to, and made my own, a number of oral traditions.

In addition to thinking about the variety of oral traditions,

EVENTS BEHIND ORAL AND WRITTEN TRADITIONS

Approximate dates	
1850 BC	Abraham experiences God's call
	Isaac
	Jacob
	Joseph
	Slavery in Egypt
1250 BC	Moses and the exodus
	Period of the Judges
	Saul
1000 BC	David
	Solomon The temple in Jerusalem
922 BC	Kingdom divides
	Prophets call the people to fidelity
721 BC	Northern kingdom falls to Assyrians
587 BC	Southern kingdom falls—beginning of the Babylonian exile
537 BC	Cyrus, a Persian, conquers the Babylonians and lets the Israelites return to the holy land
336 BC	Alexander the Great
	Hellenization
167 BC	Maccabean revolt
	Persecution
63 BC	Romans conquer near east
7–6 BC	Jesus born
30 AD	Crucifixion
100 AD	End of apostolic age

we should think about the motivations which underlie them. In the examples which I mentioned there are a variety of motivations—a joke is told to amuse, family stories could be told for a variety of reasons—to preserve the past, to instruct the young by good examples, to glorify a loved one, to build family pride and a sense of belonging. A jump rope rhyme is used to keep rhythm, to enable several people to act in unison. A creed is recited to hand on beliefs.

Accuracy of Oral Tradition

I remember very clearly the first time I learned that oral tradition lay behind the written accounts of events which we read in the Bible. I remember because the idea upset and alarmed me. It was my prejudice, and one which was wrong, that oral tradition was extremely inaccurate. I did not like to think of the Bible, which I knew to be revelation and inspired by God, as resting on traditions passed on by word of mouth.

Since so many students have shared this initial reaction I think it is very important to consider the question, "Is oral tradition accurate?" What can we expect in terms of accuracy from accounts of events which rest on oral tradition?

I think my initial prejudice dates back to a game we played as children. We called the game "gossip" but many of my students called it "telephone." In this game one person would whisper something to the next and so on down the line. The last person would repeat out loud what was heard. This was always very different from what had originally been said. The point of the game was to demonstrate the unreliability of gossip.

This game has no relationship to oral tradition. In fact, it is a useful contrast. Oral tradition is basically extremely accurate because it rests on the witness of the entire community. If "gossip" were played out loud the message would not be lost because mistakes would be corrected as they were made. When a child in our culture says, "Our Father, who art in heaven, Harold be thy name," we do not need to worry that generations after will make the same mistake. The community guards its oral traditions.

Although oral tradition is basically accurate, there are some ways in which it does not claim accuracy. To not claim accuracy is not the same as to be inaccurate. Inaccuracy enters in only if the reader has unrealistic expectations of what he or she is reading. As you read the accounts of events which are based on oral tradition you should remember that the tradition does not claim accuracy in several specific areas.

Not Exact Quotations

Oral tradition does not claim to be quoting exactly in the way that a twentieth century newspaper reporter would be quoting if that reporter used quotation marks. The expectation that you are reading exact quotations when you are reading written accounts of oral conversations is a realistic expectation only if you are reading nineteenth and twentieth century writings. As far as I have been able to discover the goal of quoting verbatim started in the late eighteenth century with James Boswell when he wrote the *Life of Samuel Johnson*. If one moves back to an earlier century and reads Isaac Walton's *Life of John Donne,* it becomes evident that Walton is composing speeches rather than quoting. If you would like to check this out for yourself you need only compare successive editions of Walton's work. For instance, Donne's deathbed speech is not identical in each edition.

Some people find the fact that oral tradition does not claim accuracy in terms of exact quotation very upsetting. They seem to understand "not exact quotation" to mean total "fabrication." This, of course, is a big mistake. Again we can demonstrate the error of this thinking by looking at our own everyday experience. If I tell you a joke which I heard yesterday, I am not quoting the person who told me the joke exactly. At the same time, you need hear only a sentence or two to know if you've heard the joke before. There is a big difference between saying, "This is not an exact quotation," and saying,

"There is no relationship at all between this account of a conversation and what actually occurred."

I myself find the fact that oral tradition does not claim exact quotations very enlightening. I can't escape the idea that I should have figured out for myself earlier that the written Scripture was not claiming exact quotations, given the facts that Jesus spoke Aramaic, the Gospel writers wrote in Greek Koine, and I am reading the Gospels in English. Since every translation is to some extent an interpretation it should have been obvious to me that I was not reading exact quotations. Those who passed on the oral traditions were interested in passing on powerful and invaluable ideas, accounts of reality, their understanding of the significance of events. We must look for this intent which the speakers and writers clothed in words. We must not center in so much on language that we expect exact quotations.

Not Historical Social Setting

A second way in which oral tradition does not claim accuracy is in what I like to call "social setting." What happened may be reported very accurately but where it happened may be of no interest. The fact that this is true is evident when we read the Bible. For instance, you may already be familiar with the popular title "The Sermon on the Mount." You may refer to the Beatitudes as part of the Sermon on the Mount. If you do, you are referring to Matthew's Gospel where he pictures Jesus saying the Beatitudes on the mountain. Luke, however, pictures Jesus saying almost exactly the same thing while standing on the plain. Before I studied literature and knew what to expect from literature which rests on oral tradition, such discrepancies used to upset me. Didn't Matthew or Luke know where Jesus was standing? Even then the answer, "Maybe Jesus said it twice," didn't seem at all satisfactory. The real answer lies in the fact that oral tradition does not claim accuracy in social setting. What Jesus said was passed on separately from where he was standing when he said it. That Matthew provided a setting is also important, and we will look into that when we discuss the Gospel as genre. For now we need only understand that oral tradition did not include the exact social setting.

Not Exact Historical Chronology

A third way in which oral tradition does not claim accuracy is in historic chronology. Again, we will draw on the Gospels for an example since they are more familiar to most people. If I were to ask you, "When did Jesus cleanse the temple?" you might have a difficult time responding. In the Gospels of Matthew, Mark and Luke this incident takes place at the end of Jesus' ministry as he enters Jerusalem right before his crucifixion. In John's Gospel the cleansing of the temple appears in the beginning of the Gospel, right after the wedding feast of Cana. How could such a discrepancy occur?

When the disciples passed on accounts of Jesus' activities, they passed them on as isolated incidents. Jesus cured a blind man, he cured a cripple, and he cured the woman with the hemorrhage. Each event was talked about as a mighty sign in its own right. No one cared in what order Jesus cured these people. The stories of Jesus' ministry were not passed on as a connected narrative with each incident in its proper historic chronology. Rather, stories of one incident or another were passed from town to town without regard to historic chronology. The Gospel writers supplied the chronology in which these incidents appear in our present-day Gospels.

As we said in regard to social setting, to say that the chronology in any given Gospel is not historical is not to say that it is unimportant. The Gospel editors arranged their inherited materials in the order in which they now appear for a reason. This reason relates to each Gospel writer's purpose in writing, to his audience and to the special theme which he chose to emphasize to meet the needs of that audience. The order of episodes in the Gospel is important, but we make a mistake if we assume that it is also historical.

When reading written accounts which rest on oral traditions, then, we should not expect accuracy in quotations, exact social settings, or historic chronology. We should expect accurate accounts of the intent of Jesus' words and the nature and significance of his actions. This is true because the accuracy of the accounts of the people's religious experiences rests not on the witness of one person but on the witness of the entire believing community.

Presumed Knowledge Not Repeated

Before we leave the topic of word of mouth transmission, we should notice one more characteristic that might help us understand what we read in the Bible. When traditions are handed on by word of mouth, the speaker and the listener are physically present to each other. They share a great deal of knowledge and a culture. Since all of this shared knowledge is taken for granted, what is presumed known is not stated. In reading written accounts which grew out of oral tradition we may find that something which was presumed known in the original interchange is totally foreign to us. We may bring twentieth century presumptions, problems, and concerns, or twentieth century knowledge to an ancient text and expect, somehow or other, that this text is addressing our point of view. Or we may presume that the author has the same presuppositions we do and be puzzled to read something which reflects that his presuppositions are different. In reading Genesis we must remember that ancient people thought the world was flat. In reading Job we must remember that the author did not know about the resurrection and had no clear understanding of life after death. In reading some of the historic books and psalms we must remember that the Israelites did not as yet understand God's love for other nations, only his love for Israel. In reading Paul we must remember that he did not realize that the second coming would not be imminent. These presuppositions are usually not explicit in the biblical text, but they are presumed known; speaker and audience, writer and audience, shared them. Twentieth century readers must always remember that we are not the original audience and that the original authors would be absolutely astounded by ideas which seem self-evident to us, as we are by ideas that seemed self-evident to them.

Oral tradition, then, does not claim accuracy in exact quotations, social setting, or historical chronology. Sometimes something very important is not clearly stated because it is presumed known. On the whole, however, oral tradition is extremely accurate because it is the product of the entire community.

We return now to the growth process which finally resulted in our written Bible. We have already discussed the first step of the process—the event—and the second step—oral tradition. The third step of this growth process is the written tradition.

Written Tradition

Written accounts of events were based on oral traditions. As word of mouth traditions were written, they were also revised. Traditional stories were appropriated, sometimes from surrounding cultures, and were made contemporary by succeeding generations. Therefore, the fact that a story was written at a particular historic time in a given culture does not mean that the whole story is contemporary with that culture. A writer might appropriate a story which already existed in his culture in oral or written form, and use it to illustrate a different theme. For instance, a story about the animosity which existed between a nomad and a person who "owned" land and grew crops might be retold to illustrate the pervasive effect of sin—Cain, the tiller of the soil, kills Abel, the shepherd. An existing story about a natural disaster, a flood, might be retold to illustrate how God acts through events, how man is responsible for his actions, and how only God can save.

The stories as they appear in the Bible, then, are "layered." A layered text might be compared to a tree. If I cut down a tree I can see its layered history by the circles which have grown around the trunk each year. A story, too, can be layered in that elements of the story reflect its passage through time, as various authors revise the story to include new emphases

GROWTH PROCESS

Events	God reveals himself through events
Oral Tradition	People talk about these events
Written Tradition	Parts of the oral tradition are gradually written down (i.e., songs, riddles, stories about individual people, etc.)
Edited Tradition	At various times in history people collect and edit oral and written traditions
Canonical	Some of these edited traditions are recognized by the worshiping community as inspired and are accepted as vehicles of revelation because they faithfully reflect the experience and beliefs of the community.

or insights. The text is layered because it is not the work of a single generation.

Stories about people or events, songs, poems, riddles, curses, blessings—all the elements of oral tradition were eventually written down. The fact that they were written down does not mean that the oral tradition stopped. The two traditions could exist side by side.

Edited Tradition

The fourth stage of this growth process is the editing stage. At various times in the history of the chosen people the inherited oral and written traditions were edited. Most Scripture scholars believe that the first five books of our present Old Testament reflect a number of editings. It is not necessary for our purposes at this time to study the historical setting and the characteristics of each editor. What is important is to understand the ramifications of the fact that we are dealing with a layered, much edited text.

The first ramification of the fact that our texts have been edited several times is that the books in the Bible do not appear in the order in which they were written. Scholars date the creation story in Genesis 1:1—2:4 to the last editing stage, the Priestly editors who reworked the traditions after the Babylonian exile (around 450 B.C.). The next story, about the man and his wife who ate the fruit of the forbidden tree, is thought to be a much older story dating to the earliest of the editors, the Yahwist editor, who organized and interpreted inherited materials during David's reign (about 950 B.C.). The present order of the stories in the Bible is an edited order.

The organization of the Old Testament, the arrangement of books, is largely thematic. First we have the law, also called the Torah or the Pentateuch. Next we have the prophets, who called their people to faithfulness to the covenant as the kingdom grew and then declined. Finally we have the writings, literature which grew up after the Babylonian exile. In each section, the order in which the books appear is not the order in which they were written. Prophetic literature, such as the Book of Hosea, reached its present form long before the first five books of the Bible reached their present form. Editing of the Pentateuch continued longer than editing of the prophetic books. Therefore, stories about the patriarchs may include insights not contemporary with the patriarchs, and even of more recent date than the prophetic literature which appears later in the Bible.

A second ramification of an edited text is that the present text contains divergent points of view. An obvious example of this is in the attitude toward Israel's having a king like other nations which appears in 1 Samuel. Some texts seem to favor the idea of kingship while others disapprove of it, since only God is king. The explanation for the lack of consistency lies in the history of the text. The editor had several traditions with which to work, and he did not choose between them but included both. The earlier tradition is probably the "pro

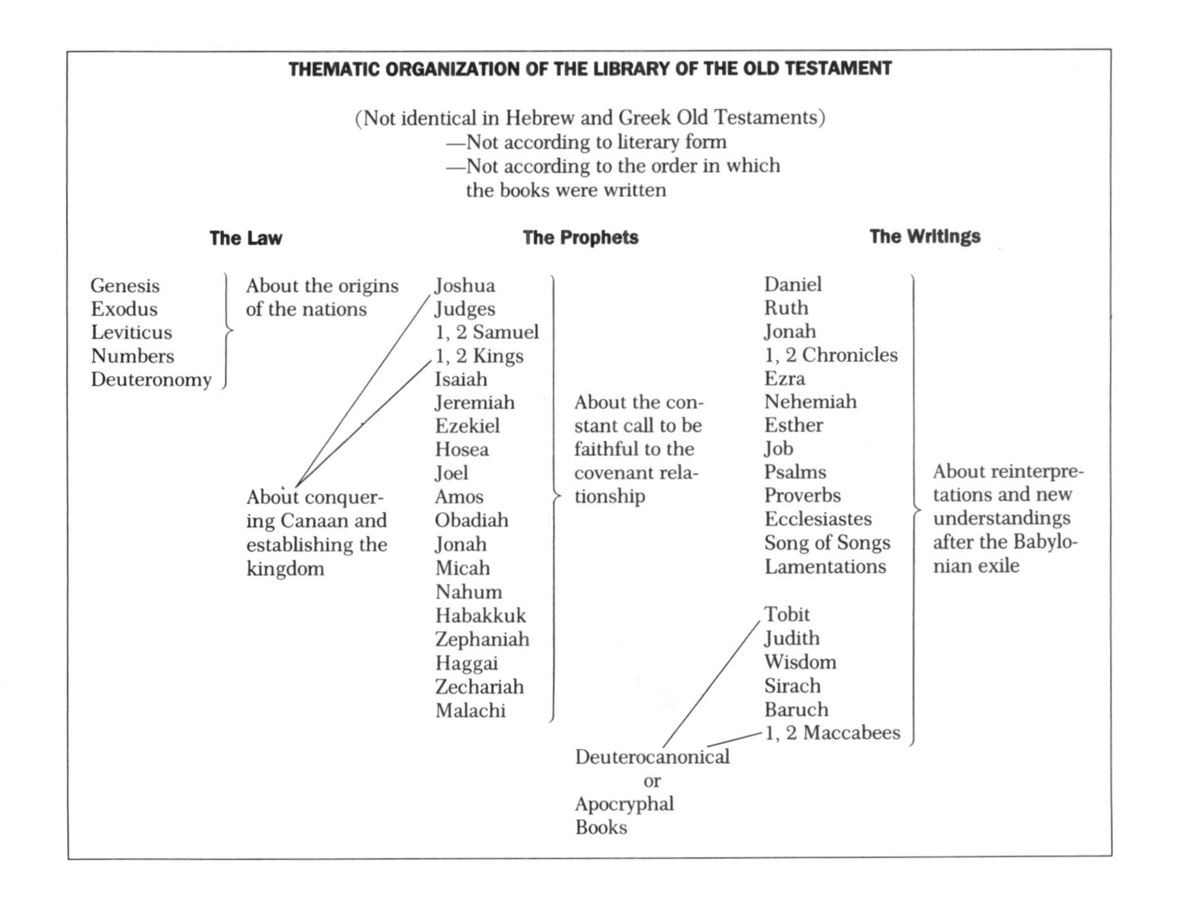
THEMATIC ORGANIZATION OF THE LIBRARY OF THE OLD TESTAMENT
(Not identical in Hebrew and Greek Old Testaments)
—Not according to literary form
—Not according to the order in which the books were written
The Law
Genesis
Exodus
Leviticus
Numbers
Deuteronomy
About the origins of the nations
About conquering Canaan and establishing the kingdom
The Prophets
Joshua
Judges
1, 2 Samuel
1, 2 Kings
Isaiah
Jeremiah
Ezekiel
Hosea
Joel
Amos
Obadiah
Jonah
Micah
Nahum
Habakkuk
Zephaniah
Haggai
Zechariah
Malachi
About the constant call to be faithful to the covenant relationship
The Writings
Daniel
Ruth
Jonah
1, 2 Chronicles
Ezra
Nehemiah
Esther
Job
Psalms
Proverbs
Ecclesiastes
Song of Songs
Lamentations
Tobit
Judith
Wisdom
Sirach
Baruch
1, 2 Maccabees
About reinterpretations and new understandings after the Babylonian exile
Deuterocanonical or Apocryphal Books

king" tradition, and the text which reflects a negative attitude toward the king probably dates to a later time when abuses had tempered the people's early idealism in regard to having a king.

This example also illustrates a third ramification of an edited text. No account which we read is an account contemporary with the event. All the accounts include hindsight. As the accounts were edited for new generations, they were made contemporary for that generation. Certain themes were emphasized for the audience whom the editor was addressing. This is clearly seen in the story of Noah. Ancient flood stories existed in surrounding cultures but this flood story is given religious significance. Details are added which reflect the religious sensibilities of later generations. Notice that in one tradition Noah takes on both "clean" and "unclean" animals, a reference to laws nowhere near as ancient as the story itself. Notice also how the story is molded into the covenant tradition through the symbolism given the rainbow, an editing technique which scholars attribute to the Priestly editors who lived after the exile.

Let us back up now and integrate what we have just said into the overall growth process which resulted in our present text. So far we have the event, oral tradition, written tradition, and editing. We know the effect oral tradition has on the written text, and we know the effect editing has on the final text. Specific examples of these effects will be explored in detail in later chapters as we look at the stories of the patriarchs and at the Gospels.

Religious Intent

It is important to remember, when reading the Bible, that we are not reading the writings of people whose primary interest is historical and whose main motivation is to keep accurate historical records for successive generations. Rather we are reading the writings of people whose interest is religious and whose purpose is to interpret the religious significance of events for successive generations. The Israelites' view of history presumes that an event is not just an event. An event is God acting. So when one records events, one is recording God's acting and man's response to God. There would be no Bible if it were not for the profound religious insight which undergirds the entire work. Events are not haphazard. People are not wanderers without purpose or direction. The Israelites saw themselves as created and loved by a God who was interacting every moment with his beloved people, and each person as a member of the community who had a responsibility for his or her actions within the context of that loving relationship. The past is remembered in order to understand the present and is repeated to help the younger generation remain faithful to God's love. To pass on the details of the event and never mention the religious significance of the event or what could be learned from the event in terms of the covenant relationship would have been a totally useless undertaking to those who passed on the biblical traditions. In Scripture we are reading history, but it is history interpreted religiously.

Canonical Accounts of Traditions

The fifth and final step in the growth process which resulted in our present Bible is that some books became "canonical." When a book became canonical it became an accepted part of Scripture. In other words, the community recognized and acknowledged that this book accurately reflected its religious experience and religious beliefs. Again, the Gospels might serve as a good example since they are so familiar to us. We have four Gospels in our New Testament. These four Gospels are not the only Gospels in existence. If you would like to read other gospels, such as the Gospel of Thomas or the Gospel of Jude, you could check them out of the library. Some Gospels are canonical—they made it into the Bible—and some are not. Gospels became canonical not through legislation but through use. In the early Church, the writings which emerged during the life of the Church were read at worship services. By the end of the second century some were accepted and loved by all the churches while others fell into disuse. You may read that the Gospel canon was closed by the end of the second century and you may read that it was closed at the Council of Trent in 1546. In terms of usage, however, the Gospel canon was "decided" through consensus by the end of the second century. The Council of Trent "closed" the New Testament canon in the sense that it legislated what had already been decided through traditional usage. The Council of Trent did this in response to Martin Luther who questioned whether certain books should be accepted as canonical. The books of the Bible were born through the experience and beliefs of the community and they reached canonicity through the experience and beliefs of the community. In every way the Bible exists because of God's acting in and through his people.

Inspiration

It has been my experience that a first understanding of "how the Bible came to be" often results in a person's having to rethink exactly what is meant by the words "inspiration" and "revelation." This five step growth process which involves generations of human beings' misunderstandings as well as their understandings seems to some incompatible with the notion that God is the author of the Bible. So, before we move on to a look at a number of different literary forms which appear in the Bible, we will first say a few words about inspiration and revelation.

When we claim that the Bible is inspired, what are we claiming? No one responds to that question by saying that God put pen to paper—or chisel to rock—wrote the Bible, and years later someone dug it up. So we don't mean that God is the author of the Bible in the sense that he actually "wrote" it. Nor do people defend the idea that one human author went into a trance and when he came back to himself the job was done. Most believers have accepted the idea of inspiration without ever defining for themselves what the experience might have been for the writer. Did he know he was inspired? Did he hear voices? What did happen?

Instead of thinking of inspiration as something that occurred between God and one writer it is better to think of inspiration as occurring between God and each member of the community. The Bible, from beginning to end, is the product of God's acting in and through his people. God's inspiration, God's acting in the hearts and minds of his people, was present at every stage of the growth process which resulted in the Bible. At the time of the event it was God's inspiration which allowed the people to experience and interpret the event as a religious event. Those who were moved to speak and write about their religious experiences were inspired. Those who were moved to pass on, reinterpret and make contemporary the lessons from the past were inspired. The communities which accepted and responded to these written works, integrating them into their worship services and establishing them in a unique place of honor in their religious traditions, were inspired. A reader today who reads Scripture, who finds that it speaks to his or her heart, who allows it to take root, to form conscience, and to shape action, is also inspired. God acts in and through his people, he breathes in and with them, he inspires them. The Bible is a fruit and a channel of inspiration.

Revelation

In addition to claiming that the Bible is inspired we claim that the Bible is revelation. This claim has led to a great deal of misunderstanding and wrongheadedness, as history confirms. What do we mean when we say that the Bible is revelation? I prefer to say that the Bible is about revelation. God revealed himself to the Israelites through events, just as he reveals himself to us through events. We read about the process of the Israelites' coming to a knowledge of the God who revealed himself through events in the Bible. Notice that the revelation is about God, not about any other subject. It is not revelation about the relationship of the planets or about the order or time frame in which material forms became present on the surface of the earth. It is not revelation about the shape of the earth or even about future events. The Bible is revelation in that it reveals the relationship between God and man. It tells us who God is, what our relationship with God is, and what we need to know in order to grow in that relationship.

I was once asked, "What will you do if when you get to heaven Jesus asks you, 'How many unblemished lambs did you offer to me in burnt holocaust?' " I thought that was a very interesting question. Reworded it is asking, "What will you do if when you get to heaven you find out that you never knew what it was God wanted of you, you never knew who he was, how to act to cooperate with him and please him? What if you never understood the spiritual order after all?" Because I believe that the Bible is revelation I don't have to worry about such a situation occurring. My belief that the Bible is revelation is my belief that it will not lead me astray when I look to it for understanding about spiritual realities. Because I believe it is revelation, I believe I know what I am to do. Even an Old Testament person would be able to say, "I am to act justly, love tenderly, and walk humbly with my God." A New Testament person would add, "And the knowledge and the power to do this rests in my union with the risen Lord, Jesus Christ."

The Bible is not revelation on any other topic. We now realize our mistake with Galileo, yet despite this many Christians continue to repeat that mistake. They try to read the Bible in such a way that it becomes revelation on topics which it actually never addresses, revelation on questions whose answers will be found not in Scripture but in scientific study. Those who make this mistake are totally blind to the concept of literary form and to the significance that knowledge of literary form has in interpreting various books of the Bible. Let us now proceed to an examination of a variety of literary forms which are the vehicle for revelation.

Review Questions

1. Why is the Bible comparable to a library?
2. What is the first step in the growth process which resulted in Scripture? Explain.
3. Name some events which underlie Scripture.

4. What is the second step in this growth process? Explain.
5. Is oral tradition basically accurate? Why?
6. In what ways does oral tradition not claim accuracy?
7. What is the difference between not claiming accuracy and being inaccurate?
8. What is the third step in the growth process which resulted in Scripture? Explain.
9. What does it mean to say that a text is layered?
10. What is the fourth step in the growth process which resulted in Scripture? Explain.
11. Name three effects of having an edited text.
12. What was the interest and purpose of those who handed on the traditions which we read about in the Bible?
13. What is the fifth step in the growth process which resulted in the Bible? Explain.
14. How did Gospels become canonical?
15. What do we mean when we claim that the Bible is inspired?
16. What do we mean when we claim that the Bible is revelation?

Discussion Questions

1. Imagine a single Saturday on which you pass a playground of children playing, attend a wedding, and go to some form of evening entertainment. If you were to give a friend a detailed description of all you heard, what literary forms might be embedded in your oral account? How does this relate to the Bible?
2. Are exact quotations necessary in order to explain to a third party the content and intent of something which has been explained to you? How does this relate to the Bible?
3. Think of what you do in the course of a normal weekday. If, in a time warp, you recounted your day to a person who lived in Jesus' time, what might you have to explain which, to a twentieth century listener, would be presumed known? How does this relate to the Bible?

4. How does God reveal himself today? Is this the same method he used in past history?
5. What role does the community play in inspiration? Can you see any relationship between the small group sharing going on right now and the process of revelation which resulted in Scripture?
6. What are some questions which the Bible can't answer but which some claim that the Bible does answer? Why can't the Bible answer these questions?
7. Has reading this chapter caused you to revise your understanding of inspiration or revelation? In what way?

2

Myth

The word "myth" has an alarming effect on many people of faith. They see no relationship at all between the Bible and myth. One reason for this is that they take the word "myth" to mean "something once believed to be true but now known to be false." For instance, I recently saw an article entitled, "Myths about Old Age." The article outlined a number of misperceptions about old age and attempted to dispel them. The word "myth," used to name a literary form, has an entirely different meaning.

Having said what "myth," when referring to a literary form, does not mean, I shall now attempt to say what it does mean. The genre "myth" is defined in a number of ways. Some define myth in terms of its characters and say that a myth is a story in which gods and goddesses play a role as characters in the action. Others define myth in terms of its function and say that myth reconciles what is otherwise unreconcilable—for instance, it reconciles the human and the divine. Still others define myth in terms of its psychological source and say that myth is a human being's attempt to come to grips with his or her place in the universe. For those who are just beginning to understand myth as a literary form, I recommend the following definition: A myth is an imaginative story which uses symbols to speak about reality, but a reality which is beyond a person's comprehension. Societies compose myths to orient themselves in a moral and spiritual world.

Let us look at the elements of this definition. A myth is about reality. This is very important. Myth is not a synonym for fiction. When we say something is a myth we are not saying it is "untrue." In fact, we are not commenting on the truth or falsity of the content of the myth at all. We are talking about the form. A myth reflects a very serious attempt to come to grips with reality. The myths which are revelation have succeeded in coming to grips with the reality of God's relationship with man in a profound way.

If a myth is about reality, why is it an imaginative story which uses symbols? Because the reality which the myth is exploring is one which is beyond our comprehension.

In this chapter we will examine two myths—the creation of the world in six days and the man and woman in the garden. What realities are these myths about?

Let us back up just a moment and remember what was said in the last chapter about the growth process which resulted in the Bible. The first step was an event. In Chapter I, when we outlined the events which underlie the Old Testament, we started with the call of Abraham around 1850 B.C. We did not start with Adam. A myth is dealing with reality but not an event in recorded history. So instead of saying that myth grows out of an event let us say that it grows out of an experience—an experience of trying to understand realities which are beyond our comprehension. For instance—I am here. I know I am here from experience. I also know that others are here and that we live in a world full of other realities. The question is, "How did we get here?" How did all that exists come into being? Now this is a very important question. It is about reality but a reality which is beyond our comprehension. If I were to say something on this subject, I would not have the option of reporting historic events which I or others had witnessed because creation was pre-historic. No one witnessed creation. Instead, I would have to write an imaginative story using symbols to come to grips with this profound reality. So one reality with which myth might deal is the reality that we came from somewhere.

A second experience which we have all had is that we experience suffering. We suffer ourselves and we see others suffer. There are all kinds of suffering which are inescapable—death, pain in childbirth, drought. It makes one wonder:

"Why?" Why do people suffer? Once again we have a reality but a reality which is beyond our comprehension. So to address this problem we can't simply describe an event objectively. We must use an imaginative story and symbols to try to come to an answer. A second reality which myth might address is the reality that we suffer and we want to know why.

The mystery of our origins and the mystery of our suffering are the two realities which are dealt with through myth in the first chapters of Genesis.

We will now look at each myth, at its use of symbols, at its message, and at why each myth is considered to be revelation.

The Myth about Creation

> In the beginning God created the heavens and the earth. Now the earth was a formless void, there was darkness over the deep, and God's spirit hovered over the water.
>
> God said, "Let there be light," and there was light. God saw that light was good, and God divided light from darkness. God called light "day," and darkness he called "night." Evening came and morning came: the first day.
>
> God said, "Let there be a vault in the waters to divide the waters in two." And so it was. God made the vault, and divided the waters above the vault from the waters under the vault. God called the vault "heaven." Evening came and morning came: the second day.
>
> God said, "Let the water under heaven come together into a single mass, and let dry land appear." And so it was. God called the dry land "earth" and the mass of waters "seas," and God saw that it was good.
>
> God said, "Let the earth produce vegetation: seed-bearing plants, and fruit trees bearing fruit with their seed inside, on the earth." And so it was. The earth produced vegetation: plants bearing seed in their several kinds, and trees bearing fruit with their seed inside in their several kinds. God saw that it was good. Evening came and morning came: the third day.
>
> God said, "Let there be lights in the vault of heaven to

divide day from night, and let them indicate festivals, days and years. Let them be lights in the vault of heaven to shine on the earth." And so it was. God made the two great lights: the greater light to govern the day, the smaller light to govern the night, and the stars. God set them in the vault of heaven to shine on the earth, to govern the day and the night and to divide light from darkness. God saw that it was good. Evening came and morning came: the fourth day.

God said, "Let the waters teem with living creatures, and let birds fly above the earth within the vault of heaven." And so it was. God created great sea serpents and every kind of living creature with which the waters teem, and every kind of winged creature. God saw that it was good. God blessed them, saying, "Be fruitful, multiply, and fill the waters of the seas; and let the birds multiply upon the earth." Evening came and morning came: the fifth day.

God said, "Let the earth produce every kind of living creature: cattle, reptiles, and every kind of wild beast. And so it was. God made every kind of wild beast, every kind of cattle, and every kind of land reptile. God saw that it was good.

God said, "Let us make man in our own image, in the likeness of ourselves, and let them be masters of the fish of the sea, the birds of heaven, the cattle, all the wild beasts and all the reptiles that crawl upon the earth.

God created man in the image of himself.
In the image of God he created him,
male and female he created them.

God blessed them, saying to them, "Be fruitful, multiply, fill the earth and conquer it. Be masters of the fish of the sea, the birds of heaven and all living animals on the earth." God said, "See, I give you all the seed-bearing plants that are upon the whole earth, and all the trees with seed-bearing fruit; this shall be your food. To all wild beasts, all birds of heaven and all living reptiles on the earth I give all the foliage of plants for food." And so it was. God saw all he had made, and indeed it was very good. Evening came and morning came: the sixth day.

Thus heaven and earth were completed with all their array. On the seventh day God completed the work he had

> been doing. He rested on the seventh day and made it holy, because on that day he had rested after all his work of creating.
>
> Such were the origins of heaven and earth when they were created (Gen 1:1–2:4).

We have here a myth which can only be described in superlatives. As we shall see in our further discussion, this myth reflects profound wisdom in its religious insights and profound simplicity in its structure. The organizing metaphor, a work week, reflects the theme. Let us go step by step and see why such conclusions are true.

How Ancient a Story?

One misperception which many beginning students of the Bible have is that they presume this story is as old as creation itself. Without being a scholar in any field at all, you can see that the story is not terribly ancient. How? Because the story reflects a society which is organized into a six day work week and a sabbath day.

An example will make this observation obvious. Bill Cosby has a wonderful record entitled "The Best of Bill Cosby" which includes several episodes about Noah. In Cosby's recounting of this ancient story, Noah is at work in his rec room, he lives in a house with a driveway, and he fears that he might be on Candid Camera. If you heard this record one thousand years from now you would know that Cosby's account is not contemporary with the actual deluge, which is thought to have taken place about 3000 B.C. Cosby dates his account with references which reflect his own society. The first creation story in the Book of Genesis comes from a well organized, civilized society, as is reflected in the established six day work week and sabbath rest.

Structure and Theme

The story has a very clear organizational structure, and one which reflects its theme. If the question behind the story is, "How did all that exists come to exist?" the answer is, "It is God's work." So what better organizational structure could be used than a work week? Thus the structure reflects the theme.

Notice the obvious ordering within the basic structure. The author has six days in which to divide up all of the reality which he knows from experience. So he gives God three days to divide and three days to populate what has been divided. On the first day God divided light from darkness, on the second he divided the waters above the vault from the water under the vault, and on the third day he divided the water from the dry land. On the fourth day God populated the vault of heaven with the sun, the moon, and the stars. On the fifth day he populated the waters with fish and put birds under the vault, and on the sixth day he populated the dry land with every kind of vegetation and with human beings. Then God kept the sabbath, just as the author's society keeps the sabbath.

Taught or Presumed?

This seems a good time to bring up another distinction which is very important. There is a difference between what is presumed and what is taught. The subject about which something is being taught in this myth is the relationship between God and man. The author understands that all of creation is an expression of God's activity in man's life. Human beings exist because God freely chose to make them with great dignity—in God's own image—and they are not just good but "very good." The author presumes things about his world that we now know were inaccurate from a scientific point of view, a view totally unrelated to his purpose or method. We know now that the dome of heaven is not a solid vault holding back waters. If this story were written today the author might have God roll the earth in his hands and make it round. Such details are not part of what is being taught. The author presumes that his society's understanding of the cosmos is accurate and so pictures God forming the cosmos as he understands it to exist.

To allow the author's ideas of the cosmos to distract us from his religious insight is a big mistake. Imagine you are with a much loved person who says, "As long as the sun rises in the east and sets in the west, so long will I love you." Would you respond, "Since the earth is round and spinning in space the sun isn't actually rising and setting." This would be a ridiculous response, totally off the point. If you miss the expression of love because you have your mind on extraneous details you have missed a great deal. Exactly the same is true when reading this creation myth. We must always keep our mind on the intent of the author, on his or her religious insights. That's what the story is about.

People who read this myth as though the author's intent were historic or scientific find themselves in a hopeless muddle. One person who represents this dilemma in my mind is William Jennings Bryan, the prosecuting attorney in the Scopes trial. Here we have a highly educated man, apparently of deep faith, who had evidently never heard that there are a variety of literary forms to be found in Scripture. He thus found himself in the position of trying to explain the inexplicable. Bryan was put on the stand and asked by the defense attorney, Clarence Darrow, "How could there be three days and three nights before there was a sun?" Poor Bryan collapsed and died several days later. I have always wished that he had been able to say, "The question reflects a misunderstanding of the literary form of the creation story. The order in which material forms appear in the story reflects the author's literary, organizational technique and not any attempt to describe the historic or scientific order."

We now know the literary form of this story—myth. We know the reality which the story explores—we exist so we must have arrived here somehow. We know the literary technique used to organize the story—a work week. And we know the theme—we exist because God made us on purpose and with love.

HEAVEN AND EARTH WITH ALL THEIR ARRAY

Heavens

God said, "Let there be a vault in the waters to divide the waters in two" (Gen. 1:6).

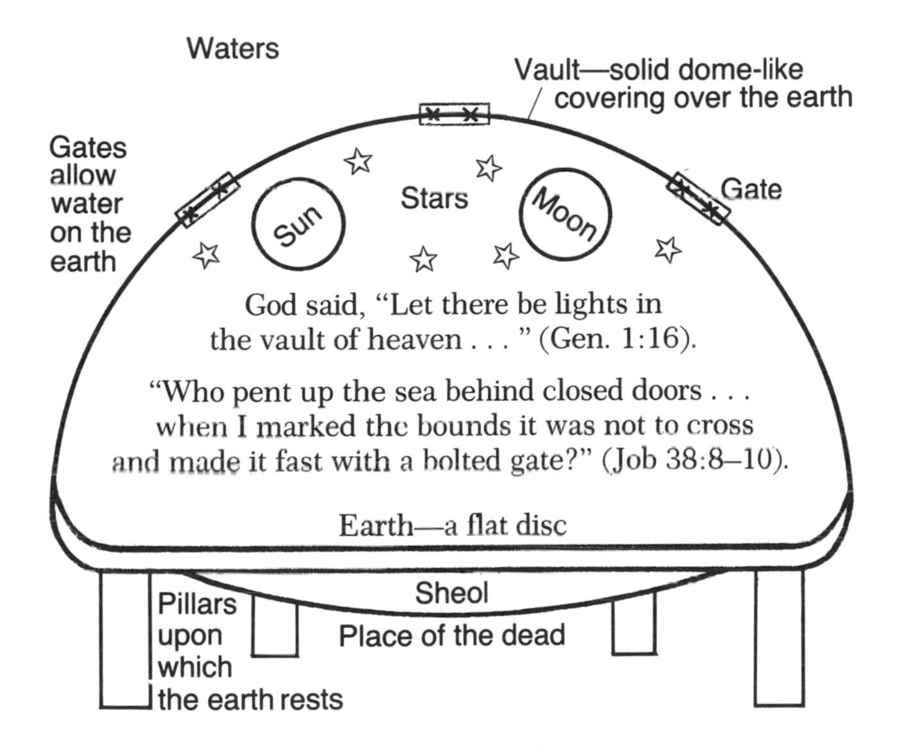

"Where were you when I laid the earth's foundations . . . What supports its pillars at their bases?" (Job 38:5).

Myth as a Vehicle for Revelation

Let us now try to understand why this myth has become part of the Bible while other creation myths have not.

As was mentioned in the first chapter, scholars date this story to about 450 B.C., to the period in Israel's history when their traditions were being re-edited in the light of the Babylonian exile. When seen in this cultural setting the religious wisdom in the story becomes even more evident. In Babylon the Israelites were exposed to beliefs very foreign to their own. We can compare the beliefs of the Babylonians because we have their creation myth too, entitled *Enuma Elish*.

In *Enuma Elish* the creation of man is accomplished by the god Marduk. Marduk, although himself a god, is created by other gods in order that he might defend them in a fight. *Enuma Elish* does not begin with the creation of the universe and man, but rather with the story of the gods embroiled in wars with each other. Apsu, the sea god, wants to kill some gods who are bothering him. Instead he is killed himself. In defense of her sea god husband, Apsu's wife, Tiamet, and another god, Kingu, intend to destroy the gods who killed Apsu. It is in order to defend themselves against these two that the gods create the wise god Marduk. After successfully slaying Tiamet, Marduk creates the universe from her corpse. Next he decides to create man out of the corpse of Tiamet's rebellious partner, Kingu. The reason Marduk creates man is so that man might serve the gods.

The idea that human beings are created from the corpse of a rebellious and defeated god is, of course, very different from the Genesis creation myth and reflects an entirely different concept of our nature. Are we basically good or basically bad? In the Babylonian myth, even though there is something god-like about us, we are essentially rebellious and defeated because we are made from the body of a god who had rebelled and was slain. In the Genesis myth we are very good. All of creation is good, as the author emphasizes by having God see everything's goodness at the end of each day. God sees that man and woman are very good. We are made in the image of the one God himself who made us not for the purpose of being his lackies, as in the Babylonian myth, but to be masters of the rest of creation.

If a person were able to accept the revelation which the Genesis myth contains he or she would be free of many worries which burdened the Babylonians. Since there is only one God, one wouldn't have to worry about inadvertently displeasing one god while honoring another. There is no need to worry about getting caught in the crossfire of the gods' jealousies. One wouldn't have to worry about the sun and the moon controlling his or her life. The sun and the moon are material creations, provided by a loving God to serve man, not rule him. They measure his day and his night. One would know that he or she is essentially good. There would be no negative duality—spirit may be good but matter isn't. Human bodies are also essentially good. God made them, and he said so. If a Babylonian had a fault which seemed to be part of his nature, say a murderous temper, he might say, "Well, what can I expect? Look what I'm made from. This is just the way I am and this is the way I'll always be." An Israelite, on the other hand, might say, "I was made in God's own image. That means I am capable of love, I am capable of tempering my anger." These are very different attitudes, very different self-concepts indeed.

Because the Israelite creation myth contains profound religious truth about our nature and our relationship with God, the community of believers has come to recognize that the author was truly inspired and that his insights are God's revealing himself to his people. His insights contain revelation.

The Myth about the Reason for Suffering

What is popularly referred to as the second creation story is not primarily about creation at all. Let us familiarize ourselves with the story.

> At the time when Yahweh God made earth and heaven there was as yet no wild bush on the earth nor had any wild plant yet sprung up, for Yahweh God had not sent rain on

the earth, nor was there any man to till the soil. However, a flood was rising from the earth and watering all the surface of the soil. Yahweh God fashioned man of dust from the soil. Then he breathed into his nostrils a breath of life, and thus man became a living being.

Yahweh God planted a garden in Eden which is in the east, and there he put the man he had fashioned. Yahweh God caused to spring up from the soil every kind of tree, enticing to look at and good to eat, with the tree of life and the tree of the knowledge of good and evil in the middle of the garden. A river flowed from Eden to water the garden, and from there to make four streams. The first is named the Pishon, and this encircles the whole land of Havilah where there is gold. The gold of this land is pure; bdellium and onyx stone are found there. The second river is named the Gihon, and this encircles the whole land of Cush. The third river is named the Tigris, and this flows to the east of Ashur. The fourth river is the Euphrates. Yahweh God took the man and settled him in the garden of Eden to cultivate and take care of it. Then Yahweh God gave the man this admonition, "You may eat indeed of all the trees in the garden. Nevertheless of the tree of the knowledge of good and evil you are not to eat, for on the day you eat of it you shall most surely die."

Yahweh God said, "It is not good that the man should be alone. I will make him a helpmate." So from the soil Yahweh God fashioned all the wild beasts and all the birds of heaven. These he brought to the man to see what he would call them; each one was to bear the name the man would give it. The man gave names to all the cattle, all the birds of heaven and all the wild beasts. But no helpmate suitable for man was found for him. So Yahweh God made the man fall into a deep sleep. And while he slept, he took one of his ribs and enclosed it in flesh. Yahweh God built the rib he had taken from the man into a woman and brought her to the man. The man exclaimed:

"This at last is bone from my bones,
and flesh from my flesh!
This is to be called woman,
for this was taken from man.

This is why a man leaves his father and mother and joins himself to his wife, and they become one body.

Now both of them were naked, the man and his wife, but they felt no shame in front of each other.

The serpent was the most subtle of all the wild beasts that Yahweh God had made. It asked the woman, "Did God really say you were not to eat from any of the trees in the garden?" The woman answered the serpent, "We may eat the fruit of the trees in the garden. But of the fruit of the tree in the middle of the garden God said, 'You must not eat it, nor touch it, under pain of death.' " Then the serpent said to the woman, "No! You will not die! God knows in fact that on the day you eat it your eyes will be opened and you will be like gods, knowing good and evil." The woman saw that the tree was good to eat and pleasing to the eye, and that it was desirable for the knowledge that it could give. So she took some of its fruit and ate it. She gave some also to her husband who was with her, and he ate it. Then the eyes of both of them were opened and they realized that they were naked. So they sewed fig-leaves together to make themselves loin-cloths.

The man and his wife heard the sound of Yahweh God walking in the garden in the cool of the day, and they hid from Yahweh God among the trees of the garden. But Yahweh God called to the man. "Where are you?" he asked. "I heard the sound of you in the garden," he replied. "I was afraid because I was naked, so I hid." "Who told you that you were naked?" he asked. "Have you been eating of the tree I forbade you to eat?" The man replied, "It was the woman you put with me; she gave me the fruit, and I ate it." Then Yahweh God asked the woman, "What is this you have done?" The woman replied, "The serpent tempted me and I ate."

Then Yahweh God said to the serpent,
"Because you have done this,
be accursed beyond all cattle,
all wild beasts.
You shall crawl on your belly and eat dust
every day of your life.
I will make you enemies of each other:
you and the woman,
your offspring and her offspring.
It will crush your head
and you will strike its heel."

To the woman he said:
"I will multiply your pains in childbearing,
you shall give birth to your children in pain.
Your yearning shall be for your husband,
yet he will lord it over you."
To the man he said, "Because you listened to the voice of your wife and ate from the tree of which I had forbidden you to eat,
Accursed be the soil because of you.
With suffering shall you get your food from it
every day of your life.
It shall yield you brambles and thistles,
and you shall eat wild plants.
With sweat on your brow
shall you eat your bread,
until you return to the soil,
as you were taken from it.
for dust you are
and to dust you shall return."
The man named his wife "Eve" because she was the mother of all those who live. Yahweh God made clothes out of skins for the man and his wife, and they put them on. Then Yahweh God said, "See, the man has become like one of us, with his knowledge of good and evil. He must not be allowed to stretch his hand out next and pick from the tree of life also, and eat some and live for ever." So Yahweh God expelled him from the garden of Eden, to till the soil from which he had been taken. He banished the man, and in front of the garden of Eden he posted the cherubs, and the flame of a flashing sword, to guard the way to the tree of life (Gen 2:5–3:24).

If I were to ask you to summarize the plot of this story you would not say, "It was about God's making man and woman." This describes only an early plot element. You would be more likely to say, "It was about a man and a woman who lived in a garden where everything was perfect. But then they sinned and had to leave the garden and from then on they suffered." With Genesis 2:5 we have moved into a separate story probing a different mystery—the mystery of suffering.

One might well ask, "Why don't the chapter divisions reflect the fact that we have begun a different story?" We must remember that the chapter divisions were not in the original texts. The chapter divisions we use were made in the Middle Ages. They do not reflect the understanding of the original authors or editors. The purpose of the chapter and verse divisions is to facilitate reference to the text. If I say Chapter 2, verse 4, we can each quickly turn to the same place.

In order to understand this story we will use the same method we used with the creation myth. We will define the genre, look at the way the author uses symbols to develop the theme, and pinpoint why this particular myth is accepted as revelation.

The Form of the Story

The story of the man and the woman in the garden is a myth. It is an imaginative story which uses symbols to explore a reality which is beyond our comprehension. The reality being explored is, "Why do human beings suffer?" In its present position, coming after a story which is nowhere near as old, the question becomes even more mysterious. Given the beliefs that God is all loving and all powerful, that God made human beings in his own image, and that we are very good, why do we suffer? You would think God would have created things in an order that didn't involve suffering. Why pain in childbirth? Why death? Suffering appears to be part of the order of things. All of this is very mysterious. How can our belief that God is all loving and all powerful be made compatible with our experience of suffering?

Symbols

Once more the author who chooses to explore this question does not have the option of giving an historical explanation. He doesn't know an historical explanation. The author makes it very evident that his genre is not historical reporting by his obvious use of symbols.

What in the story is an obvious symbol? Every reader, once he or she thinks about it, recognizes the tree of a knowledge of good and evil as a symbol. Such a tree does not in fact exist in the order of reality. Notice there is no apple tree in this story. There is a tree of a knowledge of good and evil and a tree of life—another obvious symbol. If one can eat every day from the tree of life one will not die. A third obvious symbol is the talking snake. Notice too that the snake is not referred to as the devil. The snake is a character in the plot, just as God, the man, and the woman are characters in the plot.

It is not unusual for a student to ask, "How do you know that these are symbols? Maybe back at the beginning of creation there were trees like that and snakes could talk." This question flows from the same misunderstanding which we discussed in regard to the creation myth. The story does not date back to the beginning of time. The author is not contemporary with the dawn of creation. This is a very sophisticated story. At the dawn of civilization society did not have a highly sophisticated view of marriage as is expressed in Genesis 2:24. Neither farming nor the establishment of towns was an early development in pre-historic man's life, yet the fourth chapter of Genesis reports that Cain, who tilled the soil, married and built a town, all while separated from the family of his birth. This story, like the story in which God creates the world in a work week, reflects a much more highly sophisticated society than would a story about the actual first human beings on the face of the earth. However, when we understand the literary form of the story, questions which presume historicity appear irrelevant. The text will simply not support a claim of historicity.

We return now to the symbols which are used. Now that we know we are dealing with a symbol story, we can interpret the symbols and ferret out the author's meaning.

In the beginning of this story God creates "the man." Notice in this translation the man is not called Adam. This is good because Adam has come to be a proper noun, a masculine singular noun, to English speaking readers. The Hebrew word which is translated "the man" is not a masculine singular noun but a collective noun. "The man" is each of us—all of us.

Notice in this story the man is created first, before the animals, unlike the creation story we just read in which man is created last. The editors who placed these two stories side by side were not in the least concerned about this inconsistency since neither story is in any way addressing the order in which material forms appear on the earth.

A Place of No Suffering

The man is placed in the garden of Eden and is told not to eat of the tree of a knowledge of good and evil, for on the day he eats of this tree he will die. God then makes a very profound observation, "It is not good that the man should be alone." Notice the description of God is anthropomorphic—that is, God is described as though he were a human being. God tries out lots of helpmates for the man which prove to be unsuccessful. It is only after all the wild beasts, the birds, and the cattle do not solve the problem that God tries creating the woman. The man and the woman are both naked but unashamed. This symbolizes their self-acceptance and comfort with who they are. There is not yet any self-alienation. The man and his wife love each other dearly. They are as one. The garden is a lovely place in which to live, and all their relationships are well ordered—their relationship with themselves, with each other, with the earth which feeds them abundantly and with God who comes in the evening for a walk and a talk.

Temptation

Enter the villain. The serpent is the most subtle of all the wild beasts which God created. He tempts the woman to eat the fruit of the tree of a knowledge of good and evil. She eats. The man eats. They both realize they are naked and try to cover themselves with fig leaves.

Again let us digress for a moment in order to respond to a question which often comes up. "Why," some ask, "did God make a tree which was forbidden? If God hadn't put that tree in the garden then the woman and the man wouldn't have sinned." The question reflects a misunderstanding of the genre. God didn't make a tree of a knowledge of good and evil. The question should be, "Why did the author of this story choose to have a tree of a knowledge of good and evil be part of the garden?" This is a question which can be answered. The tree of a knowledge of good and evil is a symbol for the author's belief that there is a spiritual order in the universe. If there is a spiritual order (the alternative would be no order—chaos), then there is a possibility of acting contrary to that order. We are used to the idea of order in the natural world. It is part of the natural order that I must eat if I want to live. If I act contrary to the order I suffer—I am in pain and eventually die. The author believes that spiritual reality is also ordered by God. People may act in accordance with God's order and prosper, or they may act contrary to God's order, suffer, and eventually die. So the order—the word acts as a pun in English—not to eat of the tree of a knowledge of good and evil is the author's symbolic way of representing the possibility of man's choosing to act contrary to the spiritual order which God has established.

Sin

The word "sin" is not used in this story but the author has done a magnificent job of representing sin. Sin is committed when a person knows the spiritual order and chooses to act contrary to it. The author dramatizes sin perfectly. Through the dialogue between the serpent and the woman we are able to see that the woman does know the spiritual order. She tells the snake that God told them not to eat of this one tree. It is interesting that she doesn't quote God's order exactly, but makes it stricter than God did—we may not eat it "nor touch it." The serpent tempts the woman by misrepresenting God's motivation in telling the man and woman not to eat of the tree. The woman does not trust God's love, and because the fruit looks desirable to her, she eats it. Her husband is with her, and he eats it too. The eating symbolizes the sin, and a wonderful symbol it is.

Sin is something we choose to do. Eating is something we choose to do too. As every parent of a young child knows, you can't force another person to eat. So eating is a good symbol for sin. What we eat becomes a part of us. This is literally true. The food becomes a part of what we are. Sin too becomes a part of us; it becomes a part of who we are. We can be forgiven sin, but we are not, by forgiveness, returned to the state of being we had before we sinned. What is the difference? The difference is knowledge. Through sin we grow in our knowledge of evil. Knowledge of sin affects our idea of ourself, our perceptions of others, and our relationship with God. When we sin we do eat of the tree of a knowledge of good and evil.

Some people, when they read this story, want to narrow in on the type of sin which is depicted. Was the sin a sexual sin? Was it the sin of pride? What exactly was the sin? A symbol story does not lend itself to such a specific interpretation. Eating of the tree of knowledge of good and evil symbolizes any sin which a person might commit, any action which a person chooses despite knowing that the action is contrary to God's will.

Suffering

The first change which the man and woman experience as they come to know good and evil is shame. They realize that they are naked and try to cover themselves with fig leaves. Self-alienation has become part of their world.

A person's relationship with self is not the only relationship which becomes disordered when he or she sins. This is symbolized by the fact that the man and the woman hide from God when they hear him walking in the garden. Again we have an anthropomorphic description of God. God appears not to know that the sin has been committed. He comes expecting a pleasant walk, as usual. By sinning, and by experiencing shame, the man and the woman have lost the ability to relate to God in the same way they did before. God does not prevent their walking and talking as usual. Their shame destroys their capacity to relate openly and lovingly with God.

In addition to ruining their self-concepts and their ability to love God, the man and the woman have ruined their relationship with each other. The man, instead of loving the woman, blames her for his own sin.

The author then dramatizes in dialogue form what he understands to be the effect of sin—human suffering. He has God describe the suffering which the author, and every human being, knows to exist from personal experience. The woman will bear her children in pain and will be in a subservient position to her husband. This is a reflection of the position of women in the Israelite society of 1000 B.C. Woman was considered to be property. This is seen even more clearly in Exodus 20:17 when men are commanded not to covet another man's property. "You shall not covet your neighbor's house. You shall not covet your neighbor's wife, or his servant, man or woman, or his ox, or his donkey, or anything that is his."

Occasionally, someone will interpret the fact that God is pictured as saying "Your husband shall lord it over you" as meaning that woman's subservient position is ordained by God and is part of the order of creation. This is a misinterpretation based on a misunderstanding of the literary form. The author is not reporting observed historical events, nor is he quoting God. Rather he is, through the speech he composes for God, naming the experiences in life which cause suffering. The author believes this suffering is not the way God ordered things, and he attributes such disorder to the fact that human beings have sinned. Far from thinking that God created human beings to lord it over one another, the author is insightful enough to see that such a state of affairs is a symptom of sin.

The man's suffering is that he will work by the sweat of his brow in order to obtain food and he will suffer physical death. Notice that this physical death is not the death which God said would result from eating of the tree of knowledge of good and evil. That death happened, as God warned, on the day on which the man and woman ate. That death was a spiritual death which separated the man and woman from their loving relationship with God and from their loving relationship with each other. Physical death is symbolized by the man and woman's being rejected from the garden so that they are no longer able to eat from the tree of life.

The author recognizes that all human beings are enmeshed in sin. He universalizes his symbol story by saying that the man named his wife "Eve" because she is the mother of all those who live.

God's Steadfast Love

Despite the fact that all are enmeshed in sin, the author is not without hope. He pictures God as remaining loving and solicitous. "God made clothes out of skins for the man and his wife." He also pictures God as speaking with supreme tragic irony—"See, the man has become like one of us, with his knowledge of good and evil." One can hear the profound regret and sorrow in these words. God is deeply disappointed in man's fall from grace.

It is important to see that the author does picture God as continuing to love and care for his creatures even after the creatures have destroyed their capacity to respond. Some who don't understand the literary form of this story see it as representing a very harsh and unforgiving God. I once had a student remark, "I don't understand how you can keep saying that the Bible reveals a God who is all loving. Here we see that God is so unloving that just because one man made a mistake and took one bite of an apple when he was told not to, God has been punishing everyone ever since. That's not what I call loving!"

This student, too, misunderstood the literary form of the story. He was presuming historicity and understanding the story as an historical account of cause and effect. One historic person sinned and a big bully God has been taking out his anger on everyone ever since. The story is not describing historical chronology—cause and effect. Rather the story was born from the experience of living in a world where people suffer. The author is aware of suffering and asks, "Why?" He then composes a story through which he expresses his belief—God

INTERPRETING A MYTH

Through concrete symbols and a concrete plot the author speaks about what is beyond comprehension.

Adam	Each person—all of us
Eve	The other person whom we need to love and by whom we need to be loved
Garden	A place of no suffering
God's instructions	Moral and spiritual order
Tree of knowledge of good and evil	The possibility of acting contrary to the spiritual order
Tree of life	Avoid physical death—one kind of suffering
Naked but unashamed	Self-acceptance
Serpent	Temptation
Eating	Sin
Naked but ashamed	Self-alienation
Hiding	Loss of capacity to respond to God's love
Punishments	Suffering, known from experience, which is seen as the natural consequence of disobeying the spiritual order
Expelled from garden and unable to return	Man is powerless to undo the effects of sin

PLOT: No suffering—sin—suffering

THEME: Suffering is due to sin

is loving. Man suffers because man sins. Suffering is the natural result of acting contrary to the spiritual order.

By the time this story, in the form we now have it, became part of the written religious heritage of the Israelites—around 950 B.C.—salvation history through the chosen people had been progressing for some nine hundred years. Jerusalem, the holy city, had recently been established under David. It is in that historic context that many commentators interpret God's words to the serpent, "I will make you enemies of each other, you and the woman, your offspring and her offspring. It will crush your head and you will strike its heel." The author has inserted his understanding that God has been working through his chosen people (personified as a woman, as both Israel and Jerusalem often are) to overcome evil. With this interpretation the passage can be read as a messianic prophecy. Such an interpretation is supported by the use of "it" rather than "she" when reference is made to the woman. In New Testament times Christian artists have seen in this passage a reference to Mary, the mother of Jesus, and have thus depicted her crushing the head of a serpent with her foot.

The Stage Is Set

The story of Adam and Eve is the first of four stories in these early chapters of Genesis which set the stage for salvation history by showing the snowballing effect of sin. In the present order in which the stories in Genesis appear we have first a story which establishes the fact that all of creation is ordered and good because God made it that way. We then have the belief expressed that the reason human beings do not always experience creation as being ordered and good is that we have totally disrupted the spiritual order by sinning. Suffering is the result of sin. The stories of Cain and Abel, Noah and the flood, and the tower of Babel all show how sin grows and totally separates people from one another and from God. "The man" only blamed the woman, but Cain killed Abel. In the story of the tower of Babel, people are completely separated

SINS' EFFECTS GROW

Human beings' relationships are destroyed

Relationship	Adam and Eve	Cain and Abel	Story of Noah	Tower of Babel
With self	Adam is ashamed	Cain must master sin—like a crouching beast hungering for him	Man's thoughts fashion wickedness	
With God	Adam hides from God	Cain leaves the presence of Yahweh	Yahweh regrets making man	Man powerless to reach God
With others	Adam blames Eve	Cain murders Abel	Man makes violence	Men cannot even speak to each other
With environment	Adam is expelled from the garden and must work by the sweat of his brow	Cain wanders as a stranger on the earth	The earth is corrupt	

Therefore, human beings need to be redeemed! "Yahweh said to Abraham . . ."

from God and from each other and are totally helpless to do anything about it. Thus, in terms of its theme, the Bible's stage is set for the beginning of salvation history. God calls Abraham, and salvation history begins.

In our next chapter we will examine the genre with which we need to be acquainted in order to better understand the accounts of Abraham, Moses, and the other great leaders whom we read about in the Old Testament.

In still a later chapter we will look at yet another genre when we read the Book of Job. I mention that fact now because, while the author of Job does not dispute the revelation contained in the story of the man and woman in the garden—sin does cause suffering—he does not think that this insight completely solves the mystery of why people suffer. It appears to him that innocent people suffer too. The story of Adam and Eve is a good example of the process of coming to knowledge which is evident in Scripture. While its author's insight is a profound and true revelation—sin causes suffering—the story does not contain all the revelation we find in Scripture about the mystery of our suffering. After six hundred years' more experience, six hundred years' more reflection on the religious significance of events, further insights are gained.

But first to Abraham, and to the dawn of salvation history.

Review Questions

1. What does "myth" mean when used in general conversation?
2. What does "myth" mean when used as the name of a literary form?
3. Why is myth a very different form from fiction?
4. Name two realities known from experience which myth might explore.
5. What is the structure of the creation myth in Genesis?
6. How is the structure of this myth related to its theme?
7. What is the difference between what is taught in a

story and what is presumed by the author? How does this distinction relate to the Genesis creation myth?

8. What religious truths does the Genesis creation myth teach which are not present in *Enuma Elish*?

9. With what problem is the story of the man and woman in the garden grappling? How does the plot reflect this concern?

10. How do the symbols in the story reflect such ideas as self-acceptance, sin, and shattered relationships?

11. What does the story of the man and woman in the garden teach?

12. Does the story of the man and woman in the garden reflect any hope? How?

13. How do the first chapters of Genesis set the stage for the call of Abraham?

Discussion Questions

1. Why is the word "myth" confusing and upsetting for many when it is used to refer to some part of the Bible? What is the source of such misunderstanding?
2. What is the difference between saying that a story has at its root an event or a story has at its root a reality known from experience? Can stories from these two roots be written in the same form? Why or why not?
3. What problems would arise for a person who mistook the creation myth in Genesis for an historic or scientific account?
4. How might an Israelite and a Babylonian of the fifth century B.C. differ in their understanding of who they are? How would this affect each person's relationship with God?
5. How does the author of the story of the man and woman in the garden make it obvious that he is writing an imaginative story and using symbols?
6. Does the story of the man and woman in the garden reflect a loving God or a petty, punishing God? How?

7. Do you believe that God has created a spiritual order and that if we violate that order the result will be pain and suffering? What evidence do you see for or against this idea in the world around you?

3

Legend

In our first chapter we answered the questions, "What is the Bible?" and "How did the Bible reach its present form?" The information discussed in that chapter is an essential background for understanding the sections of the Bible we will now examine: stories about Abraham, Lot, Isaac, Moses, and Samson.

In our second chapter we defined the genre "myth" and interpreted two stories in Genesis in the context of that literary form: the story of the creation of the world in six days and the story of the man and the woman in the garden.

In this chapter we will move on to another kind of writing, that of legend. A myth and a legend are not identical, so it is a mistake to use the two words interchangeably. We will begin by exploring the definition of legend. Next we will apply concepts introduced in the first chapter to the Genesis accounts of the patriarchs—that is, we will notice the effect that a background of oral tradition and a layered, edited text have on the written text. Next we will look at the characteristics of legend and how these characteristics are manifest in stories about Lot and his wife, Moses, and Samson and Delilah. Last, we will integrate the idea of revelation with legend by looking at the story of the sacrifice of Isaac.

Definition of a Legend

The main difference between a legend and a myth is that a legend is more firmly based in history. The story about "the man" in the garden who could eat from the tree of life was not about an identifiable person within the scope of history. Many people have trouble understanding the difference between "the man" and Abraham in terms of their historicity because they do not understand what the word "history" means. The following statement shows a lack of understanding about the meaning of the word "history." "There must have been a first person and so the first person is an historical person." History does not include all of past reality. In addition to historic events and people, there were pre-historic events and people, those before history. History deals with those past events about which we have some oral or written records. The events have been observed, and those who observed them spoke or wrote about them. The story about the man in the garden at the time of creation is not a story based on observed events about which people spoke or wrote, but the stories about Abraham and his society are. These stories are about an identifiable group of people within the bounds of history.

The Genesis accounts of the "nationality" of the patriarchs, the part of the world in which they lived, their movement to Canaan, their occupations, and their ways of relating to each other socially all have their roots in history. The studies of historians and archeologists both confirm that the underlying political, geographic, social and religious conditions in the biblical accounts are accurate pictures of the second millennium B.C.

Having claimed that the stories about the patriarchs have their roots in history we must now reiterate two statements which clarify just what kind of history we mean. First, the stories about the patriarchs are folk history, that is, they were originally based on oral tradition rather than on written records. Second, the stories are a religious history, that is, they are a religious interpretation of events. It takes time to understand the ramification of these statements.

The Effect of Oral Tradition

Since the written legends which we will now study are based on oral tradition, we must integrate what we learned in the first chapter about the accuracy of oral tradition, and how such a background affects a written text. We know from Chapter I that oral tradition does not claim accuracy in exact quotation, in social context, or in historic chronology. These characteristics of oral tradition are evident in the accounts of the patriarchs.

On "Quotations"

First, we will see how the fact that oral tradition does not claim exact quotations affects the text.

> Yahweh said to Abram, "Leave your country, your family and your father's house, for the land I will show you. I will make you a great nation; I will bless you and make your name so famous that it will be used as a blessing.
>
> 'I will bless those who bless you;
> I will curse those who curse you.
> All the tribes of the earth
> shall bless themselves by you' " (Gen 12:1–3).

It is a surprise to many people to realize that God is pictured as saying, "I will bless those who bless you. I will curse those who curse you." That doesn't sound like the God in whom we believe, who loves all people and who wouldn't curse anyone.

Once we understand the literary form of this story—a legend based on oral tradition—and understand that we are never reading quotations when we are reading legends based on oral traditions, then the solution to this problem becomes clearer. The question is not "Why did God say this?" but "Why does the legend picture God as saying this?"

Blessings and Curses

This rephrasing of the question allows us to look at the culture and at the beliefs of the people of the time for our explanation. Curses and blessings were customary among most primitive people. Curses and blessings were originally magic words and actions which the people firmly believed caused the good or bad which they expressed. The Israelites, like all the people of the ancient near east, retained vestiges of this primitive idea. However, the Israelites adapted the belief to their own religious experience and attributed the power of the blessing or curse to the power of God. What was originally a primitive belief in magic became an expression of belief in the power and presence of Yahweh. So when God is pictured as saying, "I will bless those who bless you; I will curse those who curse you," he is pictured as expressing himself in a way common to the culture. Blessings and curses appear throughout the Old Testament. In the New Testament Jesus teaches his followers to love rather than curse their enemies, although Paul apparently retained this form of expression, for in 1 Corinthians 16:22 we read, "If anyone does not love the Lord, a curse on him."

On Chronology

In addition to not expecting exact quotation, we already know that we should not expect exact historic chronology when reading legends based on oral traditions. Stories about the patriarchs were told and retold to many audiences in a variety of situations for a variety of reasons. The stories were episodic—self-contained units about a particular episode—not long narratives with smooth transitions joining one to another. The present order of the stories is the arrangement of various editors who did not always attempt to bridge gaps between the inherited legends. This is evident in many instances but one obvious example is the beginning of Genesis 25. In chapter 24 Abraham is an old man, preparing for his death by arranging for the marriage of his son, Isaac. Chapter 25 begins with the news that Abraham married another wife and had another whole line of descendants by her. Then, in verse 8, we are told that Abraham dies. This lack of logical sequence reveals the work of an editor who is combining various sources. We are not reading events reported with exact historic chronology.

On Social Setting

The third expectation which we have learned is inappropriate when reading legends is total accuracy in social setting. This becomes evident when we read about a covenant made between the Israelites and Abimelech at a place since called Beersheba. Was this covenant made between Abraham and Abimelech or between Isaac and Abimelech? What was the exact social setting? By comparing Genesis 21:22–31 to Genesis 26:26–33 we can see that the editors had two written accounts which placed the incident in different social settings.

> At that time Abimelech came with Phicol, the commander of his army, to speak to Abraham, "God is with you in all you are doing. Swear by God to me here and now that you will not trick me, neither myself nor my descendants nor any of mine, and that you will show the same kindness to me and the land of which you are a guest as I have shown to you." "Yes," Abraham replied, "I swear it."
>
> Abraham reproached Abimelech about a well that Abimelech's servants had seized. "I do not know who has done this," Abimelech said. "You yourself have never mentioned it to me and, for myself, I heard nothing of it till today." Then Abraham took sheep and cattle and presented them to Abimelech and the two of them made a covenant. Abraham put seven lambs of the flock on one side. "Why have you put these seven lambs on one side?" Abimelech asked Abraham. He replied, "You must accept these seven lambs from me as evidence that I have dug this well." This is why they called that place Beersheba, because there the two of them swore an oath (Gen 21:22–31).

> Abimelech came from Gerar to see him, with his adviser Ahuzzath and the commander of his army, Phicol. Isaac

> said to them, "Why do you come to me since you hate me, and have made me leave you?" "It became clear to us that Yahweh was with you," they replied, "and so we said, 'Let there be a sworn treaty between ourselves and you, and let us make a covenant with you.' Swear not to do us any harm, since we never molested you but were unfailingly kind to you and let you go away in peace. Now you have Yahweh's blessing." He then made them a feast and they ate and drank.
>
> Rising early in the morning, they exchanged oaths. Then Isaac bade them farewell and they went from him in peace. Now it was on the same day that Isaac's servants brought him news of the well they had dug. "We have found water!" they said to him. So he called the well Sheba, and hence the town is named Beersheba to this day (Gen 26:26–33).

In each account the patriarch makes a covenant with Abimelech and promises not to harm him or his descendants. In each account a well becomes part of the story and an explanation is given for naming the site Beersheba, although not the same explanation. However, one account identifies the patriarch as Abraham while the other identifies him as Isaac. The editor who arranged his inherited material into a panoramic account of the religious history of his people did not choose between these two legends but included each. The fact that the legends did not identify identical social settings did not deter him, for this detail was irrelevant to his purpose in including these two legends in his larger narrative.

Some Information Presumed Known

In addition to not expecting exact quotes, historic chronology or exact social settings when reading literature based on oral tradition, we also know not to expect the story to include all the information necessary for a person from another time and culture to understand every detail. Sometimes something important is not stated because it is presumed known. We see many examples of this in the legends which are repeated in the Book of Genesis. For instance, a modern reader is amazed at how long the patriarchs lived. We presume that the motivation behind reporting someone's old age is to tell the listener how many years that person actually lived. Such a presumption is a mistake when reading Genesis. At the time these stories were originally told, to say someone lived many years was to say that the person lived a virtuous life. The statement "the number of years Abraham lived was a hundred and ninety-five" was not a statement about his longevity but about his virtue. The intent of this statement is not explained because it is presumed known; indeed it was known in the culture which originated these oral legends.

A second example of the importance of knowing a fact which is not always spelled out can be seen when reading the well-known story in which Jacob steals his father Isaac's blessing from his brother Esau. The response of many modern readers to this account in Genesis 37 is, "Once Isaac realized his mistake, why didn't he take the blessing away from Jacob and give it to Esau?" This question comes from a presumption that the beliefs of our culture are the same as the beliefs of the culture about which we are reading. In our culture a contract, or a vow which a person makes, becomes non-binding if it is later discovered that one contracting partner misunderstood what was being agreed upon due to the deliberate deceit of the other contracting partner. The idea that deceit on the part of one person would allow another person to take back his blessing would never have entered the mind of Isaac, Jacob or Esau. They shared the belief that a blessing, once given, was effective and could not be taken back. Esau, in his grief, never suggests to Isaac that he take back the blessing he had mistakenly given to Jacob, but only that Isaac give Esau a blessing too. In the culture in which this legend took form, everyone knew that blessings and curses, once spoken, could never be taken back. There was no need to explain what everyone already knew.

We have now illustrated the effect that the oral roots of legends have on the written text. In the process of this discussion two topics have been referred to but not clearly explained. The first is that, in addition to illustrating the characteristics of literature based on oral tradition, the text in Genesis shows the characteristics of literature which has been assembled by editors. We already noted this when we compared the two accounts of the covenant with Abimelech, but there is more to be said on this topic. A second subject which needs further amplification is the distinction between history, and history which has been interpreted religiously. This second topic will be discussed later in this chapter.

The Effects of Editing

The effect of editing can be seen by comparing several accounts of one legend. It is not unusual, as we saw in the two accounts of the covenant between the Israelites and Abimelech at Beersheba, for the same legend to become attached to two patriarchs. A second example of this is in the story of a patriarch claiming that his wife is actually his sister in order to assure his own safety. This story is told of Abraham and Sarah in Genesis 12:10–20 and in Genesis 20:1–18.

> When famine came to the land Abram went down into Egypt to stay there for the time, since the land was hard pressed by the famine. On the threshold of Egypt he said to his wife Sarai, "Listen! I know you are a beautiful woman. When the Egyptians see you they will say, 'That is his wife,' and they will kill me but spare you. Tell them you are my sister, so that they may treat me well because of you and spare my life out of regard for you." When Abram arrived in Egypt the Egyptians did indeed see that the woman was very beautiful. When Pharaoh's officials saw her they sang her praises to Pharaoh and the woman was taken into Pharaoh's palace. He treated Abram well because of her, and he received flocks, oxen, donkeys, men and women slaves, she-donkeys and camels. But Yahweh inflicted severe plagues on Pharaoh and his household because of Abram's wife Sarai. So Pharaoh summoned Abram and said, "What is this you have done to me? Why did you not tell me she was your wife? Why did you say, 'She is my sister,' so that I took her for my

wife? Now here is your wife. Take her and go!" Pharaoh committed him to men who escorted him back to the frontier with his wife and all he possessed (Gen 12:10–20).

Abraham left there for the land of the Negeb, and settled between Kadesh and Shur, staying for the time being at Gerar. Of his wife Sarah, Abraham said, "She is my sister," and Abimelech the king of Gerar had Sarah brought to him. But God visited Abimelech in a dream at night. "You are to die," he told him, "because of the woman you have taken, for she is a married woman." Abimelech however had not gone near her; so he said, "My Lord, would you kill innocent people too? Did he not tell me himself, 'She is my sister,' and did not she herself say, 'He is my brother'? I did this with a clear conscience and clean hands." "Yes I know," God replied in the dream, "that you did this with a clear conscience, and it was I who prevented you from sinning against me. That was why I did not let you touch her. Now send the man's wife back; for he is a prophet and can intercede on your behalf for your life. But understand that if you do not send her back, you will most surely die, and all your people too."

So Abimelech rose early next morning and summoning all his servants told them the whole story, at which the men were very much afraid. Then summoning Abraham Abimelech said to him, "What have you done to us? What wrong have I done you that you bring so great a sin on me and on my kingdom? You have treated me as you should not have done." "Because," Abraham replied, "I thought there would be no fear of God here, and the people would kill me because of my wife. Besides, she is indeed my sister, my father's daughter though not my mother's; and she became my wife. So when God made me wander far from my father's home I said to her, 'There is a kindness you can do me: everywhere we go, say of me that I am your brother.' "

Abimelech took sheep, cattle, men and women slaves, and presented them to Abraham, and gave him back his wife Sarah. And Abimelech said, "See, my land lies before you. Settle wherever you please." To Sarah he said, "Look, I am giving one thousand pieces of silver to your brother. For you this will be compensation in the eyes of all those

> with you. . . ." At Abraham's prayer God healed Abimelech, his wife and his slave-girls, so that they could have children, for Yahweh had made all the women of Abimelech's household barren on account of Sarah, Abraham's wife (Gen 20:1–18).

The same story is told of Isaac and Rebekah in Genesis 26:1–14.

> There was a famine in the land—a second one after the famine which took place in the time of Abraham—and Isaac went to Abimelech, the Philistine king at Gerar. Yahweh appeared to him and said, "Do not go down into Egypt; stay in the land I shall tell you of. Remain for the present here in this land, and I will be with you and bless you. For it is to you and your descendants that I will give all these lands, and I will fulfill the oath I swore to your father Abraham. I will make your descendants as many as the stars of heaven, and I will give them all these lands; and all the nations in the world shall bless themselves by your descendants in return for Abraham's obedience; for he kept my charge, my commandments, my statutes and my laws." So Isaac stayed at Gerar.
>
> When the people of the place asked him about his wife he replied, "She is my sister," for he was afraid to say, "She is my wife," in case they killed him on Rebekah's account, for she was beautiful. When he had been there some time, Abimelech the Philistine king happened to look out of the window and saw Isaac fondling his wife Rebekah. Abimelech summoned Isaac and said to him, "Surely she must be your wife! How could you say she was your sister?" Isaac answered him, "Because I thought I might be killed on her account." Abimelech said, "What is this you have done to us? One of my subjects might easily have slept with your wife, and then you would have made us incur guilt." Then Abimelech issued this order to all the people: "Whoever touches this man or his wife shall be put to death."
>
> Isaac sowed his crops in that land, and that year reaped a hundredfold. Yahweh blessed him and the man became rich; he prospered more and more until he was

very rich indeed. He had flocks and herds and many servants. The Philistines began to envy him (Gen 26:1–14).

On Emphasizing a Theme

Scholars believe that the earliest version of the story is the one in which Isaac and Rebekah are the main characters. The story then became associated with Abraham because it served as an example that God was being faithful to his promise to Abraham. He was protecting Abraham and blessing those who blessed him.

On Moral Implications

It is interesting to compare the two versions of this legend in which Abraham and Sarah are the main characters (Gen 12:10–20 and Gen 20:1–18) because we can see a growth in moral sensitivity between the two accounts. Shock is a common response of students when they first read Genesis 12:10–20. They are shocked because Abraham, who has experienced God's power and presence, does not trust God to protect him. Instead he lies in order to protect himself, and encourages his wife to commit adultery in order to secure his own safety. Also, students are shocked at the way God acts. After all, Pharaoh is innocent in his wrong-doing since he did not know that Sarah was Abraham's wife. Why would Yahweh inflict severe plagues on an innocent man?

The second legend about the same event seems to reflect some of the same religious sensibility which a twentieth century reader brings to the story. In this second account (Gen 20:1–18), Abraham is deceitful but not an outright liar, Sarah is protected from committing adultery, and God, while he threatens to punish an innocent man, does not carry out his threat because Abimelech reminds God of his innocence. The second legend is more sophisticated not only in its religious sensibilities but in its literary technique. Through the use of dialogue Abimelech is given the opportunity to claim his innocence before God, and Abraham is given an opportunity to explain that he didn't actually lie because he and Sarah have the same father. The religious motivation behind the legend is made clear when Abimelech's household is blessed for blessing Abraham. This is divine confirmation of the promise made in Genesis 12:3, "I will bless those who bless you." These two legends illustrate the fact that the Bible reveals a growth process in revelation and in religious sensibility. As legends were told and retold they were reworked to reflect the growth in understanding about God's nature and about ethical behavior which was constantly taking shape among the chosen people. By comparing two accounts of the same legend, then, we can see this growth process and the effect of editing.

Thus far we have seen the effects which oral tradition and which an edited, layered text have had on our accounts of the patriarchs. Next we will look at how history is interpreted religiously and then at some characteristics of legend which are evident in our biblical texts.

Religious Interpretation or Exaggeration?

To say that events are interpreted religiously in Scripture is not another way of saying that legends include exaggeration. However, we will discuss religious interpretation and exaggeration together in order to distinguish between them, and we will turn to the Book of Exodus for our example.

The stories in the Book of Exodus of the call of Moses, the plagues in Egypt and the exodus are familiar to most adults. However, many have seen a Hollywood version starring Charlton Heston and have not actually read the accounts as they appear in the first eighteen chapters of the Book of Exodus. As you read these chapters you will notice many of the characteristics of literature based on oral tradition which we have already explained. Thus we are no longer wondering if God actually said, "I myself will make Pharaoh's heart stubborn" (Ex 7:2). We are no longer lost when the chronology does not seem perfect and we read several accounts of the call of Moses and Aaron (Ex 4:10–17; 5:2–13). Nor are we puzzled by the

LEGENDS

I. Have an historical base

II. Have an oral history
   A. Not quotations
   B. Not exact historical chronology
   C. Not exact historical social setting
   D. Some information presumed known

III. Are edited narratives
   A. Emphasize a theme
   B. Reflect growth in moral sensitivity
   C. Include religious interpretation

IV. Are characterized by:
   A. Exaggeration
   B. Magical details
   C. Etiologies
   D. Folk customs appropriated for religious purposes

V. Can be the vehicle for revelation
   A. Revelation about God
   B. Revelation about our relationship with God

question, "Who had the magic rod?" (Ex 4:17 cf. 7:10–13). The problem we do want to address is the marvelous nature of what occurs in these chapters. There are two factors operating at the same time, each of which we will isolate and discuss. The first is the religious interpretation of events. The second is the exaggeration which is inherent to legend.

Religious Interpretation of Events

In Chapter I we discussed the Israelites' view of history. We said that they believed an event is not just an event. An event is God acting. This brings us to a distinction which is very important for a twentieth century reader to understand. When speaking of the cause of an event we speak in terms of its proximate cause. The Israelites always spoke in terms of its ultimate cause. If it rained, God made it rain. An explanation based on cumulus clouds, rising warm air, or jet streams would have been totally foreign to them. In order to appreciate the Israelites' understanding of God it is absolutely essential to realize that their God was a present, powerful, loving God who acted through events. Thus their whole life was an interaction with their God who was present in everything that occurred.

The Israelites felt God's saving presence and power in a profound way in the events of the exodus. God intervened and freed them from slavery in Egypt.

Sign vs. Miracle

A twentieth century reader might look on the plagues as natural rather than supernatural events. Again, we are bringing an idea to the Scripture which is not shared by those who experienced, talked about and wrote about the events that occurred at the time of the exodus. The word "miracle" is not used. Rather, we read the word "sign." The Israelites experienced these events as signs of God's power and presence.

Since twentieth century readers view a miracle as a supernatural occurrence, let us look for a moment at our distinction between natural and supernatural. These are point of view words and not real distinctions. When we say "supernatural" we mean above our nature or above what we understand, with our present knowledge, as being within the order of nature. From God's point of view nothing that exists or happens is supernatural.

Perhaps an example would make the point clearer. Suppose an ant is carrying a large crumb from one place to another. I am watching the ant and can clearly see its destination. Suppose I admire the ant for its industriousness and so decide to help it out. I pick up the ant and place it, crumb and all, exactly where it was going. From the ant's point of view something supernatural has occurred. From my point of view what occurred was well within my understanding of the natural order of events. What is supernatural to the ant is not supernatural to me and what is supernatural to me is not supernatural to God. The distinction is simply a point of view, and one which the Israelites did not utilize.

So when we read the accounts of the plagues we are not understanding the intent of the author if we keep asking, "Are these natural or supernatural events?" Rather we should understand that the Israelites experienced the events as God acting, and it is this experience which they are passing on to their children.

Exaggeration

This religious interpretation of events is not the same as the exaggeration which one expects to find in legend. The difference between the two is easily demonstrated in the present text because we have the work of several traditions combined, all of which interpret events religiously but one of which adds exaggeration to the religious interpretation.

Most scholars agree that three edited traditions are combined in our present account of the plagues and the exodus. The traditions are alike in that they all include the first and the last plagues. However, they differ in the number of plagues—from eight to five—and in certain emphases. One tradition gives Aaron a more prominant role and embellishes events by dramatically emphasizing the marvelous nature of what is occurring. If one reads Exodus 14 carefully, one can see that, while both traditions agree that God has acted, one pictures God acting by using the east wind to drive back the waters while the other has God acting by using Moses and his rod to divide the waters.

> Yahweh said to Moses, "Why do you cry to me so? Tell the sons of Israel to march on. For yourself, raise your staff and

stretch out your hand over the sea and part it for the sons of Israel to walk through the sea on dry ground. I for my part will make the hearts of the Egyptians so stubborn that they will follow them. So shall I win myself glory at the expense of Pharaoh, of all his army, his chariots, his horsemen. And when I have won glory for myself, at the expense of Pharaoh and his chariots and his army, the Egyptians will learn that I am Yahweh."

Then the angel of Yahweh, who marched at the front of the army of Israel, changed station and moved to their rear. The pillar of cloud changed station from the front to the rear of them, and remained there. It came between the camp of the Egyptians and the camp of Israel. The cloud was dark, and the night passed without the armies drawing any closer the whole night long. Moses stretched out his hand over the sea. Yahweh drove back the sea with a strong easterly wind all night, and he made dry land of the sea. The waters parted and the sons of Israel went on dry ground right into the sea, walls of water to the right and to the left of them. The Egyptians gave chase; after them they went, right into the sea, all Pharaoh's horses, his chariots, and his horsemen. In the morning watch, Yahweh looked down on the army of the Egyptians from the pillar of fire and of cloud, and threw the army into confusion. He so clogged their chariot wheels that they could scarcely make headway. "Let us flee from the Israelites," the Egyptians cried, for Yahweh was fighting for the Israelites against the Egyptians. "Stretch out your hand over the sea," Yahweh said to Moses, "that the water may flow back on the Egyptians and their chariots and their horsemen." Moses stretched out his hand over the sea, and as day broke, the sea returned to its bed. The fleeing Egyptians marched right into it, and Yahweh overthrew the Egyptians in the very middle of the sea. The returning waters overwhelmed the chariots and the horsemen of Pharaoh's whole army, which had followed the Israelites into the sea; not a single one of them was left. But the sons of Israel had marched through the sea on dry ground, walls of water to the right and to the left of them. That day, Yahweh rescued Israel from the Egyptians, and Israel saw the Egyptians lying on the shore. Israel witnessed the great act that Yahweh had performed against the Egyptians,

> and the people venerated Yahweh; they put their faith in Yahweh and in Moses, his servant (Ex 14:15–31).

The two traditions are interwoven, like strands in a braided rope, but the separate strands are indentifiable.

A twentieth century reader might ask, "Well, which was it? Was this a natural event, a wind, or a supernatural event, Moses and his rod?" The question ignores the intent of the authors. The distinction between natural and supernatural is irrelevant. In both accounts we are dealing with an event in which God's presence was experienced. The difference between the methods through which God acted—through the wind or through the more dramatic and marvelous action in which Moses raised his rod—illustrates the exaggeration which is characteristic of legend. In the later version the author has embellished the story, using exaggeration to make Moses' role more dramatic.

Motivation

Remember that the legends were told and retold not merely to recall the past but to affect a present audience. To embellish a legend with marvelous details is to make it all the more interesting and inspiring to the next generation. In most legends exaggeration is used to build up a human hero. In these legends, however, the religious purpose of the author is always present. It is not really Moses, but God acting through Moses, who is being glorified. The author wishes to inspire his audience with the marvelous nature of God's intervention in the history of his people. Their God is a God who saves.

Magic

A second characteristic of legends is that legends sometimes go beyond exaggeration and include magical touches. In reading the early chapters of Exodus we can see this characteristic in the magic rod which turns into a snake. In order to understand this characteristic of legend and the way it is appropriated for a religious purpose, we will now turn to the story of Samson and Delilah which appears in the book of Judges.

> After this, Samson fell in love with a woman in the Vale of Sorek; she was called Delilah. The chiefs of the Philistines visited her and said to her, "Cajole him and find out where his great strength comes from, and how we can master him and bind him and reduce him to helplessness. In return we will each give you eleven hundred silver shekels."
>
> Delilah said to Samson, "Please tell me where your great strength comes from, and what would be needed to bind you and tame you." Samson answered, "If I were bound with seven new bowstrings that had not yet been dried, I should lose my strength and become like any other man." The chiefs of the Philistines brought Delilah seven new bowstrings that had not yet been dried and she took them and bound him with them. She had men concealed in her room, and she shouted: "The Philistines are on you, Samson!" Then he snapped the bowstrings as a strand of tow snaps at a touch of the fire. So the secret of his strength remained unknown.
>
> Then Delilah said to Samson, "You have been laughing at me and telling me lies. But now please tell me what would be needed to bind you." He answered, "If I were bound tightly with new ropes that have never been used, I should lose my strength and become like any other man." Then Delilah took new ropes and bound him with them, and she shouted, "The Philistines are on you, Samson!" She had men concealed in her room, but he snapped the ropes round his arms like thread.
>
> Then Delilah said to Samson, "Up to now you have been laughing at me and telling me lies. Tell me what would be needed to bind you." He answered, "If you wove the seven locks of my hair into the warp of the web and fixed the peg firmly, I should lose my strength and become like any other man." She lulled him to sleep, then wove the seven locks of his hair into the warp, fixed the peg and shouted, "The Philistines are on you, Samson!" He woke from his sleep and pulled out both stuff and peg. So the secret of his strength remained unknown.
>
> Delilah said to him, "How can you say you love me

when you do not trust me? Three times now you have laughed at me and have not told me where your great strength comes from." And day after day she persisted with her questions, and allowed him no rest, till he grew tired to death of it. At last he told her his whole secret; he said to her, "A razor has never touched my head, because I have been God's nazirite from my mother's womb. If my head were shorn, then my power would leave me and I should lose my strength and become like any other man." Then Delilah realized he had told his whole secret to her; she had the chiefs of the Philistines summoned and given this message, "Come just once more; he has told his whole secret to me." And the chiefs of the Philistines came to her with the money in their hands. She lulled Samson to sleep in her lap, and summoned a man who sheared the seven locks off his head. Then he began to lose his strength, and his power left him. She cried, "The Philistines are on you, Samson!" He awoke from sleep, thinking, "I shall break free as I did before and shake myself clear." But he did not know that Yahweh had turned away from him. The Philistines seized him, put out his eyes and took him down to Gaza. They fettered him with a double chain of bronze, and he spent his time turning the mill in the prison.

But the hair that had been shorn off began to grow again.

The chiefs of the Philistines assembled to offer a great sacrifice to Dagon their god and to rejoice. They said:

> "Into our hands our god has delivered Samson our enemy."

And as soon as the people saw their god, they acclaimed him, shouting his praises:

> "Into our hands our god has delivered Samson our enemy."

And as their hearts were full of joy, they shouted, "Send Samson out to amuse us." So Samson was brought out of prison, and he performed feats for them; then he was put to stand between the pillars. But Samson said to the boy who was leading him by the hand, "Lead me where I can touch the pillars supporting the building, so that I can lean against them." Now the building was crowded with men and women. All the chiefs of the Philistines were there, while about three thousand men and women were watch-

> ing Samson's feats from the roof. Samson called on Yahweh and cried out, "Lord Yahweh, I beg you, remember me; give me strength again this once, and let me be revenged on the Philistines at one blow for my two eyes." And Samson put his arms round the two middle pillars supporting the building, and threw all his weight against them, his right arm against one and his left arm against the other; and he cried out, "May I die with the Philistines!" He thrust now with all his might, and the building fell on the chiefs and on all the people there. Those he killed at his death out-numbered those he had killed in his life. His brothers and his father's whole family came down and carried him away. They took him up and buried him between Zorah and Eshtaol in the tomb of Manoah his father. He had been judge in Israel for twenty years (Jgs 16:4–31).

Again, what we have already learned makes it unnecessary to address some common questions. Since we know the literary form we are reading we need no longer ask "Was Samson really strong enough to seize the town gate and two posts?" or "Why didn't Samson realize that he couldn't trust Delilah after her first or second attempt to trick him?" or "Was Samson's strength really in his hair?" But we might still want to ask, "Why does the legend picture Samson's strength as being in his hair?" This is a good question because it leads us right to the heart of the story. The legend of Samson and Delilah has been included in the Book of Judges because it perfectly illustrates the religious theme of the book. In the second introduction to the Book of Judges we read, "Then the sons of Israel did what displeased Yahweh and served the baals. . . . They bowed down to these; they provoked Yahweh. . . . Then Yahweh's anger flamed out against Israel. He handed them over to pillagers who plundered them; he delivered them to the enemies surrounding them, and they were not able to resist them" (Jgs 2:11–15).

The theme of the Book of Judges is didactic. The examples from history are all chosen to illustrate the fact that infidelity to Yahweh brings destruction while fidelity to Yahweh brings peace and success. This theme is repeated by means of a preface and conclusion to the story of each judge (see 3:7, 4:1, etc.).

The story of Samson, a judge who became a folk hero, perfectly illustrates this theme. Samson was known for his strength. He was also a nazirite. You may be familiar with the fact that a nazirite is one who is dedicated to God in a special way. The outward signs of this internal dedication are that the nazirite never cuts his hair or drinks wine. Samuel and John the Baptist, as well as Samson, were nazirites from birth. Knowing that Samson is a nazirite allows us to see the real significance of his words to Delilah. "A razor has never touched my head, because I have been God's nazirite from my mother's womb. If my head were shorn, then my power would leave me and I should lose my strength and become like any other man" (Jgs 16:17).

In these words Samson is telling Delilah that his strength lies in his total commitment to Yahweh. His hair, his strength, is a symbol of this commitment. Should he stray from his total commitment to God, symbolized by cutting his hair, he would lose his strength.

The plot of the story confirms the truth of Samson's statement. When his commitment to God is broken, when his hair is cut, he loses his strength and is delivered into the hands of his enemies. When he returns to the Lord, when his hair grows back, his strength returns. He is thus able to overpower his enemies once more.

As was mentioned in Chapter I, editors appropriated stories already existent in the culture and retold them to suit their own purposes. In the Book of Judges we have a variety of appropriated literary forms: the song of Deborah (ch. 5), riddles which, whatever their original purpose, have been woven into the story of Samson (14:14; 14:18–19), and an old parable poem which has also been woven into the story, in addition to this delightful legend of Samson and Delilah. In each case material which grew up in oral literature, and which originally may not have had its present meaning, has been retold as part of Israel's religious history. It is certainly easy to see why the legend of Samson and Delilah was included since it embodies so clearly the central theme of the Book of Judges—infidelity to Yahweh brings disaster.

We have now discussed two characteristics of legend—the glorification of a hero through exaggeration and the inclusion of magical details which, in Scripture, are appropriated as symbols for religious truths. A third characteristic of legends is that they often include etiologies.

Etiologies

An etiology is a story which is told to explain the origin of something which is well known to the listener. In the Bible we see etiologies that purport to tell the origins of names of people and places (we have already read two explanations of why Beersheba is called Beersheba), the origins of institutions, ceremonies, nations and natural phenomena.

I recently read a column in Dear Abby which illustrated the way etiologies function. A reader, who described himself as a bird lover, had written in to complain about the derogatory nature of the phrase, "for the birds." He asked Abby to find out the origin of the phrase. Some time later Abby printed a number of explanations which her readers had sent her, all delightfully imaginative, all plausible, all different. Abby did not choose among these explanations—she printed several. When the editors arranged their inherited materials various etiologies already existed in the culture, and many were included. Here, too, those which are included are often given religious significance.

Genesis is full of etiologies. One very well known example of an etiological explanation in a legend is found in the legend about the destruction of Sodom.

> When the two angels reached Sodom in the evening, Lot was sitting at the gate. As soon as Lot saw them he rose to meet them and bowed to the ground. "I beg you, my lords," he said, "please come down to your servant's house to stay the night and wash your feet. Then in the morning you can

continue your journey." "No," they replied, "we can spend the night in the open street." But he pressed them so much that they went home with him and entered his house. He prepared a meal for them, baking unleavened bread, and they ate.

They had not gone to bed when the house was surrounded by the men of the town, the men of Sodom both young and old, all the people without exception. Calling to Lot they said, "Where are the men who came to you tonight? Send them out to us so that we may abuse them."

Lot came out to them at the door and, having closed the door behind him, said, "I beg you, my brothers, do no such wicked thing. Listen, I have two daughters who are virgins. I am ready to send them out to you, to treat as it pleases you. But as for the men, do nothing to them, for they have come under the shadow of my roof." But they replied, "Out of the way! Here is one who came as a foreigner, and would set himself up as a judge. Now we will treat you worse than them." Then they forced Lot back and moved forward to break down the door. But the men reached out, pulled Lot back into the house, and shut the door. And they struck the men who were at the door of the house with blindness, from youngest to oldest, and they never found the doorway.

The men said to Lot, "Have you anyone else here? Your sons, your daughters and all your people in the town, take them out of the place. We are about to destroy this place, for there is a great outcry against them, and it has reached Yahweh. And Yahweh has sent us to destroy them." Lot went to speak to his future sons-in-law who were to marry his daughters. "Come," he said, "leave this place, for Yahweh is about to destroy the town." But his sons-in-law thought he was joking.

When dawn broke the angels urged Lot, "Come, take your wife and these two daughters of yours, or you will be overwhelmed in the punishment of the town." And as he hesitated, the men took him by the hand, and his wife and his two daughters, because of the pity Yahweh felt for him. They led him out and left him outside the town.

As they were leading him out they said, "Run for your life. Neither look behind you nor stop anywhere on the plain. Make for the hills if you would not be overwhelmed."

> "No, I beg you, my Lord," Lot said to them, "your servant has won your favor and you have shown great kindness to me in saving my life. But I could not reach the hills before this calamity overtook me, and death with it. The town over there is near enough to flee to, and is a little one. Let me make for that—is it not little?—and my life will be saved." He answered, "I grant you this favor too, and will not destroy the town you speak of. Hurry, escape to it, for I can do nothing until you reach it." That is why the town is named Zoar.
>
> As the sun rose over the land and Lot entered Zoar, Yahweh rained on Sodom and Gomorrah brimstone and fire from Yahweh. He overthrew these towns and the whole plain, with all the inhabitants of the towns, and everything that grew there. But the wife of Lot looked back, and turned into a pillar of salt (Gen 19:1–26).

In this account we once again see many of the characteristics of legend which we have noted before. The story, in its present form, has a very clear theological intent. The destruction of the town, even if it historically resulted from an earthquake, is not viewed as a haphazard event but as an act of God and as a punishment for sin. Because of God's promise to Abraham, Lot is saved. God is always faithful to his promises. A modern reader is shocked by Lot's offer to send his virgin daughters out to the men instead of his guests. In our culture women are not just property, to be used in whatever way serves the needs of hospitality. This lack of moral sensitivity shows that the roots of the legend are very old. Included in the legend are etiologies, one in verse 22 to explain the name of the town Zoar and the second in verse 26 to explain the presence of a boulder or rock formation which was undoubtedly well known to the listeners.

> But the wife of Lot looked back, and was turned into a pillar of salt.

Many students, upon reading this verse, ask, "Why would God turn Lot's wife into a pillar of salt?" Such a question flows from a lack of knowledge about the literary form. The pertinent question is, "Why did the editor retain this etiological detail in the legend of the destruction of Sodom?" This dramatic touch not only added interest for generations of audiences, but it gave them a concrete symbol of the danger of "looking back," of not being totally committed to the ways of God. Lot's wife becomes a symbol in the legend for those who remain "on the fence," who are undecided and ambivalent about choosing God over evil. Once more the author is calling his audience to total commitment and fidelity to their God.

Legend as a Vehicle for Revelation

In all that we have said about legend we have constantly emphasized the fact that the biblical authors and editors use the genre as a vehicle for revelation. These legends appear in the Bible because they reflect man's growing understanding of God and man's relationship with God. We must never forget, when reading the Old Testament or the New, that this coming to knowledge occurred slowly over time. A well known legend which clearly shows this step by step coming to knowledge about God and how he wants us to act is the story of the sacrifice of Isaac.

> It happened some time later that God put Abraham to the test. "Abraham, Abraham," he called. "Here I am," he replied. "Take your son," God said, "your only child Isaac, whom you love, and go to the land of Moriah. There you shall offer him as a burnt offering, on a mountain I will point out to you."
>
> Rising early next morning Abraham saddled his ass and took with him two of his servants and his son Isaac. He chopped wood for the burnt offering and started on his journey to the place God had pointed out to him. On the third day Abraham looked up and saw the place in the distance. Then Abraham said to his servants, "Stay here with the donkey. The boy and I will go over there; we will worship and come back to you."
>
> Abraham took the wood for the burnt offering, loaded it on Isaac, and carried in his own hands the fire and the knife. Then the two of them set out together. Isaac spoke

> to his father Abraham. "Father," he said. "Yes, my son," he replied. "Look," he said, "here are the fire and the wood, but where is the lamb for the burnt offering?" Abraham answered, "My son, God himself will provide the lamb for the burnt offering." Then the two of them went on together.
>
> When they arrived at the place God had pointed out to him, Abraham built an altar there, and arranged the wood. Then he bound his son Isaac and put him on the altar on top of the wood. Abraham stretched out his hand and seized the knife to kill his son.
>
> But the angel of Yahweh called to him from heaven. "Abraham, Abraham," he said. "I am here," he replied. "Do not raise your hand against the boy," the angel said. "Do not harm him, for now I know you fear God. You have not refused me your son, your only son." Then looking up, Abraham saw a ram caught by its horns in a bush. Abraham took the ram and offered it as a burnt-offering in place of his son. Abraham called this place "Yahweh provides," and hence the saying today: On the mountain Yahweh provides.
>
> The angel of Yahweh called Abraham a second time from heaven: "I swear by my own self—it is Yahweh who speaks—because you have done this, because you have not refused me your son, your only son, I will shower blessings on you. I will make your descendants as many as the stars of heaven and the grains of sand on the seashore. Your descendants shall gain possession of the gates of their enemies. All the nations of the earth shall bless themselves by your descendants, as a reward for your obedience."
>
> Abraham went back to his servants, and together they set out for Beersheba, and he settled in Beersheba (Gen 22:1–19).

The legend of the sacrifice of Isaac is recognized as one of the most powerful and poignant stories in all Scripture. It has two levels of meaning, each of which involves the human heart in an unbearably difficult choice.

God and Child Sacrifice

At one level we see in the story of Abraham a man coming to the realization that his God is not one who wants or demands child sacrifice. In the Canaanite culture children were sacrificed by burning. The Israelites offered all their first fruits to Yahweh, but they came to the realization that their God did not want child sacrifice. While they sacrificed the first born males of animals, they redeemed or bought back the first born males of people (Ex 13:11).

Even though Abraham came to realize that God did not want child sacrifice, and prohibitions against it were eventually written into the law, child sacrifice was occasionally practiced by the leaders in Israel. In 2 Kings we read of two kings of Judah, Ahaz and Manasseh, who did not do what was pleasing to Yahweh but had their sons "pass through fire" (2 Kgs 16:1–4; 21:6). King Josiah, who was a great reformer, "removed the furnace in the Valley of Ben-hinnon so that no one could make his son or daughter pass through fire in honor of Molech" (2 Kgs 23:10).

To a twentieth century reader it often comes as a surprise to realize that Abraham's contemporaries and descendants might have struggled with the question of whether or not it would please God to sacrifice to him the first fruits of the womb. We often take our New Testament view of God and presume that the patriarchs had just the same ideas. For Abraham, it was a huge step forward in understanding to realize that his God was present, powerful, loving, and able to move around with him. Abraham's religious experience convinced him that God knew him personally, cared about him personally, and acted in his life with power and purpose. He believed that God would protect him and his descendants in order to fulfill his promise and his purpose. Abraham's concept of God represents a mind-boggling leap forward in revelation. But Abraham's contemporaries and immediate descendants were not yet clear on monotheism, they did not realize that their God loved all people, not just them, and they had not come to a realization of the kind of unconditional love which God not only offered them but required that they offer one another. We see these latter insights develop over time and come to clear definition with the prophets who lived about one thousand years after Abraham. As we appreciate Abraham's profound religious insights we must also be aware of the insights which belong to later generations and which should not be projected back onto Abraham.

Faith Forced To Grow

While the question of child sacrifice did not continue to remain a moral dilemma through the centuries, the legend of Abraham's struggle did continue to be told and retold. To this day, this story has not lost its power and universal appeal. The legend has universal significance in that it so poignantly portrays the dilemma of a man of faith confronted with a situation which challenges that faith to its deepest roots.

The background for the legend of the sacrifice of Isaac would have been familiar to those who listened to the story over the years. They would be fully aware of God's promise to Abraham, which depends on Isaac's existence, and of the trials of faith already endured by Abraham while awaiting the birth of Isaac.

Legends were often told to contemporary audiences for the purpose of instruction. The didactic purpose for which this legend was told is revealed in the opening verse, "It happened some time later that God put Abraham to the test." The narrator wants his audience to view Abraham's experience as a test of faith because that is the part of the experience which is applicable to them.

Abraham, from his first "Here I am," is presented as a perfect model of a faithful man. Abraham has no idea in the world how God's purpose can and will be fulfilled in him. But Abraham does not need to understand; he needs only to rely completely on his God, trust in him, be obedient to him, have faith in his goodness, his purpose, his truthfulness and his covenant.

Now we hear the narrator tell us of Abraham's terrible dilemma, for he pictures God as saying, "Take thy son, thy only son Isaac, whom thou lovest." The sparsity of language in the Hebrew legend accounts for some of its power. What does Abraham think as he struggles with this terrible duty? What does he say? We are not told any of this. The silence portrays Abraham's numbness more than any long description could. No relief is given Abraham or the listener as Abraham rises early in the morning and makes his three day journey in the time it takes to say so.

That Abraham arose early is only one of the many details which portray so clearly the fact that Abraham's faith never falters. He says to his servants, "The boy and I will go over there; we will worship and come back to you." If his voice cracked and his heart broke with the ". . . and come back to you." we are not told of it. Abraham's unswerving faith is again shown in his "God himself will provide the lamb for the burnt offering." Abraham could not know how Isaac was to be saved, or even that Isaac was to be saved, but he knew God's promise to his seed. Somehow, God would provide. Again we notice the power in the sparsity of language. All that we learn of Abraham's character we learn through action and conversation. There are no narrative descriptions of his character.

Without delay Abraham builds an altar, lays the wood, binds Isaac to the wood, and stretches forth his hand with the knife to slay his son. Did they speak? Did Isaac struggle? We do not know. We know only that Abraham is walking in faith. Where will it lead him?

But the angel of Yahweh called to him from heaven. "Abraham, Abraham," he said. "I am here," he replied. The same words were said in answer to God's voice. Hebrew style often repeats phrases word for word, but more than style is at work here. Abraham is still here, still in God's sight and unwaveringly fulfilling his commands as he understands them. "Here I am" fully expresses Abraham's presence before his God, his willingness to do God's bidding.

The divine messenger then replies, "Do not raise your hand against the boy. Do not harm him, for now I know you fear God. You have not refused me your son, your only son." The relief of tension, not only for Abraham but for the listening audience, is immense. The poignant words, "your son, your only son," which originally weighed our grief now add to our relief. The minor inconsistency in the identification of the voice (was it an angel or God?) would not have bothered the listeners. All through the legends of Genesis and Exodus we see God's presence represented in different traditions with different imagery. Sometimes an anthropomorphic God appears himself, sometimes an angel is pictured as his messenger, sometimes God is a cloud or a pillar of fire. While the image varies the faith behind the image does not. God is with his people.

Abraham's test of faith is over. He offers a ram as a burnt offering in place of his son. The narrator reminds his listeners of God's promise to Abraham, a promise which they experience as being made to them too.

> I will shower blessings on you. I will make your descendants as many as the stars of heaven and the grains of sand on the seashore. Your descendants shall gain possession of the gates of their enemies. All the nations of the earth shall bless themselves by your descendants, as a reward for your obedience (Gen 22:17–18).

As the listeners hear the words of the promise once more, words which fill them with feelings of awe, purpose, hope and courage, they also recognize that they must try to emulate Abraham's faith under the most difficult of circumstances. Like Abraham, they too must walk in darkness, struggling to understand the ways of God as he reveals himself to them in the events of their daily lives. They too must walk in faith and obedience during difficult times when the ways of God are totally beyond their comprehension. And so must we. This legend about Abraham and Isaac is revelation because it reveals the truth about who God is: he is a loving God who does not demand child sacrifice. The legend also reveals the truth about how we must act in our relationship with our God—we must faithfully trust his love no matter what the circumstances.

Review Questions

1. What is a legend? How does it differ from a myth?
2. What is history?
3. What effect does a background of oral tradition have on "quotations"?
4. How can we account for the fact that the stories about the patriarchs often lack logical connections and sometimes seem to lack reasonable chronology?
5. How can we account for the fact that we might read two accounts of the same story but not always with the same characters?
6. What did the claim of longevity mean to the Hebrews?
7. What effects does editing have on a text?
8. How do the two accounts about Abraham asking Sarah to say she is his sister show a growth in religious sensibilities?
9. What does the phrase "a religious interpretation of events" mean? How does this concept relate to the account of the patriarchs?
10. What is the difference between interpreting an event religiously and claiming the event is a miracle? Are these two points of view identical?
11. Why might exaggeration be included in a legend? Is exaggeration the same as a religious interpretation of events? Why or why not?
12. Religious systems appropriate customs or beliefs from previous cultures and redefine them to express new religious understandings. How is this fact illustrated by the Hebrews' use of magical details or curses and blessings? For what religious purpose are these ideas appropriated?
13. What is the theme of the Book of Judges?
14. What is an etiological story?
15. In the story of the destruction of Sodom, what religious purpose is served by including the etiological detail of Lot's wife being turned into a pillar of salt?

16. In the legend about the sacrifice of Isaac, what does Abraham learn about God's desires and demands?

17. To what purpose does the narrator continue to retell the legend of the sacrifice of Isaac?

Discussion Questions

1. What basis do we have for claiming an historic base to the stories about Abraham but not to the story about Adam?
2. Why would the Bible picture God as cursing other nations?
3. Can you think of some ways Americans have of communicating which depend on presumed knowledge and which would not be understood by a person from another culture? Name several.
4. Can you think of Old Testament accounts which surprised you because they reflect some moral insensitivity? How can such accounts be explained?
5. Do you interpret events religiously? Give some examples.
6. What is the difference between seeing an event as a sign of God's presence and seeing it as a miracle?
7. When you tell a story about events in your life do you ever use exaggeration? Why? How might this experience of yours relate to biblical accounts?
8. Can you think of practices which have religious significance in our lives which have been appropriated from a non-Christian culture and have been redefined to express Christian beliefs?
9. Can you think of any etiological explanations for rituals, phrases, or physical phenomena in our culture? How do you think such explanations come about? What motivation would account for including some etiologies in Scripture?
10. Have you ever been in a situation which forced you to grow in faith? What similarities are there between your experience and Abraham's?

4

Debate

The Book of Job introduces us to a literary form substantially different from myth or legend. However, what we have learned about the story of the man and the woman in the garden in Chapter II and what we have learned about legend in Chapter III are helpful backgrounds for understanding both the form and the meaning in the Book of Job.

The Problem of Suffering

The Book of Job is related to the story of the man and the woman in the garden, not because they are the same literary form (they are not) but because they are addressing the same problem. Both works are about the problem of suffering.

In order to understand the content and form of the Book of Job it is important to know what the original audience of this work thought about the problem of suffering.

It is no wonder that the Israelites had continued to struggle with this problem over the centuries. Each time the nation met with disaster or destruction the problem of suffering and its meaning once more came to the surface. When the Book of Job was composed the Jewish people had been forced to re-examine and redefine all of their sacred traditions because of the experience of the Babylonian exile. But earlier re-examinations had occurred throughout the history of the chosen people.

Perhaps you remember, when reading the legends of Abraham in the Book of Genesis, that Abraham is pictured as interceding with God on behalf of the just in the town of Sodom (Gen 18:16–32). Abraham asks God, "Are you really going to destroy the just man with the sinner?" This is a very important question because it reflects the belief that there would be something wrong if an innocent person were to suffer. As in the story of the man and woman in the garden, we can understand that a sinner might suffer, but that a just person would suffer doesn't seem right. Abraham's question also reflects a strong sense of collective responsibility. Abraham never asks God if he might take the innocent out of the town before he destroys it, but only if God would refrain from destroying the town for the sake of the just. In his dialogue with God, Abraham asks if the town would be saved for the sake of fifty, forty-five, forty, thirty and ten just men. In each instance God says he will not destroy the city for the sake of that number. However, Abraham never goes below ten. The question of how much further God would go in withholding punishment from the wicked for the sake of the just is left up to our imagination.

Like Abraham, we can see the problem. We find it difficult to believe that a loving, all powerful God would allow an innocent person to suffer. We understand the outrage in Abraham's tone when he says:

> Do not think of doing such a thing, to kill the just man with the sinner, treating just and sinner alike! Do not think of it! Will the judge of the whole earth not administer justice? (Gen 18:25–26).

When it comes to the question of an innocent person's suffering, God's reputation is at stake. Could a just God allow such a thing?

Although the legend about Abraham never gives us an answer to the question of whether God would refrain from destroying a town for the sake of a single just person, the prophet Ezekiel does. Ezekiel was a prophet during the exile.

Ezekiel believed that God would spare a town for the sake of one just man, but one just man was nowhere to be found. Ezekiel, in his prophetic oracle, laments this fact as he pictures God saying, "I have been looking for someone among them to build a wall and man the breach in front of me, to defend the country and prevent me from destroying it; but I have not found anyone. Hence I have discharged my anger on them; I have destroyed them in the fire of my fury. I have made their conduct recoil on their own heads—it is the Lord Yahweh who speaks" (Ez 22:30–31).

Ezekiel saw man not just as a member of a community, but also as an individual who bears personal responsibility for sin. In Ezekiel's view, an innocent person would not have suffered had an innocent person been found. God would not punish the innocent. Ezekiel believed this so strongly that he taught against the generally accepted belief that a person might suffer, not for his own sins, but for the sins of his parents. In Ezekiel 18:1–4 we read:

> The word of Yahweh was addressed to me as follows, "Why do you keep repeating this proverb in the land of Israel:
>
> The fathers have eaten unripe grapes;
> and the children's teeth are set on edge?
>
> As I live—it is the Lord Yahweh who speaks—there will no longer be any reason to repeat this proverb in Israel. See now: all life belongs to me; the father's life and the son's life, both alike belong to me. The man who has sinned, he is the one who shall die."

It is interesting to note that while Ezekiel denied that children suffer for the sins of their parents, there is evidence that the Jewish people still held this view when Jesus was alive. In John's Gospel the people ask Jesus the reason why a man was born blind: "Rabbi, who sinned, this man or his parents, for him to have been born blind?" (Jn 9:2). It is still inconceivable to them that an innocent person might suffer.

The author of Job is writing later than Ezekiel but well before John, probably from 400–300 B.C. The author is well acquainted with the thinking of his people in regard to an innocent person's suffering. He knows that his audience would reject such an idea out of hand. But the author of Job does not agree with this thinking. It is his observation of life that the innocent do suffer. He wants to confront his audience with this excruciatingly painful mystery. But how to do it? The author of Job picks a literary technique which today we would call a debate. He frames his debate with a legend which he uses to set the stage and to draw to a conclusion the profound problem he has raised. In order to understand the power and purpose of the Book of Job we must understand both the prose legend which forms the frame and the poetic debate which forms the body of the book.

Frame—Prose Legend

> There was once a man in the land of Uz called Job: a sound and honest man who feared God and shunned evil. Seven sons and three daughters were born to him. And he owned seven thousand sheep, three thousand camels, five hundred yoke of oxen and five hundred she-donkeys, and many servants besides. This man was indeed a man of mark among all the people of the East. It was the custom of his sons to hold banquets in each other's houses, one after the other, and to send and invite their three sisters to eat and drink with them. Once each series of banquets was over, Job would send for them to come and be purified, and at dawn on the following day he would offer a holocaust for each of them. "Perhaps," Job would say, "my sons have sinned and in their hearts affronted God." So that was what he used to do after each series.
>
> One day the sons of God came to attend on Yahweh, and among them was Satan. So Yahweh said to Satan, "Where have you been?" "Round the earth," he answered, "roaming about." So Yahweh asked him, "Did you notice my servant Job? There is no one like him on the earth; a sound and honest man who fears God and shuns evil." "Yes," Satan said, "but Job is not God-fearing for nothing, is he? Have you not put a wall round him and his house and all his domain? You have blessed all he undertakes, and his flocks throng the countryside. But stretch out your hand and lay a finger on his possessions: I warrant you, he

will curse you to your face." "Very well," Yahweh said to Satan, "all he has is in your power. But keep your hands off his person." So Satan left the presence of Yahweh.

On the day when Job's sons and daughters were at their meal and drinking wine at their eldest brother's house, a messenger came to Job. "Your oxen," he said "were at the plough, with the donkeys grazing at their side, when the Sabaeans swept down on them and carried them off. Your servants they put to the sword: I alone escaped to tell you." He had not finished speaking when another messenger arrived. "The fire of God," he said, "has fallen from the heavens and burnt up all your sheep, and your shepherds too: I alone escaped to tell you." He had not finished speaking when another messenger arrived. "The Chaldaeans," he said, "three bands of them, have raided your camels and made off with them. Your servants they put to the sword: I alone escaped to tell you." He had not finished speaking when another messenger arrived. "Your sons and daughters," he said, "were at their meal and drinking wine at their eldest brother's house, when suddenly from the wilderness a gale sprang up, and it battered all four corners of the house which fell in on the young people. They are dead: I alone escaped to tell you."

Job rose and tore his gown and shaved his head. Then falling to the ground he worshiped and said:

"Naked I came from my mother's womb,
naked I shall return.
Yahweh gave, Yahweh has taken back.
Blessed be the name of Yahweh!"

In all this misfortune Job committed no sin nor offered any insult to God. Once again the sons of God came to attend on Yahweh, and among them was Satan. So Yahweh said to Satan, "Where have you been?" "Round the earth," he answered, "roaming about." So Yahweh asked him, "Did you notice my servant Job? There is no one like him on the earth: a sound and honest man who fears God and shuns evil. His life continues blameless as ever; in vain you provoked me to ruin him." "Skin from skin!" Satan replied. "A man will give away all he has to save his life. But stretch out your hand and lay a finger on his bone

> and flesh; I warrant you, he will curse you to your face." "Very well," Yahweh said to Satan, "he is in your power. But spare his life." So Satan left the presence of Yahweh.
>
> He struck Job down with malignant ulcers from the sole of his foot to the top of his head. Job took a piece of pot to scrape himself, and went and sat in the ashpit. Then his wife said to him, "Do you now still mean to persist in your blamelessness? Curse God, and die." "That is how foolish women talk," Job replied. "If we take happiness from God's hand, must we not take sorrow too?" And in all this misfortune Job uttered no sinful word.
>
> The news of all the disasters that had fallen on Job came to the ears of three of his friends. Each of them set out from home—Eliphaz of Teman, Bildad of Shuah and Zophar of Naamath—and by common consent they decided to go and offer him sympathy and consolation. Looking at him from a distance, they could not recognize him; they wept aloud and tore their garments and threw dust over their heads. They sat there on the ground beside him for seven days and seven nights. To Job they spoke never a word, so sad a sight he made (Job 1:1–2:13).

After reading the first two chapters of the Book of Job a person who knows nothing about its literary form often finds himself or herself totally puzzled. Why was Satan attending Yahweh? Why would God be so petty and weak as to give in to Satan's taunting and allow Job to suffer? What does all this mean? Such questions flow from a misunderstanding about the literary form.

The frame of the Book of Job could be described as a legend. Job was a legendary person to the Israelites, one who probably lived at the time of the patriarchs and had a reputation for being a just man. Job's name appears in Ezekiel as one known for his personal integrity (Ez 14:14, 20). In its original form, this legend seems to be grappling with the same problem which the Book of Job addresses. Can an innocent man suffer? However, the legend embraces a solution which the Book of Job, as a whole, rejects. Job's suffering is merely a test. Because Job is virtuous he is rewarded on earth. In the end Job has double what he had before (see Job 42:7–17).

Purpose of Frame

The debate which is framed by the legend raises much more serious questions, and offers much less of an easy answer to the problem of an innocent person's suffering. Since there is some tension between the point of view offered in the frame and the point of view put forth by the body of the Book of Job, one must ask why the author of the book framed his debate with this legend.

The legend is used as a literary device to set the scene for the debate. The way in which the legend functions might be compared to the way the narrator functions at the beginning of the play *Our Town*. The narrator comes out on a completely empty stage. He informs the audience that there are two houses on the stage, and tells us something about who lives in each of them. No one in the audience mentions that he or she doesn't see any houses. We all accept what the narrator says because he is merely setting the stage for what is to follow. The frame of the Book of Job sets the stage in the same way. The legend is used to say, in a dramatic and interesting way, that for the sake of what is to follow the audience must accept two facts: Job is innocent, and Job is suffering. That these two facts are simultaneously true is an impossibility for the audience. Such a situation would be tantamount to denying that God is all loving and all powerful. But the author gets his audience to accept the two facts through the literary technique of using a traditional legend to set the stage.

The audience would not have a modern day reader's question about why Satan is in God's presence. The word "Satan" would not have meant "devil" or "fallen angel" to the contemporary audience. Rather, the word would have been understood to refer to a good angel whose job it was to police the earth and report man's offenses to God. An American reader can understand the role of this "Satan" or "adversary" by comparing him to a prosecuting attorney. Satan, in this legend, is a good angel who is doing God's will.

One benefit which this concept of an angel assigned the role of adversary offers to the author of the Book of Job is that it allows him to separate God, to some degree, from the sufferings which Job is to endure. God is pictured as allowing the sufferings but not as causing the sufferings. To the author, this slight disassociation on God's part from actually inflicting the sufferings is no real defense, but to an audience who has accepted the idea of a short test of faith, the concept becomes a useful one. For the time being the audience will accept that Job is innocent and suffering.

In addition to using the legend to set the scene and cajole the audience into accepting as compatible two ideas which it really considers incompatible, the author of the Book of Job uses his framing device to establish dramatic irony in the debate which will follow. Dramatic irony exists when the audience or reader knows something which the characters in the story do not know. In the debate, Eliphaz, Bildad, Zophar, and Elihu debate with Job about the meaning of his suffering. As the debate continues Job's four friends lose faith in his innocence. The audience never loses faith in Job's innocence. The legend framing device has established Job's innocence beyond all doubt. We know Job is innocent because God said he was.

As the debate proceeds we will notice other ways in which the framing device interacts with the debate. But before going on to the debate we should notice that the frame is used to dismiss one other problem. Some people, when confronted with suffering, do not, like Job, try to search out the meaning of the suffering. Instead they simply get angry. Job's wife's response represents and dismisses this angry, irrational response. A person who neglects to look for meaning, but merely gives up, will never come to grips with the problem which the author of the Book of Job is going to explore.

The Debate

We move now to the body of the Book of Job, a debate which consists of three series of speeches. In each series each friend speaks and Job responds to each. After the friends have spoken for the third time, another character, Elihu, appears and he also rebukes Job. Finally Yahweh appears and responds to Job and his dilemma. We will not go into a discus-

**STRUCTURE OF DEBATE
IN THE BOOK OF JOB**

Eliphaz's Three Speeches	**Job's Responses**
Chapters 4–5	Chapters 6–7
Chapter 15	Chapters 16–17
Chapter 22	Chapters 23–24

Bildad's Three Speeches	**Job's Responses**
Chapter 8	Chapters 9–10
Chapter 18	Chapter 19
25:1–6; 26:5–14	26:1–4; 27:1–12

Zophar's Three Speeches	**Job's Responses**
Chapter 11	Chapters 12–14
Chapter 20	Chapter 21
24:18–24 ?;27:13–23 ?	Chapters 29–31

The debate consists of three cycles of arguments. The third cycle presents problems and various attempts have been made to reconstruct it. Chapters 32–37 are Elihu's rebuke of Job.

sion of whether or not the debate, in its present form, is the work of a single author, or whether editorial changes have been made, such as the insertion of Elihu into the narrative. Rather, we will accept the work as it now stands in the canon.

The debate starts with Job expressing his misery. Job is so miserable that he would rather be dead. Job asks:

> Why give light to a man of grief?
> Why give life to those bitter of heart,
> Who long for a death that never comes,
> and hunt for it more than for a buried treasure?
> They would be glad to see the grave mound
> and shout with joy if they reached the tomb. (Job 3:20–22).

Retribution

Eliphaz is the first to try to help Job understand his suffering. He believes in the traditional doctrine of retribution. Eliphaz asks Job:

> Can you recall a guiltless man that perished,
> or have you ever seen good men brought to nothing?
> I speak of what I know: Those who plow iniquity
> and sow the seeds of grief reap a harvest of the same kind
> (Job 4:7–8).

Job does not accept Eliphaz's understanding of what is happening to him. Job is very miserable and his misery is increased by his feelings of disillusionment toward his friends.

> My brothers have been fickle as a torrent,
> as the course of a seasonal stream (Job 6:15).

> So, at this time, do you behave to me:
> one sight of me, and then you flee in fright (Job 6:21).

> Put me right, I will say no more;
> show me where I have been at fault.
> Fair comment can be borne without resentment,
> but what is the basis for your strictures?
> Do you think mere words deserve censure,
> desperate speech that the wind blows away? (Job 6:24–26).

Job resents the traditional theory of retribution because it is accusing him of wrong-doing when he believes he has done no wrong. By solving the problem of Job's suffering with the pat answer of retribution, Job's friends have misjudged and hurt him at the very time when he desperately needed their faith, understanding and support.

In addition to being disappointed with his friends, Job is disappointed with God. Job's sufferings are so intense that even if Job had sinned, which he hasn't, the suffering could never be understood as a just punishment. What kind of God is this who would inflict or allow such suffering even as a punishment?

> Will you never take your eyes off me
> long enough for me to swallow my spittle?
> Suppose I have sinned, what have I done to you,
> you tireless watcher of mankind?
> Why do you choose me as your target?
> Why should I be a burden to you? (Job 7:19–20)

The next speaker is Bildad who agrees with Eliphaz that all suffering must be due to sin.

> Is there no end to these words of yours,
> to your long-winded blustering?
> Can God deflect the course of right
> or Shaddai falsify justice?
> If your sons sinned against him,
> they have paid for their sins;
> So you too, if so pure and honest,
> must now seek God, plead with Shaddai.
> Without delay he will restore his favor to you,
> will see that the good man's house is rebuilt.
> Your former state will seem to you as nothing
> beside your new prosperity (Job 8:1–7).

When Eliphaz spoke the audience's initial response was probably to agree with him. With Job's claims of innocence, though, they can see that Eliphaz is wrong. The frame puts Job's innocence beyond question. Now, as Bildad supports Eliphaz's point of view, the doctrine of retribution becomes less and less tenable in the audience's mind. Because they know that Job is truly innocent and truly suffering, Bildad's response makes him seem judgmental and unsympathetic. To suggest that Job's dead sons have merely paid for their sins is cruel. After all, when all was well with Job he used to offer sacrifice just in case his sons might have sinned, although he had no reason to think they had. Surely Job cannot view his son's deaths as the punishment of a just God for sin. Nor can he view his own suffering as a test which will soon end. These explanations no longer satisfy Job or the audience. Bildad's question, "Can God deflect the cause of right or Shaddai falsify justice?" is meant to be rhetorical. The answer should be, "Of course not!" But given the context in which the question is asked, the audience is confronted with the possibility that God is deflecting the course of right. Job's suffering brings God's justice into question.

Is God Just?

In response to Bildad's easy answers, Job puts into words the terrible question which has formed in the minds of the audience. He asks God:

> Is it right for you to injure me,
> cheapening the work of your own hands
> and abetting the schemes of the wicked? (Job 10:2–3).
>
> You who inquire into my faults
> and investigate my sins.
> You know very well that I am innocent,
> and that no one can rescue me from your hand (Job 10:6–7).

The implication of Job's words is that God should stop inquiring into Job's faults and Job's sins since God's virtue is itself being called into question. Job wants only for this unjust God to leave him alone since he is too powerful to fight or defeat.

> And if I make a stand, like a lion you hunt me down,
> adding to the tale of your triumphs.
> You attack and attack me again,
> with stroke on stroke of your fury.
> Relentlessly your fresh troops assail me (Job 10:16–17).
>
> Turn your eyes away, leave me a little joy,
> before I go to the place of no return,
> the land of murk and deep shadow . . . (Job 10:21–22).

The author of the Book of Job cannot have his character look forward to a reward in the next life because at the time this debate was written, the Israelites had no clear idea of a life after death in which the good are rewarded and the evil are punished. The Israelites did develop this belief some one hundred and fifty years before the time of Christ, as we know from reading the Book of Wisdom and 2 Maccabees. But at the time the author of the Book of Job is writing he cannot suggest the future hope of "heaven" as a possible solution for Job's suffering.

Zophar, the third of Job's friends, can add nothing to the arguments of his friends. He too believes that Job must have sinned or he would not be suffering. He accuses Job:

> These were your words, "My way of life is faultless,
> and in your eyes I am free from blame."
> But if God had a mind to speak,
> to open his lips and give you answer,
> Were he to show you the secrets of wisdom
> which put all cleverness to shame—
> you would know it is for sin he calls you to account (Job 11:3–6).

Intellectual Honesty

Job's response to Zophar is absolute outrage. He accuses Zophar and his friends of being willfully dishonest because they refuse to face reality but continue to repeat pat answers that are obviously inadequate. Job says:

> As for you, you are only charlatans,
> physicians in your own estimation.
> I wish someone would teach you to be quiet,
> the only wisdom that becomes you!
> Kindly listen to my accusation,
> pay attention to the pleading of my lips.
> Will you plead God's defense with prevarication,
> his case in terms that ring false? (Job 13:4–7).

Job believes that while his friends seem to be defending God, since they have to be dishonest to do it, they are actually sinning. Job doesn't believe that God would want a defense such as this.

> Will you be partial in his favour,
> and act as his advocates?
> For you to meet his scrutiny, would this be well?
> Can he be duped as men be duped?
> Harsh rebuke you would receive from him
> for your covert partiality (Job 13:8–10).

Since Job believes that God can see the truth of everything, he believes God knows he is innocent. If God knows he is innocent then God must himself be guilty because he is treating Job unfairly. Job wants to accuse God, put him on trial, reveal God's unjust treatment in order to justify himself.

> Let him kill me if he will; I have no other hope
> than to justify my conduct in his eyes (Job 13:15).

> You shall see, I will proceed by due form of law,
> persuaded, as I am, that I am guiltless.
> Who comes against me with an accusation?
> Let him come! (Job 13:18–19).

Job has put God in contradictory roles. On the one hand he sees God as all knowing and honest, as one who does not want to be defended with lies. Job believes that God finds his agonized questions more pleasing than his friends' shallow answers because the questions are more honest than the answers. On the other hand Job sees God as guilty himself, not one who sets the standards for good but one who fails to live up to those standards himself. In the trial God seems to be both the just judge and the one standing accused. Job has probed truth as far as he can. He has asked a profoundly troubling question but he can offer no answer. The answers his friends offer are grossly inadequate.

As the debate continues the audience becomes more and more impressed with the shallowness of the answers which previously they had accepted as adequate. As Eliphaz, Bildad and Zophar continue to misjudge Job, thus continuing to evade the problem which Job presents, the real evil of their position becomes more evident. Job's friends are not defending God with their shallow dishonest responses. Rather, they are defending their own security. They are afraid to face Job's question because they don't know the answer. Their fear of the unknown causes them to misrepresent God. In seeming to defend God, they are actually accusing him of being the kind of God who would punish man's infractions with horrible diseases and unbearable grief. What kind of a God is that? The debate exposes the friends as judgmental, unsympathetic, intellectually dishonest, and as terrible advocates for a loving God.

God's Answer

Neither Job nor his friends, Elihu included, can solve the dilemma with which they have been confronted by Job's suffering. Now that all human wisdom has been exhausted, the author has God appear to respond to all that has preceded.

> Then from the heart of the tempest Yahweh gave Job his answer. He said:
>
> Who is this obscuring my designs
> with his empty-headed words?
> Brace yourself like a fighter;
> Now it is my turn to ask questions, and yours to inform me (Job 38:1–2).

God then proceeds to ask Job question after question, the answers to which are all totally beyond Job's comprehension. We can see immediately that God's questions are the composition of the author as they reflect his idea of the earth's shape.

> Where were you when I laid the earth's foundation?
> Tell me since you're so well informed.
> Who decided the dimensions of it, do you know?
> Or who stretched the measuring line across it?
> What supports its pillars at their bases? (Job 38:4–6).

After reading the Book of Job, chapters 38–42, many students feel some disappointment and even some outrage. There are two problems to be addressed. One is the tone of God's response. The other is the content—where is Job's answer?

Many students feel that the character of God as he appears in this debate is as unsympathetic to Job as were Job's friends. They think of God's tone as being sarcastic and belittling. It is sometimes difficult to determine tone of voice in a written rather than a spoken dialogue. However, to correctly interpret the tone is very important because the tone influences the meaning. One way to determine tone is to see how the person being addressed responds. We know Job is not afraid to confront God with what Job understands to be his faults. If God had belittled Job, Job would have pressed God for an honest response as he did his four friends. Job does not respond as one who has been belittled or as one who has been treated dishonestly or vaguely. Rather Job responds as one full of reverence and awe.

> I have been holding forth on matters I cannot understand,
> on marvels beyond me and my knowledge. . . .
> I knew you then only by hearsay,
> but now, having seen you with my own eyes,
> I retract all I have said, and in dust and ashes I repent (Job 42:5–6).

Job has not taken offense at God's questions. Rather, he has become aware that there is a great deal that he does not understand. Previously Job had acted as though the problem of suffering was the only thing in all of creation which was beyond his comprehension. Now Job understands that this is only one of a myriad of things which he is incapable of understanding.

So, part of the "answer" Job receives is that the answer to his question is beyond his comprehension. However, this is not all Job learns from God's questions. God asks Job:

> Who carves a channel for the downpour,
> and hacks a way for the rolling thunder,

> So that rain may fall on lands where no one lives,
> and the deserts void of human dwelling,
> Giving drink to the lonely wastes
> and making grass spring where everything was dry? (Job 38:25–27).

God reminds Job that the world and all of creation is ordered. There is order and beauty even where no human beings live. Job is trying to figure out the order of creation with himself as the center. He wants everything to make sense to him as it impinges on his life, his experience, his feelings. If Job, or even human beings, were the center of creation, why would God create, water, and allow to flourish lands on which no person lives? Job will never understand the order and purpose of creation as long as he views himself as the center of that order, as long as he views himself as the point from which all else must find its meaning. Job is part of a created, ordered world which he did not create and did not order. He is able to perceive only a tiny part of reality. It is no wonder he doesn't understand the mystery of suffering.

Since the order of creation is beyond Job's comprehension and he is not the center of that order, does that mean that Job understands no more after God appears to him than he did before? No, Job's peace of mind rests on the fact that he does learn something from all that God has to say which satisfies him. What does Job learn?

First, Job learns that despite the mystery of his suffering, God is not only present and powerful but God is loving. While Job was blessed he believed that God was present, powerful and loving. After he suffered he never lost faith that God was present and powerful, but he did begin to question whether or not he was loving. How could a loving God allow an innocent person to suffer? By the very fact that the author has God appear to Job and respond to his questions, he pictures a God who loves Job and wants Job to know that he is loved. Job recognizes God's love once he is in his presence and never asks God the question he intended to ask nor charges God with what he had previously perceived to be God's failings. Why does Job not ask? Because the question has become insignificant. Once he is in God's presence Job no longer needs to ask.

Not only has Job experienced God's caring love, but he has grown in faith. Through God's questions Job not only realizes that he is incapable of understanding the order and purpose of all that exists, but he also realizes that all that exists does have order and purpose. The fact that Job doesn't understand what that purpose is does not mean that the purpose doesn't exist. The fact that Job does not, indeed cannot, understand the purpose of his suffering does not mean that his suffering has no purpose. Job comes to believe that his suffering does have purpose, but Job does not know what that purpose is.

Revelation a Process

"Why," students ask, "did the author of the Book of Job not have God tell Job the purpose of his suffering? Why did the author not have God tell Job that there is life after death and that suffering has a redemptive role in the coming of the kingdom?" The reason the author did not have God tell Job these truths is that the author did not know them. The author could not reveal what had not been revealed to him. A belief in life after death and a belief in the redemptive power of suffering are both later developments in the process of revelation.

"Why, then," we might ask, "is this book considered revelation?" Because the book does not contain the fullness of revelation which later books contain, we should not dismiss the role this book plays in the process of coming to that fullness of revelation.

The author of the Book of Job was an inspired writer of great courage and honesty. He understands the connection between suffering and sin which is clearly taught in the story of the man and the woman in the garden. The author does not dispute this connection. But he strongly rejects the idea that all suffering is due to sin. He believes that such an idea reflects a God who is not really loving, a God who is guilty of totally

A PROCESS OF REVELATION

Coming to Knowledge by Reflecting on Experience

Question: Why do we suffer?

	Understanding
Account: Adam and Eve Date: 1000 B.C. Experience: We experience suffering	We suffer because we sin.
Account: Ezekiel Date: 593–571 B.C. Experience: Is each of us personally responsible for whatever destruction comes?	People don't suffer for their parents' sins but for their own. No innocent person is to be found.
Account: Second Isaiah Date: 540 B.C. Experience: Why are we in exile in Babylon?	This is a terribly painful mystery. An individual or a community might suffer to save the sinner.
Account: Job Date: 400 B.C. Experience: Innocent people do suffer	Innocent people do suffer. There must be a reason since there is a reason for everything. The reason isn't a test or punishment.
Date: 30 A.D. Event: Jesus is crucified and dies, and many experience the presence of the risen Christ	A totally innocent person has suffered. Why? What was its effect?
Account: Paul to Colossians Date: 62 A.D. Experience: Paul in captivity in Rome	Christ's suffering redeemed us. We are honored to share in his suffering, to participate in the process of redemption.

inappropriate "overkill" when it comes to punishment. The author of the Book of Job does not believe in a punishing policeman in the sky who constantly watches to see if man steps a little out of line and then zaps him. In his view, the traditional theory of retribution is teaching just such a God. Although the author does not know the purpose for suffering, he rejects the explanation of punishment and asserts some other purpose. He does not know what that purpose is—this is beyond his comprehension. But since he knows God is loving and all powerful, he knows that suffering is not punishment and that suffering does have a purpose.

Some people, after reading the Book of Job, wonder if the author's agonizing questions, which he presents through the character of Job, were not leading him to a glimmer of belief in life after death. In Chapter 17 Job seems to have no hope for a life after death when he says:

> All I look forward to is dwelling in Sheol,
> and making my bed in the dark.
> I tell the tomb, "You are my father,
> and call the worm my mother and my sister.
> Where then is my hope?
> Who can see any happiness for me? (Job 17:13–15).

But in Chapter 19 Job says:

> This I know: that my Avenger lives,
> and he, the Last, will take his stand on earth.
> After my awaking, he will set me close to him,
> and from my flesh I will look on God (Job 19:26–27).

A person who has read the New Testament is tempted to project his or her own knowledge about the resurrection and about Christ onto this passage. In its context, though, the passage seems to reflect a hope on Job's part that he will be released from Sheol, the place of the dead, for a short while to see himself vindicated. His hope is that his reputation on earth will be cleared, even if this happens after his death, and he will know it. That Job doesn't begin to believe in a resurrection of the dead seems evident from his later hopeless accusation against God.

You carry me up to ride the wind,
tossing me about in a tempest.
I know it is to death that you are taking me,
the common meeting place of all that lives (Job 30:22–23).

The Concluding Frame

After thoroughly exhausting his audience by confronting them with the shallowness of their belief in the doctrine of retribution, the author ends his great work on a light note.

When Yahweh had said all this to Job, he turned to Eliphaz of Teman. "I burn with anger against you and your two friends," he said, "for not speaking truthfully about me as my servant Job has done. So now find seven bullocks and seven rams, and take them back with you to my servant Job and offer a holocaust for yourselves, while Job, my servant, offers prayers for you. I will listen to him with favor and excuse your folly in not speaking of me properly as my servant Job has done." Eliphaz of Teman, Bildad of Shuah and Zophar of Naamath went away to do as Yahweh had ordered, and Yahweh listened to Job with favor.

Yahweh restored Job's fortune, because he had prayed for his friends. More than that, Yahweh gave him double what he had before. And all his brothers and all his sisters and all his friends of former times came to see him and sat down at the table with him. They showed him every sympathy, and comforted him for all the evils Yahweh had inflicted on him. Each of them gave him a silver coin, and each a gold ring. Yahweh blessed Job's new fortune even more than his first one. He came to own fourteen thousand sheep, six thousand camels, a thousand yoke of oxen and a thousand she-donkeys. He had seven sons and three daughters; his first daughter he called "Turtledove," the second "Cassia" and the third "Mascara." Throughout the land there were no women as beautiful as the daughters of Job. And their father gave them inheritance rights like their brothers.

After his trials, Jobs lived on until he was a hundred and forty years old, and saw his children and his children's children up to the fourth generation. Then Job died, an old man and full of days (Job 42:7–17).

The concluding epilogue, the legend frame, gives the audience a happy ending. Job is rewarded on earth with twice as much as he had before. He receives all the material signs that the audience had previously considered rewards for virtue—prosperity and old age. The happy ending brings the Book of Job to a conclusion, but it does nothing to calm the unsettling effect of the torturous questions which have been raised by the debate. Is the doctrine of retribution false? Does it offend God rather than defend him? Do innocent people suffer? Why would a loving God permit such a thing? One judges from reading the New Testament that most of the audience were unable to come to grips with the problem with which the Book of Job confronts them. Four hundred years later the doctrine of retribution was still held as the explanation for suffering.

Review Questions

1. What view of suffering is revealed by Abraham's question to God about saving the town for the sake of just men?
2. What popular belief of his culture does Ezekiel challenge?
3. What purposes does the legend which frames the debate in the Book of Job serve?
4. What response to the mystery of suffering does Job's wife symbolize?
5. What is Eliphaz's answer to the problem of suffering?
6. What role does the frame play in understanding the idea of retribution?
7. What role does the idea of life after death play in this debate? Why?
8. Why does Job accuse his friends of displeasing God in their defense of him?
9. Why are Job's friends clinging to old inadequate answers?

10. What does Job learn as he experiences God's presence and listens to his words?

11. What does the author of the Book of Job add to mankind's understanding of the problem of suffering? What has been revealed since this book was written about the problem of suffering?

Discussion Questions

1. In your observation of life do the innocent suffer? Does the idea that an innocent person might suffer cause you to doubt God's power or goodness? Why or why not?
2. Is the response of Job's wife to the mystery of suffering common? Is it helpful? Why or why not?
3. Do you regard suffering as a test which God gives you? Would the author of the Book of Job be satisfied with this explanation?
4. Do you agree with Job that God would not be pleased with intellectual dishonesty? What relevance does this observation have on our approach to troublesome questions in our own day? What are some troublesome questions in our day?
5. What motivates Job's friends? Why are they unable to grow in understanding as they are confronted with events which challenge their thinking? Do we still behave this way today? What are some examples?
6. Job realizes that there are many things which are beyond his comprehension. What are some mysteries with which our experience confronts us that are beyond our comprehension? What effect does our limited ability to understand have on us?
7. Is the idea that Scripture reflects a process of revelation rather than bottom line answers new to you? On what other subjects besides the problem of suffering can we see this process of revelation?

5

Fiction

I have often heard Christians claim that Jesus made a terribly radical statement when he said, "Love your enemies," and that no one had ever made such a statement before. Jesus' words in Matthew's Gospel are contrasted to the "Old Testament" views, "An eye for an eye and a tooth for a tooth," (Mt 5:38) and "Love your neighbor but hate your enemy" (Mt 5:43). We know from reading the Gospels that Jesus was extremely well acquainted with the Old Testament. When he teaches his followers to "love your enemies," he teaches in the tradition of a wise and witty predecessor, the author of the Book of Jonah.

It is true that some Old Testament books reflect the attitude, "Hate your enemies." It took many hundreds of years for the chosen people to understand that their God loved the people of other nations in addition to loving them. Works that precede the Book of Jonah do not reflect this insight. We will trace this coming to knowledge in order to better understand the Book of Jonah. First, however, we will introduce the genre of the Book of Jonah.

Didactic Fiction

The Book of Jonah is a work of fiction. Fiction is a broad term, and can include subgenres. One subgenre of fiction is "didactic fiction." To say that a work is fiction is to say that it is drawn from the imagination of the author. To say a work is didactic fiction is to say that the author intends to teach something through his story. The Book of Jonah is didactic fiction in that the author wants to teach his audience exactly the same thing which Jesus taught his followers: "Love your enemies." This is a teaching which, at the time the book was written, was bound to meet with intense opposition. The author of the Book of Jonah could have chosen the same genre which was used by the author of the Book of Job—debate—to teach his audience that they should love their enemies. Both authors had to somehow work around the disagreements and defenses of their audiences. But instead of using debate, which is basically intellectual and "heavy," the author of Jonah chose didactic fiction. In this genre he could use humor, parody and irony to teach his audience a lesson which was very difficult for them to accept: God loves other nations too, and so must we.

Does God Love Other Nations?

Before going to the book itself we will first try to understand why an audience which lived between 400 and 200 B.C. would find the message "God loves other nations" difficult to accept and why, through pondering events, the inspired author of the Book of Jonah came to this realization.

The statement has often been made that the development of a nation can be compared to the development of an individual person. When a very young person realizes that he or she is loved by another, the young one establishes his or her identity in the context of that love. It is therefore a very threatening experience to suspect that the one who loves me loves others too. We are all familiar with the sensitivity and care needed toward a first-born child when a second child arrives on the scene. We are also familiar with the kind of exclusiveness, possessiveness and jealousy which often accompanies a first romantic involvement. If our sense of identity, our sense of being unique and special, has been established in the context of a loving relationship with another person, we find it very threatening indeed to realize that we are not the only one loved by that person.

The Israelites developed their sense of identity and purpose through their loving, covenant relationship with God. It was a very long time before they could recognize or accept the fact that God loved all people, not just them.

We already noticed in the call of Abraham that the Israelites perceived God as loving them above all other nations, for he is pictured as saying:

> I will bless those who bless you,
> I will curse those who curse you (Gen 12:3).

The other nations will prosper or not, depending on how they treat the Israelites.

This sense that God loves them and not other nations is evident in the Book of Exodus too, for God is pictured as saying:

> I shall spread panic ahead of you; I shall throw into confusion all the people you encounter; I shall make all your enemies turn and run from you. I shall send hornets in front of you to drive Hivites and Canaanites and Hittites from your presence (Ex 23:27–28).

Since the Israelites did not realize that God loved other nations they did not realize that they should love other nations. Indeed, they believed they were doing God's will by showing no mercy to those whom they conquered. In the Book of Deuteronomy we have a clear picture of the way the Israelites believed they were to treat other nations.

> When Yahweh your God has led you into the land you are entering to make your own, many nations will fall before you: Hittites, Girgashites, Amorites, Canaanites, Perizzites, Hivites and Jebusites, seven nations greater and stronger than yourselves. Yahweh your God will deliver them over to you and you will conquer them. You must lay them under ban. You must make no covenant with them nor show them pity. You must not marry with them: you must not give a daughter of yours to a son of theirs, nor take a daughter of theirs for a son of yours, for this would

> turn away your son from following me to serving other gods and the anger of Yahweh would blaze out against you and soon destroy you. Instead, deal with them like this: tear down their altars, smash their standing-stones, cut down their sacred poles and set fire to their idols. For you are a people consecrated to Yahweh your God; it is you that Yahweh our God has chosen to be his very own people out of all peoples on the earth (Dt 7:1–6).

Students are often shocked at the way the Israelites treated those whom they conquered. In the Book of Joshua we read exactly what being placed under the ban meant. When the chosen people conquered Jericho, they stormed the town, "every man going straight ahead; and they captured the town. They enforced the ban on everything in the town: men and women, young and old, even the oxen and sheep and donkeys, massacring them all" (Jos 6:21).

The reason for this massacre can only be understood when one realizes that the Israelites thought they were doing God's will when they slaughtered everyone. The people of other nations were seen as God's enemies, and therefore the Israelites thought they should be destroyed. The Israelites were so sure that their enemies were God's enemies and deserved only destruction that they were evidently comfortable nurturing these ideas and feelings in prayer. In Psalm 58 we read a prayer which clearly reflects the psalmist's view of how those who have been in error since birth should be treated.

> God, break their teeth in their mouths,
> Yahweh, wrench out the fangs of these savage lions!
> May they drain away like water running to waste,
> may they wither like trodden grass,
> like a slug that melts as it moves,
> like an abortion, denied the light of day (Ps 58:6–8).

This passage gives us a very clear picture of the difference in understanding which the psalmist had as opposed to the idea which Jesus had. If we accepted Jesus' teaching, "Love your enemy," and we recognized in ourselves the hate and loathing for an enemy which this psalmist felt, we would not pray for the enemy's destruction. Rather we would pray that we ourselves be healed of the inability to love another who is, after all, just as much a child of God as we ourselves are.

Students often ask how a psalm such as this could be accepted as revelation. We must remember once again that when we are reading Scripture we are reading a process of coming to knowledge. This view of God, while not as advanced as the one which Jesus gave us, is still a big step forward from ideas which preceded it. This psalmist believed in God. He believed in one God who was God of all nations, not just his. He believed this God ordered all things for good, that he acted through history, and that he held men accountable for their actions. These are all very sophisticated beliefs compared to a belief in many gods who have faults of their own, are sometimes disinterested in the affairs of men, and involve men in their own petty power struggles. The psalmist is praising a present and powerful God of justice when he says:

> What joy for the virtuous, seeing this vengence,
> bathing their feet in the blood of the wicked!
> "So," people will say "the virtuous do have their harvest;
> so there is a God who dispenses justice on earth (Ps 58:10–11).

That the psalmist did not have the same degree of insight as did Jesus should not blind us to the remarkable insights which he did have.

Revelation Through Events

The author of the Book of Jonah, who preceded Jesus by two hundred to four hundred years, realized that his God was not a God who wanted us to hate our enemies. One might well ask, "How did he come to such a radical change of understanding?" How did God reveal to him that God loved other nations as well as the Israelites?

In our first chapter we discussed the idea that God revealed himself through events. One particular event in the Israelites' history had a profound and disturbing effect on the Israelites' view that they alone were loved and chosen by God. This event revolved around the person of Cyrus, a Persian. Cyrus, who was not an Israelite at all, set God's people free in much the same way as did Moses.

The exodus, under Moses' leadership, was undoubtedly the central event in the history of the Israelites. Through their experience of being saved from slavery in Egypt and being molded into a nation during their wandering in the desert, the Israelites grew in their understanding of their own identity and purpose. From the time of the exodus on, all experiences both before and after the exodus were understood in the light of this central period in their history.

The second most important time in the history of the Israelites might well be the period of the Babylonian exile (587–529 B.C.). For the second time in their history the chosen people were a conquered people, living in a land not their own. In order to free his people from slavery in Egypt, God raised up one of the chosen people, Moses. God's will was accomplished through one of their own. But in order to free the chosen people from exile in Babylon, God raised up Cyrus, a Persian, who conquered the Babylonians and allowed the Israelites to return home. This was a mind-boggling experience. Surely it was God's will that they be freed, and God's power that had freed them. But why was the instrument of God's power not one of their own? Could Cyrus, who was a Persian, be God's chosen instrument? Events revealed that he was.

The inevitable conclusion that Cyrus, too, was a chosen one of God is clear in the Book of Isaiah. In the section of Isaiah generally referred to as Second Isaiah (Chapters 40–55) we read:

> I am he who says of Cyrus, "My shepherd,
> he will fulfill my whole purpose,"
> saying of Jerusalem, "Let her be rebuilt,"
> and of the temple, "Let your foundation be laid."
> Thus says Yahweh to his anointed, to Cyrus,
> whom he has taken by his right hand
> to subdue nations before him

> and strip the loins of kings,
> to force gateways before him
> that their gates be closed no more:
> "I will go before you
> leveling the heights.
> I will shatter the bronze gateways,
> smash the iron bars.
> I will give you the hidden treasures,
> the secret hoards,
> that you may know that I am Yahweh,
> the God of Israel, who calls you by name.
> It is for the sake of my servant Jacob,
> of Israel my chosen one,
> that I have called you by your name,
> conferring a title though you do not know me.
> I am Yahweh, unrivaled;
> there is no other God besides me.
> Though you do not know me, I arm you
> that men may know
> from the rising to the setting of the sun
> that, apart from me, all is nothing" (Is 44:28–45:6).

Here we see that Cyrus is referred to as "shepherd" and as "anointed," words which are applied to those "saviors" whom the Lord used to free his people, words which were eventually applied to Jesus himself.

When the Israelites returned to the holy land after having been freed from Babylon by Cyrus, they faced another period of severe hardship. They had to once again fight their enemies to rebuild the temple which the Babylonians had destroyed. Whenever the Israelites experienced hardship they attributed their suffering to lack of fidelity to the covenant. Ezra, a scribe who was versed in the law of Moses, called those who were now in the holy land to be faithful to the law. Part of this law we have already read. Israelites were not to marry foreigners. Under Ezra's leadership Israelites who had married foreigners had to "put away" their wives and children. Such a procedure seems immoral to us. But to most of the Israelites it seemed wrong not to obey. We read about this event in the Book of Ezra.

A PROCESS OF REVELATION

Coming to Knowledge by Reflecting on Experience

Question: Whom does God love?

Date	Understanding
1850 B.C.	Abraham understood that God is a personal and loving God. He especially loved Abraham. He promised him protection, land, and descendants.
1250 B.C.	The Hebrews understood that God was a personal and loving God. He especially loved the Hebrew people. He freed them from slavery in Egypt.
1200–1000 B.C.	The Israelites understood that God loved them. He helped them conquer Canaan.
537 B.C.	Cyrus, a Persian, conquered the Babylonians and let the Israelites return home.
500–400 B.C.	The author of Jonah understood that God must love other nations. After all, he created them just as he created the Jewish people.
30 A.D.	Jesus taught his followers to love their enemies.
34 A.D.	Peter understood that all people are invited to be God's chosen people and live in a covenant relationship with their God.

> Then Ezra the priest stood up and spoke, "You have committed treason by marrying foreign women; you have added to the sin of Israel. But now give thanks to Yahweh, the God of your ancestors, and do his will by separating from the natives of the country and from your foreign wives." In a loud voice the whole assembly answered, "Yes, our duty is to do as you say" (Ezr 10:10–12).

There were some who disagreed with Ezra's view of things, as we read in verse 15:

> Only Jonathan son of Asahel and Jahzeiah son of Tikvah, supported by Meshullam and Shabbethai the Levite, were opposed to this procedure (Ezr 10:15).

As years went on, others disagreed with this narrow nationalism too. The author of the Book of Ruth certainly disagreed, because this book's heroine is a Moabite who married an Israelite, remained faithful to Jewish custom even after her husband died, remarried another Israelite, and thus became an ancestor of the great King David. Many believe that the Book of Ruth was written to contradict the kind of narrow nationalistic thinking which was encouraged among those who lived in the holy land after the Babylonian exile.

Another dissenter from this emphasis on nationalism was the author of the Book of Jonah. We can appreciate the difficulty with which he was faced. He had come to the realization that God loved other nations. To teach such an insight would be considered nothing short of treason to God and country. How was he to confront his people with this radical insight? The author of the Book of Jonah solved his problem by composing a humorous fictional narrative as a means of teaching his audience a profound but threatening religious truth.

Why Fiction?

Many who read the Book of Jonah read it as though it were an historical narrative rather than a fictional narrative. Students will occasionally ask, "How do you know this didn't happen exactly as the author tells it? Other men have survived being swallowed by a whale."

We must look to the text itself for an answer to this question. First we will look carefully at the story to see evidence in the setting, the plot and the tone that the intent of the author is not to report history. Then we will give a direct answer to this important question.

The Book of Jonah

> The word of Yahweh was addressed to Jonah son of Amittai: "Up!" he said. "Go to Nineveh, the great city, and inform them that their wickedness has become known to me." Jonah decided to run away from Yahweh, and to go to Tarshish. He went down to Joppa and found a ship bound for Tarshish; he paid his fare and went aboard, to go with them to Tarshish, to get away from Yahweh. But Yahweh unleashed a violent wind on the sea, and there was such a great storm at sea that the ship threatened to break up. The sailors took fright, and each of them called on his own god, and to lighten the ship they threw the cargo overboard. Jonah, however, had gone below and lain down in the hold and fallen fast asleep. The boatswain came upon him and said, "What do you mean by sleeping? Get up! Call on your God! Perhaps he will spare us a thought, and not leave us to die." Then they said to each other, "Come on, let us draw lots to find out who is responsible for bringing this evil on us." So they cast lots, and the lot fell to Jonah. Then they said to him, "Tell us, what is your business? Where do you come from? What is your country? What is your nationality?" He replied, "I am a Hebrew, and I worship Yahweh, the God of heaven, who made the sea and the land." The sailors were seized with terror at this and said, "What have you done?" They knew that he was trying to escape from Yahweh, because he had told them so. They then said, "What are we to do with you, to make the sea grow calm for us?" For the sea was growing rougher and rougher. He replied, "Take me and throw me into the sea, and then it will grow calm for you. For I can see it is my fault this violent storm has happened to you." The sailors rowed hard in an effort to reach the

shore, but in vain, since the sea grew still rougher for them. They then called on Yahweh and said, "O Yahweh, do not let us perish for taking this man's life; do not hold us guilty of innocent blood; for you, Yahweh, have acted as you have thought right." And taking hold of Jonah they threw him into the sea; and the sea grew calm again. At this the men were seized with dread of Yahweh; they offered a sacrifice to Yahweh and made vows.

Yahweh had arranged that a great fish should be there to swallow Jonah, and Jonah remained in the belly of the fish for three days and three nights. From the belly of the fish he prayed to Yahweh, his God; he said:

> "Out of my distress I cried to Yahweh
> and he answered me;
> from the belly of Sheol I cried,
> and you have heard my voice.
> You cast me into the abyss,
> into the heart of the sea,
> and the flood surrounded me.
> All your waves, your billows,
> washed over me.
> And I said: I am cast out
> from your sight.
> How shall I ever look again
> on your holy temple?
> The water surrounded me right to my throat,
> the abyss was all around me.
> The seaweed was wrapped round my head
> at the roots of the mountains.
> I went down into the countries underneath the earth,
> to the peoples of the past.
> But you lifted my life from the pit,
> Yahweh, my God.
> While my soul was fainting within me,
> I remembered Yahweh,
> and my prayer came before you
> into your holy temple.
> Those who serve worthless idols
> forfeit the grace that was theirs.
> But I, with a song of praise,
> will sacrifice to you.

> The vow I have made, I will fulfill.
> Salvation comes from Yahweh."

Yahweh spoke to the fish, which then vomited Jonah on to the shore.

The word of Yahweh was addressed a second time to Jonah: "Up!" he said. "Go to Nineveh, the great city, and preach to them as I told you to." Jonah set out and went to Nineveh in obedience to the word of Yahweh. Now Nineveh was a city great beyond compare: it took three days to cross it. Jonah went on into the city, making a day's journey. He preached in these words, "Only forty days more and Nineveh is going to be destroyed." And the people of Nineveh believed in God; they proclaimed a fast and put on sackcloth, from the greatest to the least. The news reached the king of Nineveh, who rose from his throne, took off his robe, put on sackcloth and sat down in ashes. A proclamation was then promulgated throughout Nineveh, by decree of the king and his ministers, as follows: "Men and beasts, herds and flocks, are to taste nothing; they must not eat, they must not drink water. All are to put on sackcloth and call on God with all their might; and let everyone renounce his evil behavior and the wicked things he has done. Who knows if God will not change his mind and relent, if he will not renounce his burning wrath, so that we do not perish?" God saw their efforts to renounce their evil behavior. And God relented: he did not inflict on them the disaster which he had threatened.

Jonah was very indignant at this; he fell into a rage. He prayed to Yahweh and said, "Ah, Yahweh, is not this just as I said would happen when I was still at home? That was why I went and fled to Tarshish: I knew that you were a God of tenderness and compassion, slow to anger, rich in graciousness, relenting from evil. So now Yahweh, please take away my life, for I might as well be dead as go on living." Yahweh replied, "Are you right to be angry?" Jonah then went out of the city and sat down to the east of the city.

There he made himself a shelter and sat under it in the shade, to see what would happen to the city. Then Yahweh God arranged that a castor-oil plant grow up over

> Jonah to give shade for his head and soothe his ill-humor. Jonah was delighted with the castor-oil plant. But at dawn the next day, God arranged that a worm should attack the castor-oil plant—and it withered. Next, when the sun rose, God arranged that there should be a scorching east wind; the sun beat down so hard on Jonah's head that he was overcome and begged for death, saying, "I might as well be dead as go on living." God said to Jonah, "Are you right to be angry about the castor-oil plant?" He replied, "I have every right to be angry, to the point of death." Yahweh replied, "You are only upset about a castor-oil plant which cost you no labor, which you did not make grow, which sprouted in a night and has perished in a night. And am I not to feel sorry for Nineveh, the great city, in which there are more than a hundred and twenty thousand people who cannot tell their right hand from their left, to say nothing of all the animals?"

Evidence from the Plot

As we shall see, an Israelite who lived after 400 B.C. would know immediately from the plot of the Book of Jonah that he or she was not reading history. Jonah is a prophet who is told to go to Nineveh, the great city, and preach. This means that the setting for the story is before the fall of the northern kingdom, possibly in the days of King Jeroboam II (783–743 B.C.), when Nineveh was the capital of Assyria, and Assyria was threatening to destroy the northern kingdom. In other words, the audience is presented with a prophet who is told to preach not to his own people but to his greatest enemy. Jonah refuses to do as God tells him. As long as Jonah refuses he is beset by hardship and danger. He runs away from God by setting sail for Tarshish, and is thrown overboard by pagans who, despite the fact that they are pagans, realize that the gods must be obeyed. Jonah is then swallowed by a great fish. While in the belly of the fish Jonah experiences a remarkable change of heart. He sings a song of praise and gratitude for having been delivered from danger even while he is still in the fish.

God likes this new attitude on Jonah's part, so God speaks to the fish who obediently vomits Jonah on the shore. When asked a second time to preach to the Ninevites, Jonah obeys.

Evidence from the Tone

To fully appreciate the humor woven into the story of Jonah, it is helpful to be familiar with the pattern of other prophetic literature. The plot of the Book of Jonah, when seen against this background, becomes all the more obviously humorous, for it seems to be a parody of serious prophetic literature.

The prophet Jonah is called by God as Israel's historic prophets were. Like them, Jonah objects to his call. The historic prophets, however, objected to their calls because they themselves felt unworthy or they feared the persecution which would come to them when the people refused to listen to the truth which they taught. Jonah, on the other hand, refuses to accept his call not because he thinks he is unworthy but because he thinks that the Ninevites are unworthy. Although Jonah does finally preach to the Ninevites, he does not want them to repent. He is looking forward to their destruction. He thinks that when they are destroyed, which is only what they deserve, he will be recognized as the prophet he is.

Much to Jonah's dismay, the Ninevites do repent. Again, to appreciate the humor in this account we must once more see it against the background of the experience of the historic prophets. When we read the other prophets we read page after page of the content of their message. Invariably, however, their prophecy falls on deaf ears. The anguish of the prophet resides in the fact that his prophecies are ignored. Jonah, however, simply says on his first day in town, "Only forty days more and Nineveh is going to be destroyed," and the whole nation immediately repents. Even the king hears the news and immediately responds. He sends out a proclamation that all are to repent and do penance, even the animals. The exaggeration here adds to the humor and the obviously fictional nature of the work. God responds by not destroying the city after all.

The expectation would now be that Jonah would be jubilant. After all, he had been God's instrument of salavation for the Ninevites. They had responded to his words and were saved. The author humorously and ironically disappoints this expectation by having Jonah react in just the opposite way. Jonah is furious because he wanted the Ninevites to be destroyed. After all, they are the Israelites' enemies. Jonah cries out in anger to Yahweh and says, "I knew that you were a God of tenderness and compassion, slow to anger, rich in graciousness, relenting from evil." One would expect such words to be a song of praise, but our author has ironically made them an accusation. Jonah is angry that God has these characteristics, for they are the very characteristics which have resulted in God's not destroying the Ninevites.

Fictional, humorous narratives are a great way to help people see their own prejudices and foibles. When this story began, many of the Israelites who read it must have understood Jonah's reluctance to preach to the Ninevites. After all, the Ninevites were enemies who, in 721 B.C., had conquered the northern tribes. The Ninevites were responsible for the loss of ten of the twelve tribes. Who could want them to be saved? But as the story continues Jonah, as a prophet, becomes a parody. He is so "unprophet-like" that he is obviously being ridiculed by the author. Jonah's behavior is simply ridiculous, his position totally untenable. We see this very clearly in the incident with the castor-oil plant. God arranges for a castor-oil plant to grow over Jonah to give him shade. God then arranges for a worm to destroy the castor-oil plant and for the sun and wind to scorch Jonah. Again, Jonah complains bitterly and begs for death. In Scripture we can read other prophets who rail against God, particularly Jeremiah. But as the historic prophets make their complaints against God, we understand the depth of their suffering and pain. Here Jonah appears as petty and silly. Still he argues boldly with God, claiming that he has every right to be angry. God responds to Jonah's anger by comparing Jonah's fondness for the castor-oil plant to God's fondness for the Ninevites.

> You are only upset about the castor-oil plant which cost you no labor, which you did not make grow, which sprouted in a night and has perished in a night. And am I not to feel sorry for Nineveh, the great city, in which there are more than a hundred and twenty thousand people who cannot tell their right hand from their left, to say nothing of all the animals? (Jon 4:10–11).

With these words the author reveals the theme of his story. God created the Ninevites just as he created the Israelites. God is loving. Therefore, God must love the Ninevites just as he loves the Israelites, even if they can't tell their right hand from their left.

An audience who might have shared Jonah's point of view when the story began can only want to separate themselves from such a shallow and ridiculous character as the story ends. Jonah's position becomes absurd. In separating oneself from Jonah, one separates oneself from Jonah's petty nationalistic thinking. Perhaps God does love other nations. Perhaps it is narrow-minded, even ridiculous, to believe anything else.

Now that we have taken a close look at the text of the Book of Jonah, we can fully answer the question, "How do you know that this is a fictional rather than an historical narrative?" As mentioned before, the evidence is in the setting, the plot and in the tone. The setting of the book is not realistic—a prophet from Israel preaching in Nineveh before the fall of the northern kingdom. The plot of the book is obviously unrealistic. The episode with the fish, the psalm from the belly of the fish, the immediate repentance of the Ninevites, and the whole episode with the castor-oil plant are perfect for a humorous fictional narrative and ludicrous for an historical narrative. And finally the humorous tone clues us in to the fact that we are reading fiction: Jonah is not an historic prophet but a parody of an historic prophet. His total lack of concern for the Ninevites even after receiving his call, his angry and accusatory tone toward God, and his constant pettiness all make him a delightful fictional creation rather than a serious historic prophet who could only be regarded with contempt.

Fiction as a Vehicle for Revelation

Once a student recognizes that the Book of Jonah is fictional, the fact that the book is also a vehicle for revelation sometimes comes as a surprise. Many students have a preconceived notion that fiction cannot be a vehicle for revelation. It becomes necessary to once more emphasize the fact that any literary form can be the vehicle for revelation. Through a fictional narrative, the author of the Book of Jonah teaches his audience a profound and difficult religious truth: God loves other nations.

We noticed when studying the Book of Job that the revelation contained in the book had not been generally accepted by the time Jesus lived on earth. People still thought that all suffering was due to sin. The revelation which is contained in the Book of Jonah was also unaccepted during Jesus' life. During Jesus' earthly ministry, the "chosen people" were still just the Israelites. In Matthew's Gospel, Jesus tells his disciples to go only to the house of Israel, and not to go to pagan towns (Mt 10:5–6). He also says that his own mission is to the house of Israel (Mt 15:25). It is only after Jesus' resurrection that Peter learns through a vision that other nations are also chosen and are to be included in the covenant (Acts 10:1–48). In obedience to the Holy Spirit, Peter baptizes Gentiles and later has to defend his actions to the other apostles (Acts 11:1–18).

With this hindsight historic view we can appreciate even more the fact that the Book of Jonah is revelation. Through the inspired author, God was preparing his people to realize and accept the fact that he created and loves all people; he wants to be known and loved by all people, not by just one nationality.

Review Questions

1. What is didactic fiction?
2. What is the author of the Book of Jonah teaching?

3. What is the ban? Why did the Israelites believe that it was right to put people under the ban?

4. Why did Cyrus' freeing of the Israelites challenge their view that only they were God's chosen instruments?

5. What evidence do we find in the plot of the Book of Jonah that we are reading fiction?

6. In what ways does the plot of the Book of Jonah appear to be a parody of serious prophetic literature?

7. In what ways does the author turn Jonah into a caricature?

8. How does the author encourage his audience to separate themselves from Jonah's narrow nationalistic viewpoint?

Discussion Questions

1. Do we believe today that God prefers some nations over others?
2. The Israelites came to a deeper understanding of God's love by pondering the events in their lives. Is this still the way we come to know God? Can you give any examples?
3. The author of the Book of Jonah chooses humor as a vehicle to teach a serious and threatening truth. Do you think this is a wise choice? Why or why not? Can you think of modern day authors who use the same vehicle to teach?
4. Is the idea that fiction could be a vehicle of revelation new to you? Does it seem reasonable? Can you think of other ways in which fiction is used in Scripture as a vehicle for revelation?

6

What Is a Gospel?

The word "Gospel" is used as though it were the name of a literary form. We refer to "the Gospels and the Epistles." An Epistle is a letter. What is a Gospel?

Scholars argue over whether or not the earliest Gospel writer invented a new literary form, or whether he wrote in a form well known in his culture but not in ours. We will discuss the Gospel as a genre later in this chapter. But first we need some background information. We need to understand the process which resulted in our present canonical Gospels.

The word "Gospel" means "good news." Originally the word meant any good news but later it began to refer to the good news which Jesus brought. So the word "Gospel" is not referring to the form of the writing at all but to its content. We have four Gospels in the New Testament, four accounts of the "good news." These four Gospels are not all the same literary form: the Gospel according to John is a different kind of writing than the Gospels according to Mark, Matthew, or Luke. In this chapter we will be speaking only about the latter three. John's Gospel will be discussed in a later chapter.

The Gospels of Mark, Matthew, and Luke are the result of a growth process. The growth process includes the same stages which we discussed in Chapter I when we asked, "What is the Bible?" In order to understand the written Gospels, in order to have realistic expectations about what they are teaching us, we need to understand this growth process and the effect that the stages of growth have had on the final text.

Events

The written Gospels started with events. Jesus was an historical person who was born at a certain point in time, who had a profound influence on his contemporaries, and who was crucified, died and buried. If the events had ended there, we would obviously not have the Gospels. But they didn't. Jesus' disciples were astounded to find that death was not death, that Jesus was still alive and with them.

Oral Tradition

None of the Gospels was written by Jesus or by Jesus' followers during Jesus' life on earth. So the first "Gospel," the first "good news," was an oral one.

Immediately after Jesus' death and resurrection, the facts about him which were of most interest to his followers were those which revolved around the very end of his earthly ministry. If I had been alive when Jesus was on earth and I had not known him, I may well have met one of his apostles who wanted to introduce me to Jesus after Jesus' death. The apostle might have initiated a conversation with me by saying, "Did you hear about Jesus, who rose from the dead?" Naturally the oral tradition did not begin chronologically with Jesus' birth, but in the order of immediate interest, with Jesus' resurrection. In other words, Christology, the study of who Jesus is, developed backward. The later events in Jesus' life were of interest first, and the earliest events were of interest later.

When Jesus' closest associates first heard that he had risen from the dead they simply couldn't believe it. Not until they personally experienced the presence of the risen Lord did they believe that he had defeated death and was still in their midst. None of the apostles fully understood who Jesus was or what he was accomplishing during the time they were together on earth.

Once Jesus had risen from the dead, and once his followers were filled with the Holy Spirit at Pentecost, they began to see things in an entirely new light. From Pentecost on, the

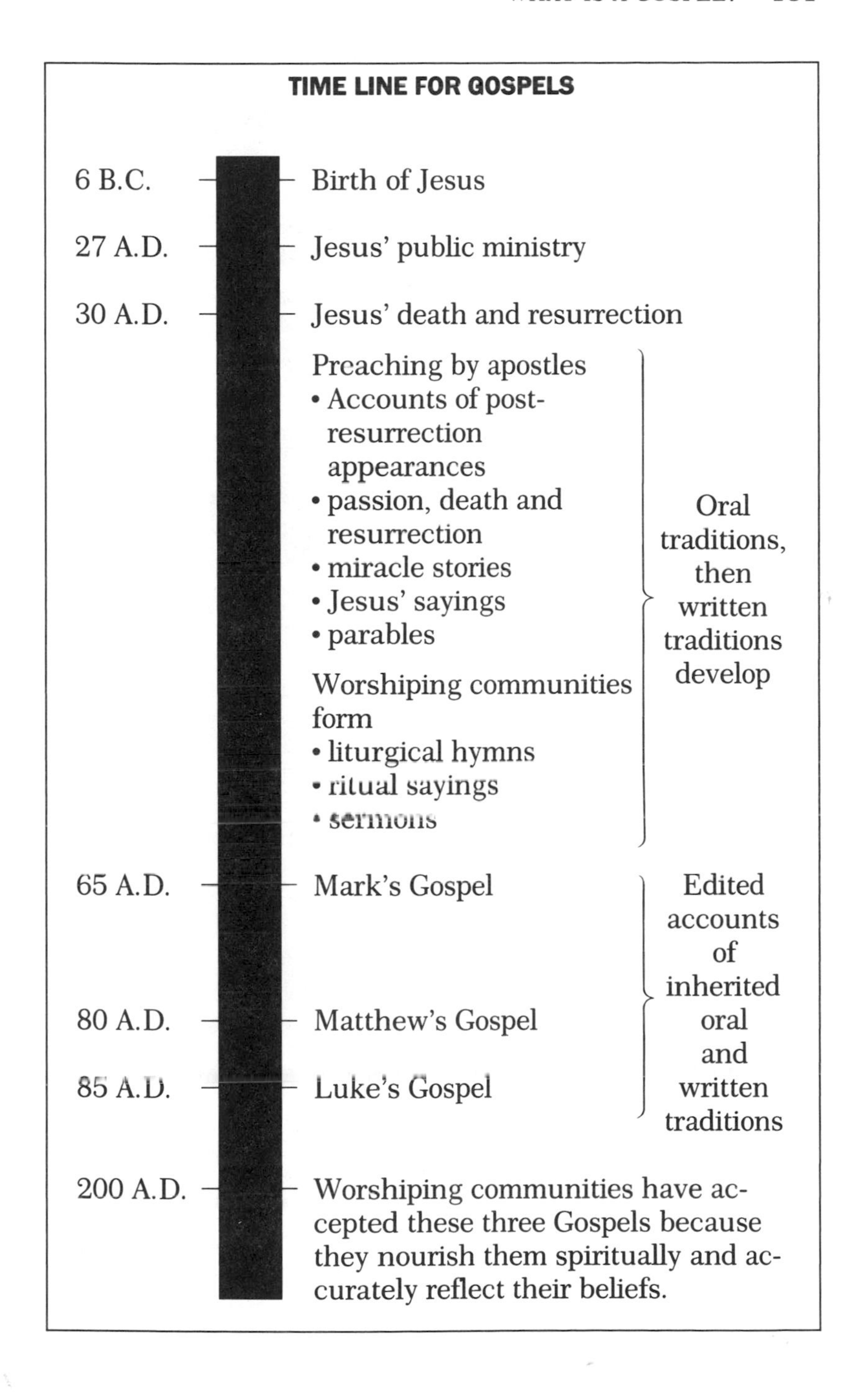
TIME LINE FOR GOSPELS
6 B.C.
Birth of Jesus
27 A.D.
Jesus' public ministry
30 A.D.
Jesus' death and resurrection
Preaching by apostles
• Accounts of post-resurrection appearances
• passion, death and resurrection
• miracle stories
• Jesus' sayings
• parables
Worshiping communities form
• liturgical hymns
• ritual sayings
• sermons
Oral traditions, then written traditions develop
65 A.D.
Mark's Gospel
80 A.D.
Matthew's Gospel
85 A.D.
Luke's Gospel
Edited accounts of inherited oral and written traditions
200 A.D.
Worshiping communities have accepted these three Gospels because they nourish them spiritually and accurately reflect their beliefs.

apostles were new creations. Not only did they understand what had been entirely beyond their comprehension earlier, but they were courageous. They now had the knowledge and the power to teach as Jesus had.

We have a good idea of the content of the earliest teachings from the Acts of the Apostles. The Acts of the Apostles is a continuation of the Gospel according to Luke. Luke gives us a good example of the earliest teaching in Peter's address to the people in the Portico of Solomon after the cure of the lame man.

> Everyone came running toward them in great excitement, to the Portico of Solomon, as it is called, where the man was still clinging to Peter and John. When Peter saw the people he addressed them, "Why are you so surprised at this? Why are you staring at us as though we had made this man walk by our own power or holiness? You are Israelites, and it is *the God of Abraham, Isaac and Jacob, the God of our ancestors, who has glorified his servant* Jesus, the same Jesus you handed over and then disowned in the presence of Pilate after Pilate had decided to release him. It was you who accused the Holy One, the Just One, you who demanded the reprieve of a murderer while you killed the prince of life. God, however, raised him from the dead, and to that fact we are the witnesses; and it is the name of Jesus which, through our faith in it, has brought back the strength of this man whom you see here and who is well known to you. It is faith in that name that has restored this man to health, as you can all see.
>
> "Now I know, brothers, that neither you nor your leaders had any idea what you were really doing; this was the way God carried out what he had foretold, when he said through all his prophets that his Christ would suffer. Now you must repent and turn to God, so that your sins may be wiped out, and so that the Lord may send the time of comfort. Then he will send you the Christ he has predestined, that is, Jesus, whom heaven must keep till the universal restoration comes which God proclaimed, speaking through his holy prophets. Moses, for example, said: *The Lord God will raise up a prophet like myself for you, from among your own brothers; you must listen to what-*

> *ever he tells you. The man who does not listen to that prophet is to be cut off from the people.* In fact, all the prophets that have ever spoken, from Samuel onward, have predicted these days.
>
> "You are the heirs of the prophets, the heirs of the covenant God made with our ancestors when he told Abraham: *in your offspring all the families of the earth will be blessed.* It was for you in the first place that God raised up his servant and sent him to bless you by turning every one of you from your wicked ways" (Acts 3:11–26).

Here we see that the oral Gospel, the oral good news, centered in on the fact that Jesus rose from the dead and is now with his Father in heaven. Jesus fulfilled the Old Testament prophecies and is the Christ, the Anointed One, the promised Messiah. This Jesus calls all to repentance. In him sins are forgiven. Everyone must repent, and then Jesus, the Christ, will come again and bring universal restoration.

Notice that Peter gives this address immediately after the cure of the lame man. It was this cure which astounded the people and which attracted their attention to Peter in the first place. The cure was a sign, just like the Old Testament signs during the time of the exodus, a sign of God's presence and power in their lives. Peter uses the cure to give authority to his words. "It is the name of Jesus which, through our faith in it, has brought back the strength of this man whom you see here and who is well known to you. It is faith in that name that has restored this man to health as you can all see" (Acts 3:16).

Imagine that you are one of those people standing in the Portico of Solomon when all of this happened. You would not be able to deny the event—the man had been cured. You would hear Peter's explanation of how this cure had been accomplished—through faith in Jesus. What would be your reaction? Perhaps you would ask, "Tell me more about this man Jesus. What was he like? Did he do anything during his life that would have made you think that he might rise from the dead?" Such a question would be most natural. If Peter had been asked such a question it would have caused him to think. Peter would remember all the mighty signs Jesus had accomplished in his sight—the calming of the storm, the cure of so many people—and he would remember how he was unable to understand the significance of those events at the time they had occurred. Peter knew, as we all do, that hindsight is so much clearer.

Written Tradition

As new converts entered the Church, then, they entered because they had been evangelized in the way Peter evangelized these people. As their conversion experience continued, as their turning to Christ continued, the new converts would be very hungry for more information about how Jesus was put to death, how he rose from the dead, and what mighty signs he had accomplished during his lifetime. In response to this hunger, the apostles and disciples would tell stories about those events. The earliest units to take form in the oral tradition, as well as in the written tradition which followed, were accounts of Jesus' passion, death and resurrection, and accounts of his miracles. The miracle stories were passed on as isolated episodes. No historical, chronological narrative of Jesus' miracles existed. Rather, isolated stories about individual events were told, retold, and eventually collected and written.

As the group of believers grew, so did an interest in Jesus' sayings. A desire to know what Jesus taught developed only after people had come to belief. The sayings and parables were not used to make converts but to deepen the knowledge and commitment of those who had already been persuaded to faith by accounts of the resurrection and miracles. Believers would gather together to remember Jesus in his word and in the Eucharist. This remembering was not just a matter of recalling past events, it was a way of making past events present and becoming a part of them. The believers united themselves to each other and to the risen Lord through repeating Jesus' teaching and Jesus' actions at the Last Supper.

Imagine for a moment that you are one of the leaders in the early Church. You would do your best to collect as many sayings and parables of Jesus as you could. When you repeated one of Jesus' parables you would not stop with the parable but would elaborate on the significance of the parable. You might compose a little sermon which applied the parable to the specific audience to whom you were speaking. Your intent in all of this would not be to teach history. Rather, you would help your listeners see the significance in what was said and done, and how they were to integrate their new beliefs into their lives.

Edited Tradition

When Mark compiled the first Gospel the Church had been in existence for a generation. Paul had already written most of his epistles. The Church had spread over a wide geographical area. The oral tradition had grown into a written tradition which included accounts of the passion, death and resurrection, collections of miracle stories, collections of sayings, and insights of the early Church. Mark was not an author in the modern sense of the word, but an editor. In his Gospel he arranged inherited materials to serve the needs of the community he was addressing.

The Gospel According to Mark

Scholars think that Mark's Gospel was probably compiled in the early 60's A.D., during the time of Nero's persecution. After the great fire, during which Nero is accused of fiddling, Christians became scapegoats and suffered severe persecution. Peter is thought to have been martyred at this time. Mark's Gospel is a book of encouragement written to a Church in the midst of persecution. Its central theme is that Christ himself set the perfect example for the necessity of suffering. Through his Gospel Mark grapples with the question which is on the minds of those who are faced with the choice of denying Christ or entering the colosseum to be eaten by lions. "Why must I die?" In order to come to an answer, Mark centers the question on Jesus. "Why did Jesus die?" The passion story dominates the narrative as it dominated the oral tradition.

Mark teaches that Jesus is the Messiah who accepted a painful and apparently premature death as the will of his Father.

In Mark's Gospel the passion narrative is preceded by some miracle stories and some sayings. The miracle stories are used, as they were in the oral tradition, to identify Jesus as the Christ, the Messiah. The sayings are presented in the form of controversies Jesus had with the Jewish leaders. The controversies answer the question "Why did Jesus die?" on the political level. The intense antagonism which the Pharisees developed for Jesus led to his death.

Mark is more accurately thought of as an editor than an author because he selected and arranged inherited materials. Mark's Gospel is an account of Jesus' life and death, in the light of Mark's own understanding about those events, and as they related to the needs of Mark's particular historic audience. Mark emphasized the significance of the events and molded the traditions to meet the needs of persecuted Christians. That is why the Gospel is called the Gospel according to Mark. It is the good news of Christ as Mark understood it in the context of his historic situation.

Revelation and Inspiration

Some students, when hearing the background of the written Gospel for the first time, find themselves upset and even disillusioned. They fear that such an explanation is robbing the Gospels of their exalted position as books which contain revelation, and denying the Gospel writers the inspiration which they had always believed lay at the root of the Gospels' composition. There is nothing incompatible about a belief in revelation and inspiration, and the knowledge that the Gospels grew from event to oral tradition, to written tradition, to the edited and canonical accounts which now appear in the Bible. The Gospels are revelation because they reveal the truth about the relationship between God and man. They reveal the truth about the fulfillment of revelation which was accomplished in the person of Jesus Christ. The Gospels are revelation because they are about those saving events through which God chose

INTERWEAVING OF MIRACLE STORIES AND CONTROVERSIES IN MARK'S GOSPEL

I. Jesus' public ministry (Chapters 1–8)
Jesus' identity is clear to the reader but not to Jesus' contemporaries

Mighty Signs	1:27	Exorcism
	1:30	Cure of Simon's mother-in-law
	1:33	Cure of many
	1:40	Cure of leper
	2:2	Cure of paralytic
Controversies	2:9	Controversy over power to forgive sin
	2:17	Controversy over eating with sinners
	2:18	Controversy over not fasting
	2:23	Controversy over picking corn on the sabbath
	3:2	Controversy over curing on the sabbath
	3:5	Pharisees want to destroy Jesus
	3:22	Controversy over exorcisms
Mighty Signs	4:40	Calming of storm
	5:1	Curing of man with Legion
	5:25	Cure of woman with hemorrhage
	5:35	Cure of Jairus' daughter
	6:37	First multiplication of the loaves
	6:45	Jesus walks on water
	6:55	Jesus heals the crowds
Controversy	7:1	Controversy over eating with unclean hands
Mighty Signs	7:24	Cure of Syro-Phoenician woman
	7:37	Cure of deaf man
	8:1	Second multiplication of the loaves
Controversy	8:10	Controversy over a "sign"
Mighty Sign	8:22	Cure of the blind man

II. Prelude to the passion (Chapters 9–13)
At Peter's profession of faith Jesus starts to prepare his followers for his passion but they still do not understand.

Mighty Signs	9:2	Transfiguration
	9:14	Cure of epileptic demoniac
Controversy	10:2	Controversy over divorce
Mighty Signs	10:46	Cure of blind Bartimaeus
	11:12	Fig tree incident
Controversies	11:16	Pharisees want to kill Jesus
	11:27	Controversy over authority
	12:1	Controversy over rejecting Jesus
	12:16	Controversy over paying taxes

III. Passion and resurrection

Controversy	14:1	Chief priests and scribes want to kill Jesus

to reveal himself to man. The Gospel writers were inspired. They were members of a community whose wisdom, power and unity came from the Holy Spirit. The Gospel writers were inspired, but so were the other members of the community who believed, recalled and united themselves to the saving events of Jesus' life. The oral tradition was no less inspired than the written tradition. God chose to work not just through a few isolated individuals but through the whole community. The whole believing community molded the traditions which we now find in Mark's Gospel.

The Gospel According to Matthew

In the years after Mark's Gospel was written, the Church continued to grow. As it grew, a variety of traditions and emphases developed in response to the needs of contemporary communities.

Matthew's Gospel is believed to have been written in Antioch, Syria around 80 A.D. Matthew's audience is different from Mark's and faces an entirely different set of problems. Far from facing persecution and imminent death, Matthew's audience is learning how to integrate Jesus' teachings into a settled community life. For this reason Matthew's audience has a much greater need to know what Jesus taught during his earthly ministry than did Mark's.

Matthew's Gospel is more systematically and logically organized than Mark's. You can understand Matthew's structure if you imagine how he might have organized his material. Imagine Matthew sitting at a desk and preparing to write his Gospel. He has before him five boxes. One box is labeled, "Old Law vs. New Law." The second box is labeled, "Instructions to Disciples," the third, "The Kingdom of God," the fourth, "Community Problems," and the fifth "Eschatological Teachings," that is, teachings about the end times. Matthew reads through all the traditions which he has inherited. If he reads something about the kingdom of God, he puts it in the third box; if he reads something about the new law, he puts it in the first. After reading all of his inherited sources, Matthew has all of the information organized thematically according to his five topics. Matthew then takes all of the information out of the first box. He molds that information into a narrative and a speech by Jesus. For each box he does the same thing—organizing his inherited materials into a narrative and a speech. Such a method of organization and composition would result in a Gospel organized exactly as Matthew's is: five thematic sections, each consisting of a narrative and a sermon, followed by an account of Jesus' passion, death, and resurrection.

Why would Matthew structure his Gospel into five thematic sections? Scholars suggest that Matthew chose to have five sections in order to reflect the five books of the Pentateuch. As Matthew pictures Jesus giving his sermon on the new law (5:1–7:29), his missionary sermon (9:35–11:1), his parables on the kingdom of God (13:1–52), his sermon on the Church (18:1–35), and his teachings on the final eschatological event (24:1–25:46), he is everywhere concerned with Jesus' teaching authority. This concern is also reflected in the social settings which Matthew supplies in his Gospel. Matthew pictures the disciples receiving authority from the risen Christ not as they eat (Mk 16:14; Lk 24:36), but on a mountain. Moses had received the old law on the mountain, Jesus taught the new law from a mountain, and the disciples are commissioned on a mountain to teach with authority (Mt 28:16–20). Matthew's hope was to give his readers a new law which would establish order and discipline within their community. It has been suggested that Matthew's Gospel may have been designed to be used for teaching, study, perhaps even memorization. It is organized as neatly and thematically as a textbook.

In addition to the five thematic sections and the account of the passion, death and resurrection, Matthew's Gospel includes a birth narrative. The birth narrative was not originally part of the written Gospel, as Mark does not have one. Mark's Gospel begins with Jesus' public ministry. The birth narrative too, like the parables, miracle stories, and sayings, was probably not composed by Matthew. Matthew made the decision to preface his Gospel with this traditional story.

When we talked about the order in which interest in, and

FIVE THEMATIC SECTIONS IN MATTHEW'S GOSPEL

I. Old law and new law
   A. Narrative 3:1—4:25
   B. Jesus' speech 5:1—7:29

II. Instructions to disciples
   A. Narrative 8:1—9:34
   B. Jesus' speech 9:35—11:1

III. The kingdom of God
   A. Narrative 11:2—12:50
   B. Jesus' speech 13:1–52

IV. Community problems
   A. Narrative 13:53—17:27
   B. Jesus' speech 18:1–35

V. Eschatology
   A. Narrative 19:1—23:39
   B. Jesus' speech 24:1—25:46

Preceded by the infancy narrative 1:1—2:23

Followed by the account of the passion, death and resurrection 26:1—28:20

stories about, Jesus developed, we said that Christology developed backward. Stories about Jesus' birth are later developments in the traditions of the Church.

"Why," one might say, "would Matthew choose to preface his Gospel with a birth narrative?" Again, the interest is not primarily historical, but Christological.

When Jesus was alive his disciples did not realize that he was divine. They realized this only after the resurrection. The question then arose: "Was Jesus always divine or was he made divine at the time of his resurrection?" Mark answers this question very clearly. Jesus was divine while he was on earth. The disciples were unable to see Jesus' divinity but it was there nevertheless. Mark emphasizes Jesus' divinity through the account of Jesus' baptism and later through the account of his transfiguration.

However, one might still ask, "When did Jesus become divine? Did he become divine at the time of his baptism?" The birth narrative reflects clearly the Church's belief that Jesus was always divine. Because the birth narrative makes such a clear Christological statement about Jesus' identity, Matthew places it at the beginning of his Gospel.

It is important to remember that Matthew is combining a number of different literary forms. The form of the birth narrative is not the same kind of writing as is the form of the account of the passion, death and resurrection. Just as the Bible as a whole is made up of many different forms, so is a single Gospel made up of many different forms. In order to understand the intent of the author correctly we must understand the form.

The Synoptic Gospels

If you were to read Mark's Gospel straight through and then read Matthew's Gospel, you would notice that Matthew's Gospel contains a great deal of Mark's account. Scholars believe that Matthew and Luke had Mark's Gospel in hand when they wrote their own accounts of the good news. In other words, Mark was one of the major sources which Matthew cut up and arranged thematically. Because the Gospels of Mark, Matthew and Luke are so similar, they are referred to as the "Synoptic" Gospels. The word "synoptic" refers to the fact that these three Gospels can be seen as one, can be presented in parallel columns and seen in a "view together". Mark, Matthew and Luke agree on the plan of each Gospel, on the emphasis on certain important facts in the public life of Jesus, and on the sequence of some events. The Gospels, however, are far from identical. Each Gospel has some material the others lack. What appears as a unit in one Gospel may be distributed through several chapters in another. In each Gospel, elements are rearranged to emphasize a different theme.

The exact relationship among these three Gospels has not been definitively explained, and may never be, since the Gospels have both an oral history and a literary history. However, scholars generally agree that the order of the Synoptic Gospels is as we have described it: Mark, Matthew and Luke. While both Matthew and Luke are dependent on Mark, they are probably not dependent on each other.

Matthew and Luke have a good deal of information in common which is not in Mark. A second common source, "Q", is posited and generally accepted, although this is pure conjecture. This source, if it existed, consisted almost entirely of words and sayings of Jesus.

In addition to information from Mark and from "Q", both Matthew and Luke have some material found only in their Gospels. No one can describe accurately the exact sources of this material, nor the exact interrelation of written and oral sources which preceded the canonical Gospels.

The three Synoptic Gospels are sometimes printed in parallel columns to facilitate comparison. A book which presents the Gospels in this way is called a harmony. The word suggests an appropriate metaphor, for the Gospels of Mark, Matthew and Luke are in harmony. While each uses the same notes, each presents us with a unique arrangement of those notes, making each Gospel an original tune composed within the frame or form imposed by the oral tradition. Mark has given us the Christ whose mighty acts turn death and suffering into resurrection and new life. Matthew has given us the Christ who dispenses the new law, and Luke, as we shall soon see, has given us the Christ who offers forgiveness and salvation to all. Each Gospel writer has arranged inherited materials to emphasize and teach what he found to be the most important element of this great and mysterious happening in order to meet the needs of his specific audience.

The Gospel According to Luke

The fact that Luke used oral and written sources to compose his Gospel is very obvious. Luke mentions that he is using the works of previous writers when he says in his preface:

> Seeing that many others have undertaken to draw up accounts of the events that have taken place among us, exactly as these were handed down to us by those who from the outset were eyewitnesses and ministers of the word, I in my turn, after carefully going over the whole story from the beginning, have decided to write an ordered account for you, Theophilus, so that your Excellency may learn how well founded the teaching is that you have received (Lk 1:1–4).

While Matthew's organization of materials reflects the orderly mind of a lawyer or teacher, Luke reveals himself to be an erudite man of letters, a gentle humanitarian who is not judgmental, is quick to forgive, and is anxious to welcome all into the new Church.

Luke's formal and proper preface, in the best Hellenistic style, was employed by him to introduce a two volume work, the Gospel according to Luke and the Acts of the Apostles. While Matthew organized his material around five sermons, Luke has used the literary technique of a journey from Galilee to Jerusalem. On this structure of a journey Luke uses his sources in alternating blocks. While Matthew's organization was thematic, Luke's appears to be geographic. Luke pictures Jesus during his Galilean ministry, on a journey to Jerusalem, and during his Jerusalem ministry. This literary technique of a journey is a much looser way to organize material than is a thematic structure. When one is on a journey there need be no obvious thematic connection between two episodes other than apparent chronology. One episode follows another as the traveler moves one step at a time toward his destination. Luke's structure allows him to include a greater variety of materials. Also, the structure reflects a process of movement through time and space to a destination. This structure reflects Luke's theme that the coming of the kingdom of God is

LUKE'S ORGANIZATIONAL STRUCTURE —A JOURNEY

In the Gospel

I. Jesus in Galilee 4:14—9:50
II. Jesus travels to Jerusalem 9:51—19:28
III. Jesus in Jerusalem 19:29—21:38

In the Acts of the Apostles

I. Early Church in Palestine 1:1—9:43
II. The Church journeys to the ends of the earth 10:1—28:31

an all-inclusive process which takes place in time—one step at a time.

Scholars believe that Luke wrote his Gospel around 80 A.D. in southern Greece for a Gentile audience. Since Luke is writing to Gentiles, it is no wonder that his Gospel seems to reach out and embrace all. Luke's Gospel alone includes the genealogy to Adam rather than to Abraham, the poor shepherds who take part in the infancy narrative, the penitent woman at Simon's house, the parable of the patient husbandman who gives the fig tree another year to bear fruit, the Samaritan lepers, the episode with Zacchaeus, the conversation with the good thief, and Jesus' words of forgiveness from the cross. Such an all-inclusive and universal theme is easily accommodated in the loose structure of a journey. As Jesus journeys, so the coming of the kingdom is in process. As Jesus' journey reaches out to more and more people in the crowd, so will the kingdom move through time to embrace all.

The Genre "Gospel"

In the process of answering the question "How did the written Gospel reach its present form?" we have mentioned genres which are included in the written Gospels: parables, miracle stories, infancy narratives, sermons, sayings, and the connected narrative of the passion, death and resurrection. We have not, however, attempted to describe the genre "Gospel" as a whole.

The literary form which Mark created as he molded traditional materials to meet the needs of his audience is unique. In striving to fulfill a particular need Mark produced a new kind of document. While we cannot point out a literary form familiar to twentieth century Americans which is closely related to a Gospel, we can understand the form more clearly by comparing it to some genres with which we are familiar.

Some claim that the Gospel genre is really biography. It is true that if studied as biography the Gospel writers show amazing skill in the revelation of character. In fact, it was centuries, possibly not until the eighteenth century, before biography caught up with the Gospels. However, the motive of the Gospel writers is not simply to describe the person of Jesus. Their theme is the significance of Jesus' identity and the fact that the act of revelation which took place in Jesus demands a response from the reader. There is no attempt to describe Jesus physically, and very little is said about the first thirty years of his life. Each Gospel writer assumes that a great deal is already known about Jesus. Disciples are introduced without the explanations of their identity that a biographer would give. In fact, the main emphasis in the Gospels is not on Jesus' life but on his death.

Neither can the Gospels be classified as history. This is not to say that the events reported in the Gospel never happened. They did. But the intent of the Gospel writers is not the intent of the historian. They are not trying to give an accurate historical account. Rather, they are trying to let the reader understand what those who were contemporary with Jesus did not understand. The Gospel writers do not limit their accounts to what was understood by Jesus' comtemporaries. Rather, they report the events which took place during Jesus' lifetime in such a way as to make the significance of those events, a significance which was realized only in hindsight, visible to their readers.

The Synoptic Gospels were written for believers. Those who read the Gospels read them not out of historical interest but out of a desire to understand more fully events in which they themselves had become intimately involved. The early Christians did not simply remember Jesus in the sense of recalling to mind someone no longer present. They remembered Jesus in the sense of once again becoming members—re-membering—uniting themselves to Jesus in order to become one with him in his life, death, and resurrection. For both the writer and the reader of the Gospels, the goal was not to learn history, not to recall past events, not simply to gain knowledge, but to achieve union and participation in a mystery through which the believer is joined to Jesus. Union and participation, not recollection, were the goals.

The written Gospel is a unique literary form called into being by a new message. Just as the birth, life, death and resurrection of Jesus are unique events in human history, so the works which make these events present to successive generations and incorporate readers into these events are also unique. The need to come to terms with a new reality resulted in a new form, the Gospel.

In this chapter we have described the process through which the written Gospels took their present form, and have named some of the literary forms which have been incorporated into the written Gospels, because this information is very helpful in interpreting the good news which Mark, Matthew, and Luke have passed on. In our next chapter we will explore what a knowledge of one form in the Gospels, the parables, can contribute to our understanding of the good news.

Review Questions

1. What events underlie the written Gospels?
2. In the weeks and months immediately after Jesus' death, what about him was of most interest?
3. At what point did the apostles begin to comprehend what they themselves had experienced?

4. How and why did written traditions about the events of Jesus' life grow in the community?

5. To whom did Mark write? What about the circumstances of his audience influenced the emphasis in Mark's Gospel? Explain.

6. What do revelation and inspiration mean when used in relation to the Gospels?

7. To whom did Matthew write? What about the circumstances of his audience influenced the emphasis in his Gospel? Explain.

8. How does Matthew organize his Gospel?

9. Why did Matthew preface his Gospel with a birth narrative?

10. What are the Synoptic Gospels? Why are they called Synoptic Gospels? How do scholars account for their similarity?

11. What is a harmony of the Gospels?

12. To whom did Luke write? What about the circumstances of his audience influenced the emphasis in his Gospel? Explain.

13. How does Luke's structure reflect his theme?

14. How does a Gospel compare to a biography?

15. How does a Gospel compare to history?

16. What is unique about the Gospel as a genre?

Discussion Questions

1. Imagine that you were an apostle who traveled with Jesus. Do you think you would have understood who Jesus was? Why or why not? What might have brought you to belief?
2. Imagine that you are the leader of a worshiping community in the first ten years after Jesus rose from the dead. What would be your motives and goals? What materials would be available to you? How does an early community's use of tradition compare to our present day community's use of traditions?
3. If you were writing to Mark's audience what would you emphasize? What would such an audience need to hear? Are

there people today who need to hear the same emphasis? Explain.

4. How can a work which grew out of oral tradition be considered inspired?
5. If, in one day, you were to visit a person on death row and a person preparing for the birth of a first child, what parts of the Gospel might you think appropriate for each? How does this relate to the New Testament?
6. Why do you think that stories about Jesus' birth were later developments in early Church traditions?
7. Have you been aware that the Gospels are different? Why or why not? Do you have a favorite Gospel passage? Which one? Why? Do you know in which Gospel this passage appears?
8. In what ways does the Gospel help you not just to remember but to re-member? What is your motive in reading the Gospels? How does your motive compare to that of the earliest Christians?

7

Parables

The word "parable" means "comparison." Parables were told to reveal, not to hide the truth. However, those who have read and interpreted parables through the centuries have not always understood the literary form of the parables and so have misinterpreted them. In this chapter we will define the parable as a literary form, looking closely at its function. We will then look at the history of parable interpretation and see how parables lend themselves to misinterpretation. Finally we will interpret a number of parables found in the Synoptic Gospels.

We can see a perfect example of the form and function of a parable in 2 Samuel 12:1–4.

> In the same town were two men, one rich, the other poor. The rich man had flocks and herds in great abundance; the poor man had nothing but a ewe lamb, one only, a small one he had bought. This he fed, and it grew up with him and his children, eating his bread, drinking from his cup, sleeping on his breast; it was like a daughter to him. When there came a traveler to stay, the rich man refused to take one of his own flock or herd to provide for the wayfarer who had come to him. Instead he took the poor man's lamb and prepared it for his guest (2 Sam 12:1–4).

At first glance a parable appears to be simply a short fictional story. Such a story might be told to amuse, to set an example, to inspire. However, a parable is not told for any of these reasons. A parable is told to personally criticize the person to whom the parable is told, to raise that person's consciousness to a new level of understanding, to call that person to conversion and reform.

In order to see the critical function of a parable, we must understand the parable within the social context in which it is told. This parable in 2 Samuel is told to David by Nathan. David has sinned. He has committed adultery with Bathsheba and has arranged for the murder of Bathsheba's husband, Uriah. Nathan is God's prophet. It is his vocation to speak for God. Nathan has to think of a way to tell this most powerful and admired king that he has sinned. How should he do it?

Nathan chooses to teach and correct David through a parable. Nathan thus reveals himself to be a skilled teacher and psychologist. It is Nathan's intent to tell David a story which appears to be merely entertaining, which appears to be about other people entirely, but which is actually about David. David will listen to the story because it is interesting, but he will not be defensive because he does not realize that the story is actually about himself.

David, like all of us, becomes involved with the characters in a good story. As he listens, he starts to form opinions and make judgments about them. When David hears about the rich man who took the poor man's only lamb he is absolutely outraged. "As Yahweh lives," he says to Nathan, "the man who did this deserves to die!"

At this point Nathan draws the comparison which is at the heart of the parable. He says to David, "You are the man." Through his apparently innocuous story, Nathan has compared David, his audience, to a character in the story, the rich man, and has thus led David to perceive and condemn his own behavior.

A parable is a comparison in that it compares someone in the story to someone listening to the story. Through the comparison the listener is criticized and challenged to conversion.

We can see from this example that a parable gets its meaning from its social context. We know the intent of the person who tells the parable by putting the parable in the context of the dramatic interaction in which it is told. Only then do we discern the intended comparison. Only then do we know the meaning of the parable.

Like Nathan, Jesus told parables to challenge, to criticize and to teach the people to whom he spoke. As we know from the last chapter, the accounts of Jesus' teaching were passed on to the early Church through oral tradition. Oral tradition, as we learned in Chapter I, passes on the core of the teaching but does not claim accuracy in social context. In other words, Jesus may have told a story to a particular person to teach that person something about himself or herself. However, when the story was passed on, the audience to whom it was originally told may not have been passed on. Thus when the Gospel editors arranged the materials which they inherited from oral tradition, that tradition included collections of parables no longer in their historical social context. The Gospel editors had to provide the social contexts.

A parable no longer in its social context does not appear to be a parable. Since the critical function of the parable, and the point of the comparison between the story and the audience, both depend on the social context in which the parable is told, the parable separated from its audience ceases to be a parable. It could be interpreted as one might interpret another kind of story entirely, an example story or an allegorical story, for instance. To interpret an exemplum or an allegory one does not need to know the social context in which the story was told.

Parables Interpreted as Allegories

Because the members of the early Church passed on parables independent of their social contexts, they sometimes chose to turn a parable into an allegory rather than to treat it as a parable. We see evidence of this in the Gospels. In all three Synoptic Gospels we read the parable of the sower (Mk 4:3–9; Mt 13:4–9; Lk 8:5–8). If we were to interpret this parable as a parable, we would compare an element in the story to the audience. Notice that when Mark repeats this parable, he makes it clear that Jesus has an urgent message for his listeners. Jesus begins, "Listen!" and ends, "Listen, anyone who has ears to hear!" Jesus is comparing his listeners to the soil. The urgent plea is, "Be good soil."

As this parable was repeated in the early Church before any of the written Gospels were compiled, it undoubtedly became the basis for a sermon. The early Church did not repeat Jesus' words as history but as living words addressed to the believing community. In making the words applicable to a contemporary audience, the early Church treated the parable as though it were an allegory. In an allegory there is not just one basic comparison between the parable and the audience. One need know nothing about the audience to understand the story. Rather, in an allegory there are numerous implied comparisons so that every element in the literal story line stands for something on the allegorical or intentional level. In an allegory there are at least two levels of meaning, one explicit and the other implicit. The intent of the story teller is that his audience understand the implicit message.

The parable of the sower, when separated from its social context, lends itself to an allegorical interpretation. The early Church did interpret it allegorically: the seed is the word, and each element of the original story stands for people who respond to the word in various ways. All three Synoptic Gospels give us an allegorical interpretation (Mk 4:13–20; Mt 13:18–23; Lk 8:11–15).

Students are often very surprised by this explanation of how allegorical interpretations of parables appear in the Gospel. The difficulty is not with understanding that a parable calls for a different kind of interpretation than does an allegory. Students are well able to understand that a parable is drawing a single comparison between the story and an audience, while an allegory is drawing many comparisons independent of any audience. The difficulty arises because, in the Gospel, the allegorical interpretation is attributed directly to Jesus. The Gospels picture Jesus giving the allegorical interpretation to his disciples himself.

To understand why words which grew up in the early Church are attributed to Jesus we must once more recall what we have learned about literature which has passed through oral tradition. Such literature is not claiming exact quotations.

The Gospel writers are not attributing to Jesus only what Jesus actually said historically. They are also attributing to him their hindsight understanding of the significance of what Jesus said and did. If historically the apostles did not understand something Jesus said, and after his resurrection they did come to understand, when they pictured Jesus explaining this they included their hindsight understanding to make the point clearer to the contemporary audience. The intent is always to make the significance of what happened historically clear to the audience being addressed at a later time in history.

This distinction between a parable and an allegory has been well known and accepted in our century, but for hundreds of years parables were interpreted as though they were puzzles—complicated and mysterious allegories whose meaning was deeply hidden and could only be unlocked by the most clever interpreters. As we have seen, the failure to distinguish between a parable and an allegory is evident in the Scripture itself. At its root, the problem probably originated because of the mixture of two cultures, the Hebrew culture and the Greek culture.

Several hundred years before Jesus was born the Hebrew Scriptures were translated into Greek. The Greek translation was called the Septuagint. In the Septuagint the Greek word παραβολή is used to translate the Hebrew word *māšāl* which means not only a comparison but also a proverbial saying. A masal could be a short pithy saying or a long, developed allegory. So the distinction between a parable and an allegory was blurred in the language. Then, when parables were passed on orally, independent of their social context, and were later used as the basis for allegorical sermons by the early Church, a further blurring took place. It is no wonder that the two have been confused for centuries.

Students sometimes ask, "If parables and allegories have been confused for centuries, why bother to make a big distinction between them now? What difference does it make if a parable is interpreted as an allegory?

The answer to that question is that it sometimes make little difference and it sometimes makes a tremendous difference. Sometimes one can interpret a parable as an allegory

INTERPRETING PARABLES AND ALLEGORIES

A Parable: Look for one basic comparison between an element in the story and the audience listening to the story. The lesson comes from this comparison. Ask yourself:

- To whom is Jesus speaking?
- What's the topic?
- With what person or thing in the story does the audience compare?
- What lesson is drawn from this comparison?

Example: *The Parable of the Sower*

- Jesus is speaking to the crowd
- Jesus is talking about being receptive
- The crowd compares to the soil
- Be good soil!

An Allegory: Look for a second level of meaning by equating each element on the literal level with an element on the allegorical level.

Example: Sower—God/a Preacher/etc.
Seed—Word of God
Those on edge of path—Those from whom Satan takes the word
Patches of rock—Those with no root
In thorns—Those in whom the world chokes out the word so there is no fruit
Rich soil—Those who accept the word and bear a rich harvest
Lesson—God's word can bear fruit only in a receptive person

Contrasting the Two Literary Forms:

1. Comparisons—	A Parable is based primarily on a single comparison. An Allegory is based on many comparisons.
2. Audience—	A Parable is addressed specifically and personally to an audience. To understand the parable you must know the audience. An Allegory is self-contained. You need not know the audience to understand it.
3. Forcefulness—	A Parable is a personal challenge to a new way of viewing reality and a new way of acting. An Allegory may be an ingenious story which entertains, which teaches a moral about life generally or about "those other guys."

and no harm is done, even if the interpretation is totally unrelated to the original intent of the parable. Other times, however, a parable is interpreted as an allegory and a harmful conclusion is drawn. The authority of Scripture is put behind a conclusion which contradicts the essence of the Gospel message. We will now give examples of allegorical interpretations of parables, one which is off the subject and several which are harmful. The value of the distinction between parable and allegory will then be made clear.

The Parable of the Good Samaritan

St. Augustine, who lived in the fourth century, thought of parables as mysterious allegorical puzzles. His interpretations show his own ingenuity, but they move totally away from the meaning which the parable has been given by the context in

SOME PARABLES IN MARK'S GOSPEL WITH WHICH JESUS CHALLENGES HIS AUDIENCE

Remember: Some sayings which are not parables came to be called parables.

Some sayings which were parables lost their parable function because oral tradition failed to pass on the social context.

4:1–9 Parable of the sower

4:21 Parable of the lamp

4:26 Parable of the seed growing by itself

4:30 Parable of the mustard seed

12:1 Parable of the wicked husbandman

which it has been placed in the Gospel. An example is Augustine's interpretation of the parable of the good Samaritan.

In Luke's Gospel the parable of the good Samaritan is told in the midst of a conversation which a lawyer is having with Jesus. The lawyer asks Jesus, "What must I do to gain eternal life?" Instead of answering the man's question himself, Jesus says, "What is written in the law? What do you read there?" (Lk 10:26). The man gives a perfect answer. He replies, "You must love the Lord your God with all your heart, with all your soul, with all your strength, and with all your mind, and your neighbor as yourself" (Lk 10:27). Jesus is pleased with his answer. The lawyer must have been feeling rather foolish that he had asked a question and then answered it, for he tries to justify himself by pressing the matter further. He asks: "Who is my neighbor?" (Lk 10:27). Jesus responds by telling the parable of the good Samaritan.

> A man was once on his way down from Jerusalem to Jericho and fell into the hands of brigands; they took all he had, beat him and then made off, leaving him half dead. Now a priest happened to be traveling down the same road, but when he saw the man, he passed by on the other side. In the same way a Levite who came saw him, and passed by on the other side. But a Samaritan traveler who came upon him was moved with compassion when he saw him. He went up and bandaged his wounds, pouring oil and wine on them. He then lifted him on to his own mount, carried him to the inn and looked after him. Next day, he took out two denarii and handed them to the innkeeper. "Look after him," he said, "and on my way back I will make good any extra expense you have" (Lk 10:30–34).

When St. Augustine interpreted this parable he did not treat it as a parable at all. He completely ignored the fact that the parable was part and parcel of a conversation which Jesus was having with the lawyer. Augustine does not ask, "What is Jesus telling the lawyer through the parable?" Rather, he looks at the parable as an allegory full of hidden meaning.

For Augustine, the parable of the good Samaritan is a story which encompasses all of salvation history. He makes the following allegorical comparisons:

The man who is going from Jerusalem to Jericho represents Adam who in turn represents the human race.

Jerusalem represents the celestial city from which the human race has fallen.

Jericho represents human mortality.

The brigands represent the devil.

The wounds which the attackers inflict represent sins which need to be forgiven.

The priest and Levite represent the people of the Old Testament who do not reach salvation.

The Samaritan stands for Jesus.

Augustine understands the story to be allegorically revealing the fact that Jesus' actions saved mankind from sin, since on the literal story level the Samaritan (Jesus) bound up the man's wounds (the sins of mankind).

No one can deny that Augustine's interpretation is very ingenious. There is nothing in the interpretation that is dangerous or "un-Christian," nothing to lead someone into error. However, the ideas in the interpretation are Augustine's. He does not help us understand what Jesus was saying to the lawyer. He has taken the parable out of its social context. His interpretation seems arbitrary and beside the point.

If instead of allegorizing the parable we look for the single comparison and the single lesson which that comparison implies we come up with a very different interpretation indeed.

After telling the parable Luke pictures Jesus asking the lawyer, "Which of these three, do you think, proved himself a neighbor to the man who fell into the brigands' hands?" With this question Jesus is helping the lawyer see that the parable was teaching him something about himself.

As the lawyer listened to the story he might be able to identify with every character but one. He might have been the man in the ditch. He might have been the priest or the Levite, respected members of the Jewish community like the lawyer himself. However, these characters did not turn out to be good, generous people. The lawyer would not want to identify with them. The one character with whom the lawyer might want to identify, because this person did what was right, was the Samaritan. But this was impossible. In the mind of the Jewish lawyer, the Samaritan was a renegade Jew, one to be avoided, one whom the lawyer would not even want to touch. Samaritans were unclean and by law the lawyer need not contaminate himself by contact with the Samaritan. The lawyer would never have considered the Samaritan a neighbor.

The lawyer had revealed a fault of his to Jesus when he asked his original question. He was looking for a law or a rule that, if he fulfilled, would guarantee him eternal life. His answer to his own question, an answer rooted in the law, seems to recognize that man's ability to enter the kingdom of God depends on his ability to love. But his second question tries to limit love by looking for a definition of the word "neighbor." Jesus outsmarts the lawyer by telling a story in which the Samaritan is the good person. The lawyer does not at first realize that the story will criticize him. But when Jesus asks which man in the story was neighbor to the man who was attacked, the lawyer realizes that he has been criticized. He can not bring himself to say, "The Samaritan." To avoid that answer he says, "The one who took pity on him" (Lk 10:37). The question was, "Who is my neighbor?" The answer is, "The Samaritan." Jesus then says to the lawyer, "Go, and do the same yourself." This is to say that in order to enter the kingdom of heaven the lawyer must love the Samaritan or any other person without exception, just as this Samaritan was willing to love the man who was robbed, presumably a Jew and his enemy. By inserting the story in the setting in which he did, Luke turns what might have been simply an example story into a parable which dramatically teaches and criticizes the lawyer to whom it is addressed.

When we compare the allegorical interpretation of the parable to the interpretation which treats the parable as a parable we can see the importance of correctly recognizing the literary form of the parable. The allegorical interpretation is arbitrary and off the point. The interpretation which treats the story as a parable is tied to the text, to the intent of the author. Through interpreting the story as a parable we are able to understand exactly how Luke uses the parable to pass on Jesus' teaching, "Love your enemy," to a lawyer who felt fully justified by the law to fail to love his enemy, the Samaritan.

Augustine's allegorical interpretation, while off the point, did not lead to outright error. Some allegorical interpretations of parables do lead to error.

The Parable of the Talents

One parable which is sometimes used to justify some un-Christian behavior is the parable of the talents. This parable appears in the midst of the long eschatological sermon which Jesus makes to the disciples.

> It is like a man on his way abroad who summoned his servants and entrusted his property to them. To one he gave five talents, to another, two, to a third, one, each in propor-

> tion to his ability. Then he set out. The man who had received the five talents promptly went and traded with them and made five more. The man who had received two made two more in the same way. But the man who had received one went off and dug a hole in the ground and hid his master's money. Now a long time after, the master of those servants came back and went through his accounts with them. The man who had received the five talents came forward bringing five more. "Sir," he said, "you entrusted me with five talents; here are five more that I have made." His master said to him, "Well done, good and faithful servant; you have shown you can be faithful in small things; I will trust you with greater; come and join in your master's happiness." Next the man with the two talents came forward. "Sir," he said, "you entrusted me with two talents; here are two more that I have made." His master said to him, "Well done, good and faithful servant; you have shown you can be faithful in small things; I will trust you with greater; come and join in your master's happiness." Last came forward the man who had the one talent. "Sir," said he, "I had heard you were a hard man, reaping where you have not sown and gathering where you have not scattered; so I was afraid, and I went off and hid your talent in the ground. Here it is; it was yours, you have it back." But his master answered him, "You wicked and lazy servant! So you knew that I reap where I have not sown and gather where I have not scattered? Well, then, you should have deposited my money with the bankers, and on my return I would have recovered my capital with interest. So now, take the talent from him and give it to the man who has the five talents. For to everyone who has will be given more, and he will have more than enough; but from the man who has not, even what he has will be taken away. As for this good-for-nothing servant, throw him out into the dark, where there will be weeping and grinding of teeth" (Mt 25:14–30).

In order to find the audience to whom Jesus is speaking when he tells this parable, one must go back to the beginning of Chapter 24.

> And when he was sitting on the Mount of Olives the disciples came and asked him privately, "Tell us, when is this

going to happen, and what will be the sign of your coming and of the end of the world?" (Mt 24:3).

Remember that Matthew organized his Gospel around five themes, each section containing a narrative and a sermon by Jesus. The sermons are collections of materials woven into a single speech.

If we interpret the parable of the talents as a parable we will look for a comparison between the characters in the story and the audience. In this instance the disciples compare to the servants who have been entrusted with their master's treasure. The lesson is the same as in the parable of the ten bridesmaids which immediately precedes it (Mt 25:1–13), except that it is expanded. Jesus draws the lesson from the parable of the bridesmaids himself: "So stay awake, because you do not know either the day or the hour" (Mt 25:13). The parable of the talents adds to that message, "And while you are awake do not, out of fear, fail to use the gifts you have been given to further the coming of the kingdom."

Harmful Misinterpretations

This parable can be misinterpreted in two ways, each of which is harmful. Both misinterpretations rest on the tendency to allegorize the parable and to make the man who had the servants symbolize God. God is then pictured as a harsh and punishing God who, in one misinterpretation, does not invite repentance, and who, in another misinterpretation, does demand a profit.

The main revelation which all of Scripture, and particularly the New Testament, emphasizes is that our God is a God who loves, who calls us to repentance, and who forgives. To allegorize this parable, to equate the master with God, and then to use the master's behavior as the basis for a hell and damnation sermon is one way to misinterpret the parable.

A second misinterpretation which sometimes results from allegorizing the parable of the talents is to mistake the subject which is being addressed. This parable is about the

SOME PARABLES IN MATTHEW'S GOSPEL WITH WHICH JESUS CHALLENGES HIS AUDIENCE

Remember: Some sayings which are not parables came to be called parables.

Some sayings which were parables lost their parable function because oral tradition failed to pass on the social context.

13:4 Parable of the sower

13:24 Parable of the darnel

13:31 Parable of the mustard seed

13:33 Parable of the yeast

13:44 Parable of the treasure in the field

13:46 Parable of the merchant looking for fine pearls

13:47 Parable of the dragnet

18:23 Parable of the unforgiving debtor

20:1 Parable of the vineyard laborers

21:28 Parable of the two sons

21:33 Parable of the wicked husbandmen

22:1 Parable of the wedding feast

24:45 Parable of the conscientious steward

25:1 Parable of the bridesmaids

25:14 Parable of the talents

coming of the kingdom. It is not about free enterprise. On occasion I have heard this parable misinterpreted to justify the profit motive in business. The person who says "Well, even God expects a profit so why shouldn't I?" has made two mistakes. He has allegorized the parable, thus equating the master with God, and he has missed the subject which the parable is addressing, the coming of the kingdom.

The Parable of the Wicked Husbandmen

Even when a parable invites allegorization, the real lesson of the parable comes from the comparison between the audience and someone in the parable. A good example of this fact is Matthew's parable of the wicked husbandmen.

> Listen to another parable. There was a man, a landowner, who planted a vineyard; he fenced it round, dug a winepress in it and built a tower; then he leased it to tenants and went abroad. When vintage time drew near he sent his servants to the tenants to collect his produce. But the tenants seized his servants, thrashed one, killed another and stoned a third. Next he sent some more servants, this time a larger number, and they dealt with them in the same way. Finally he sent his son to them. "They will respect my son," he said. But when the tenants saw the son, they said to each other, "This is the heir. Come on, let us kill him and take over his inheritance." So they seized him and threw him out of the vineyard and killed him (Mt 21:33–39).

In the Old Testament, a vineyard is used as a symbol for Israel (Is 5:1–7). When Matthew's audience read this parable they would have understood not only that the vineyard was Israel but that the vineyard owner was God, that the servants were the prophets, that the son was Jesus, and that the wicked husbandmen were the Jewish leaders who had condemned Jesus. Matthew's readers had the advantage of hindsight. To see how the parable functions as a parable, though, we should look at it from the point of view of Jesus' audience. They understood less than Matthew's audience. They did not realize that Jesus was the Son of God. Matthew pictures Jesus using this parable in exactly the same way that Nathan used the parable of the rich and poor sheep owners to lead David to condemn himself.

Matthew has Jesus tell this parable to the chief priests and elders of the temple who have asked, "What authority have you for acting like this? And who gave you this authority?" The parable is told in the context of a contentious conversation. After telling the parable, Jesus asks the Jewish leaders, "Now when the owner of the vineyard comes, what will he do to those tenants?" They answered, "He will bring those wretches to a wretched end and leave the vineyard to other tenants who will deliver the produce to him when the season arrives" (Mt 21:40–41). With these words the Jewish leaders unwittingly condemn themselves. When they answered the question they had not yet realized that Jesus was criticizing them through the story. Later they do realize this, for the Gospel writer says, "When they heard his parables, the chief priests and the scribes realized he was speaking about them but though they would have liked to arrest him they were afraid of the crowds, who looked on him as a prophet" (Mt 21:45–46). Although Jesus' parable enabled the Pharisees to see themselves and their actions as Jesus saw them, they did not respond to this new insight about themselves with repentance and conversion. Rather they remained hard-hearted and wanted only to silence their critic. Matthew has skillfully woven the parable into a dramatic context which makes the parable's function perfectly evident.

Finding the Meaning

In addition to protecting us from the errors to which allegorization might lead, a knowledge of the correct way to interpret a parable enables us to find the meaning in stories which would otherwise be extremely puzzling.

The Parable of the Crafty Steward

One parable which often puzzles students is Luke's parable of the crafty steward.

> There was a rich man and he had a steward who was denounced to him for being wasteful with his property. He called for the man and said, "What is this I hear about you? Draw me up an account of your stewardship because you are not to be my steward any longer." Then the steward said to himself, "Now that my master is taking the stewardship from me, what am I to do? Dig? I am not strong enough. Go begging? I should be too ashamed. Ah, I know what I will do to make sure that when I am dismissed from office there will be some to welcome me into their homes."
>
> Then he called his master's debtors one by one. To the first he said, "How much do you owe my master?" "One hundred measures of oil" was the reply. The steward said, "Here, take your bond; sit down straightaway and write fifty." To another he said, "And you, sir, how much do you owe?" "One hundred measures of wheat" was the reply. The steward said, "Here, take your bond and write eighty."
>
> The master praised the dishonest steward for his astuteness. For the children of this world are more astute in dealing with their own kind than are the children of light (Lk 16:1–8).

"Why," students ask, "is the dishonest steward praised and held up as an example?"

To understand what Jesus is teaching through this parable we must first notice to whom he is speaking. In this case we do not have to search for the audience, for Luke tells us that the parable is addressed to the disciples. Next we must ask, "Who in the story is like the disciples?" The disciples are like the dishonest steward, not because they are dishonest but because they too are in a temporary situation. The steward realized that his present position was temporary so that he should act now in such a way as to prepare for his next position. Jesus has been trying to teach his disciples to have the good sense to live this life with an eye to the next, as he has told them to pile up treasure in heaven rather than on earth and to always be waiting for the coming of the Son of Man. Now, through this humorous parable, he again praises the man who remembers the life to come. The dishonest steward is not praised for his dishonesty, but for his foresightedness. Even dishonest people with worldly motives show more common sense when it comes to planning for the future than do children of the light.

Applying the Lesson to Ourselves

The method of parable interpretation which we have employed stops short of involving the twentieth century audience in the action. Many parables, however, reach out and involve a modern day reader in exactly the same way in which they involved Jesus' contemporaries. As we read or hear a parable we, like Jesus' original audience, get involved with the story and start to pass judgment on the characters. As soon as we do this the parable has the potential of calling us to new insights, repentance, and conversion, just as it did its original audience.

The Parable of the Prodigal Son

One parable which very often corrects a modern day audience is the parable of the prodigal son.

> A man had two sons. The younger said to his father, "Father, let me have the share of the estate that would come to me." So the father divided the property between them. A few days later, the younger son got together everything he had and left for a distant country where he squandered his money on a life of debauchery.
>
> When he had spent it all, that country experienced a severe famine, and now he began to feel the pinch, so he hired himself out to one of the local inhabitants who put him on his farm to feed the pigs. And he would willingly have filled his belly with the husks the pigs were eating

> but no one offered him anything. Then he came to his senses and said, "How many of my father's paid servants have more food than they want, and here am I dying of hunger! I will leave this place and go to my father and say: Father, I have sinned against heaven and against you; I no longer deserve to be called your son; treat me as one of your paid servants." So he left the place and went back to his father.
>
> While he was still a long way off, his father saw him and was moved with pity. He ran to the boy, clasped him in his arms and kissed him tenderly. Then his son said, "Father, I have sinned against heaven and against you. I no longer deserve to be called your son." But the father said to his servants, "Quick! Bring out the best robe and put it on him; put a ring on his finger and sandals on his feet. Bring the calf we have been fattening, and kill it; we are going to have a feast, a celebration, because this son of mine was dead and has come back to life; he was lost and is found." And they began to celebrate.
>
> Now the elder son was out in the fields, and on his way back, as he drew near the house, he could hear music and dancing. Calling one of the servants he asked what it was all about. "Your brother has come," replied the servant, "and your father has killed the calf we had fattened because he has got him back safe and sound." He was angry then and refused to go in, and his father came out to plead with him; but he answered his father, "Look, all these years I have slaved for you and never once disobeyed your orders, yet you never offered me so much as a kid for me to celebrate with my friends. But, for this son of yours, when he comes back after swallowing up your property—he and his women—you kill the calf we had been fattening."
>
> The father said, "My son, you are with me always and all I have is yours. But it was only right we should celebrate and rejoice, because your brother here was dead and has come to life; he was lost and is found" (Lk 15:11–32).

This parable can be interpreted in its context within the Gospel, just as we have interpreted the other parables. The parable is addressed to the Pharisees and scribes who complained because Jesus was spending his time with tax collec-

SOME PARABLES IN LUKE'S GOSPEL WITH WHICH JESUS CHALLENGES HIS AUDIENCE

Remember: Some sayings which are not parables came to be called parables.

Some sayings which were parables lost their parable function because oral tradition failed to pass on the social context.

8:1	Parable of the sower
8:16	Parable of the lamp
10:29	Parable of the good Samaritan
11:33	Second parable of the lamp (Different context, so different meaning.)
13:6	Parable of the barren fig tree
13:18	Parable of the mustard seed
13:20	Parable of the yeast
14:7	On choosing places at table

tors and sinners (Lk 15:1–3). The parable is told to criticize and correct the Pharisees and scribes. As the story of the prodigal son is told, the Pharisees will naturally not identify with the younger brother. They will feel sympathetic toward the older brother who has obeyed all the rules and who resents his younger brother, who is a sinner, being welcomed so warmly back into the father's home. As the father corrects the older brother, the Pharisees will find themselves wanting to defend him. After all, the older son is right. He never did anything wrong and was taken for granted. Now his brother comes

14:15	Parable of invited guests who made excuses
14:28	Parable of the man building a tower
14:31	Parable of a king making war
14:34	Parable of the salt
15:4	Parable of the lost sheep
15:8	Parable of the lost drachma
15:11	Parable of the prodigal son
16:1	Parable of the crafty steward
16:19	Parable of the rich man and Lazarus
18:1	Parable of the unscrupulous judge
18:9	Parable of the Pharisee and the publican
19:11	Parable of the pounds
20:9	Parable of the wicked husbandmen

home and is apparently rewarded for being bad. The Pharisees will ask themselves, "Why should such a loving father reprove such a good son?" In hindsight the Pharisees will discover, if they think about it, that this simple story about a father and two sons has criticized them, for they too do not want to forgive, or to eat and drink with sinners.

Many students, particularly the conscientious and responsible ones, find themselves siding with the older brother, just as the Pharisees would have. It takes thought and prayer to recognize our own self-righteousness and failure to love those who have not been as good as we think we have been. This parable has exactly the same power to enlighten, criticize, and call to reform in the twentieth century as it had in the time of Jesus.

The parable of the prodigal son also illustrates the fact that a parable can be used in a different social setting to serve a different function and thus cease to be a parable. This parable of the prodigal son can be used as an example story rather than as a parable. If one tells the story in the context of the sacrament of reconciliation, one is expecting the audience to identify with the younger brother who is a sinner. Just as the younger brother repented and was lovingly received back into his father's home, so will we be received back if we repent. When used in this context the story of the prodigal son ceases to be a parable because it loses its critical function. Rather, the story serves as an example of a person who has repented and is forgiven. We are called to the same kind of repentance, and can be assured of the same kind of welcome.

The Parable of the Laborers in the Vineyard

Another parable which roots out a misperception that many students have is the parable of the laborers who came late to the vineyard.

> Now the kingdom of heaven is like a landowner going out at daybreak to hire workers for his vineyard. He made an agreement with the workers for one denarius a day, and sent them to his vineyard. Going out at about the third hour he saw others standing idle in the marketplace and said to them, "You go to my vineyard too and I will give you a fair wage." So they went. At about the sixth hour and again at about the ninth hour, he went out and did the same. Then at about the eleventh hour he went out and found more men standing round, and he said to them, "Why have you been standing here idle all day?" "Because no one has hired us," they answered. He said to them, "You go into my vineyard too." In the evening, the owner of the vineyard said to his bailiff, "Call the workers and pay them their wages, starting with the last arrivals and ending with the first." So those who were hired at about the

> eleventh hour came forward and received one denarius each. When the first came, they expected to get more, but they too received one denarius each. They took it, but grumbled at the landowner. "The men who came last," they said, "have worked only one hour, and you have treated them the same as us, though we have done a heavy day's work in all the heat." He answered one of them and said, "My friend, I am not being unjust to you; did we not agree on one denarius? Take your earnings and go. I choose to pay the last-comer as much as I pay you. Have I no right to do what I like with my own? Why be envious because I am generous?" (Mt 20:1–16).

Again, the parable should be interpreted in its social context. The parable is addressed to the disciples, but especially to Peter, who wants to know what he has earned. Peter has just asked Jesus, "What about us? We have left everything and followed you. What are we to have, then?" Through this parable Jesus teaches Peter that the kingdom of heaven is not earned; it is generously given. The whole idea of "What have I earned?" is totally inappropriate when speaking of the kingdom.

Just as Peter thought in terms of earning, so do many Americans. We tend to feel we deserve what we have earned, forgetting that the very power to function is a gift. The parable of the vineyard laborers involves modern readers in exactly the same way in which it involved Peter. Our presuppositions about what we deserve and earn are shattered by the landowner's words: "Why be envious because I am generous?" (Mt 20:16). In hindsight we can come to realize that we too are the recipients of generosity. Our sense that we might earn the kingdom is an illusion.

The parable of the prodigal son and the parable of the vineyard laborers illustrate the fact that the parables can enlighten, criticize, and call to conversion a twentieth century audience just as surely as they could challenge and summon those to whom Jesus spoke. To understand the literary form and function of the parables and to interpret them within their literary context does not deprive them of any of their power to affect a present day audience. Rather, such knowledge enables a twentieth century reader to correctly understand the intent behind the parables as they appear in the Gospels, and safeguards a modern day reader from drawing conclusions from the parables which are not only misinterpretations but which might also be erroneous and harmful. When we interpret parables within their dramatic contexts, they become for us just what Jesus intended them to be; they become revelatory. With an understanding of form comes an increased ability to understand meaning. Thus the prophet's words are fulfilled once more:

> I will speak to you in parables and expound things hidden since the foundation of the world (Mt 13:35).

A great deal less is hidden once we know the answer to the question, "What is a parable?"

Review Questions

1. What is a parable?
2. How should a parable be interpreted?
3. What is an allegory?
4. Why are some parables interpreted as though they were allegories in Scripture?
5. How is it possible that a sermon which grew up in the early Church might be attributed to Jesus in the Gospel?
6. In Luke's Gospel to whom does Jesus tell the parable of the Good Samaritan? What is Jesus teaching this individual?
7. To whom does Jesus tell the parable of the talents? What is Jesus teaching his audience?
8. To whom is Jesus speaking when he tells the parable of the wicked husbandmen? What is Jesus teaching?
9. To whom is Jesus speaking when he tells the parable of the crafty steward? What is Jesus teaching?
10. To whom is Jesus speaking when he tells the parable of the wedding feast? What is Jesus teaching?

shapes above the cat's head stand for a person's changing mood as he or she drinks the coffee, the heart stands for a good mood. The mug tells the story of the mood altering effects of drinking that first cup of morning coffee.

Such an allegorical frame of mind is necessary in order to understand much of John's Gospel. On the surface John's Gospel appears to be about the historic Jesus who lived on earth for thirty-three years, was crucified, and rose from the dead. However, this literal level becomes a means of revealing another level of reality entirely, the reality that the risen Christ is just as present, powerful and active in the Church of John's contemporaries as the historical Jesus was in the group of disciples to whom he was physically present during his short life on earth. On the surface John's Gospel appears to be about Jesus' historic actions. On the allegorical level, however, the Gospel is about not the past but the present. John's Gospel is about the Christ of faith who is sacramentally present and active in the contemporary Church.

In this chapter we will look closely at the seven mighty signs which Jesus performs in John's Gospel in order to probe a spiritual reality which underlies those seven signs, the spiritual journey of the contemporary Christian from baptism to resurrection. We will also look closely at the dialogues which are interwoven with the signs in order to understand how John enables his readers to move from an understanding of the past and material realities to an understanding of the present and the spiritual realities which are his allegorical theme. Before looking at each sign individually, however, it might be helpful to see an overview of the spiritual journey which John's audience and we experience in our sacramental life in the Church. This will enable us to see each of the mighty signs in context.

Our spiritual birth takes place at baptism (first sign) through which we are cleansed (cleansing of the temple) and become part of Christ's body, the Church. To continue in our new life we must have faith in Christ (second sign). We must believe in his power to forgive sins (third sign), be nourished through the Eucharist (fourth sign), know that he is with us (fifth sign), and walk in his light (sixth sign). Our spiritual journey ends not in death but in eternal life (seventh sign). On the allegorical level, John's book of signs is about this spiritual journey. One must move beyond the literal level, the level of the material world and events which take place in that world, to understand what John is saying to his audience.

An Allegory about New Birth

The first mighty sign in John's Gospel occurs at the wedding feast at Cana.

> Three days later there was a wedding at Cana in Galilee. The mother of Jesus was there, and Jesus and his disciples had also been invited. When they ran out of wine, since the wine provided for the wedding was all finished, the mother of Jesus said to him, "They have no wine." Jesus said, "Woman, why turn to me? My hour has not come yet." His mother said to the servants, "Do whatever he tells you." There were six stone water jars standing there, meant for the ablutions that are customary among the Jews: each could hold twenty or thirty gallons. Jesus said to the servants, "Fill the jars with water," and they filled them to the brim. "Draw some out now," he told them, "and take it to the steward." They did this; the steward tasted the water, and it had turned into wine. Having no idea where it came from—only the servants who had drawn the water knew—the steward called the bridegroom and said, "People generally serve the best wine first, and keep the cheaper sort till the guests have had plenty to drink; but you have kept the best wine till now."
>
> This was the first of the signs given by Jesus: it was given at Cana in Galilee (Jn 2:1–11).

On the literal level, this account appears to be about Jesus, his mother, and his disciples attending a wedding in Cana. However, to an audience familiar with Scripture, a wedding is a most familiar metaphor used to describe the relationship between Yahweh and his chosen people. Both the Old Testament and the New employ this imagery regularly. One need only recall Hosea, the Song of Songs, Jesus' parables comparing the kingdom of God to a wedding feast, and Paul's profound understanding of the sign value of marriage in order to realize that John is using a well-worn and easily understood image.

Let us look at John's account again, then, and presume that we are reading something more than an account of a wedding. We are reading an allegorical story about the relationship between God and his people.

At the wedding are six stone water jars which hold the water used for the Jewish ritual washings. These jars represent the old law, the old method through which God and his people had been united. Jesus has the servants fill these jars with water. The water does not remain mere water. Through Jesus the water becomes something completely different—wine. Water and wine are familiar symbols to a Christian audience, the water of baptism and the wine which becomes Jesus' blood in the Eucharist. Instead of reaffirming the old covenant with its ritual washings, Jesus has initiated a new covenant, one which is entered through baptism and which is continually celebrated and reaffirmed through the Eucharist. This is truly the best wine.

Mary is a guest at the wedding. It is through her that Jesus receives the request to reveal his glory. Jesus addresses his mother as "woman," both here and at his crucifixion. Many students are terribly puzzled by this impersonal reference. The question is often asked, "Why is Jesus so rude to his mother?" If we recognize the allegorical level of this account, John's reason for having Jesus address his mother as "woman" becomes evident. The wedding at Cana is about a new order of creation, a spiritual order. Just as in the Genesis account "the woman," Eve, is the mother of all the living, so in this new creation Mary becomes the mother of all the living because she gave birth to Jesus who brought new life to all of creation. The word "woman" is an allusion to Genesis which calls Eve to mind. Mary, as an allegorical symbol, is multivalent; there is more than one level of meaning implied by her presence. In addition to representing Eve, Mary represents the Church.

Just as Jesus became physically present to his contemporaries through Mary, so does he become sacramentally present to John's contemporaries through baptism and the Eucharist.

John is teaching his audience that Jesus is just as present to them in the Church and in the sacraments as he was to his contemporaries through Mary and through the Word having become flesh and having dwelt among them. Just as at Cana Jesus worked the first of his signs and let his glory be seen so that his disciples believed in him, so too by his allegorical recounting of this story John has presented the first of his signs. He has revealed Jesus' sacramental presence in order that his disciples might believe in him.

The Danger of Arbitrariness

It is a very common reaction among students to be angry at this allegorical interpretation. "You're reading things into this story that aren't there!" is a common accusation. "John didn't intend you to see all that," they argue. "You're letting your imagination run wild."

One of the difficulties with allegorical interpretations is that they sometimes seem totally arbitrary. The danger of departing completely from the intent of the author when interpreting a passage allegorically was made clear in our last chapter when we quoted St. Augustine's allegorical interpretation of the parable of the good Samaritan. In addition to offering an allegorical interpretation of John's signs, I must also, in order to avoid arbitrariness, demonstrate that the invitation to understand the account allegorically comes from John.

The literary technique which John uses to help the reader see the allegorical significance of his signs is dialogue. Through dialogue John creates situation after situation in which Jesus speaks of a concrete reality in order to teach a spiritual reality. In each instance the person to whom Jesus is speaking misunderstands. The listener takes Jesus' words literally rather than symbolically. This misunderstanding gives Jesus, and John, the opportunity to clarify the deeper meaning of Jesus' words.

Dialogue Clarifies the Allegory

The wedding feast of Cana is followed by two conversations in which Jesus is misunderstood because his audience is not able to think allegorically. The first conversation comes immediately after the cleansing of the temple.

> Just before the Jewish Passover Jesus went up to Jerusalem, and in the temple he found people selling cattle and sheep and pigeons, and the money-changers sitting at their counters there. Making a whip out of some cord, he drove them all out of the temple, cattle and sheep as well, scattered the money-changers' coins, knocked their tables over and said to the pigeon-sellers, "Take all of this out of here and stop turning my Father's house into a market." Then his disciples remembered the words of Scripture: *Zeal for your house will devour me*. The Jews intervened and said, "What sign can you show us to justify what you have done?" Jesus answered, "Destroy this sanctuary, and in three days I will raise it up." The Jews replied, "It has taken forty-six years to build this sanctuary: are you going to raise it up in three days?" But he was speaking of the sanctuary that was his body, and when Jesus rose from the dead, his disciples remembered that he had said this, and they believed the Scripture and the words he had said (Jn 2:13–22).

The cleansing of the temple is the cleansing of the covenant people who no longer are to unite themselves to God by offering sacrifice in the temple but are to unite themselves to the Father through their union with the risen Christ in his mystical body.

The fact that temple worship is replaced by union with the risen Christ is made clear through the dialogue. The Jews ask Jesus, "What sign can you show us to justify what you have done?"

Jesus answers, "Destroy this sanctuary and in three days I will raise it up." John tells us that Jesus' listeners understood him to be referring to the Jewish temple. This is evident, for they say, "It has taken forty-six years to build this sanctuary:

are you going to raise it up in three days?" The misunderstanding of the Jews gives John the opportunity to point out to his readers that they need an allegorical frame of mind to understand Jesus' intent. "But he was speaking of the sanctuary that was his body." By the time John is writing his Gospel, by the end of the first century A.D., Paul's analogy of the Church as Christ's body has been treasured by the Church for nearly half a century. John's audience would know that they themselves are now the temple of God.

> Didn't you realize that you were God's temple and that the Spirit of God was living among you? . . . The temple of God is sacred, and you are that temple (1 Cor 3:16–17).

Through this dialogue between Jesus and the Jews, John is teaching his readers to interpret the historical level—Jesus' cleansing of the temple—allegorically. Jesus' cleansing of the temple becomes, in John's Gospel, an allegorical reminder of an important step in the spiritual journey—cleansing. Just as the temple is cleansed through Jesus' actions, so are Christians, the new temple, cleansed in the new spiritual order.

John places the incident of Jesus' cleansing of the temple at the beginning of Jesus' public ministry while all three of the Synoptic Gospels place this incident at the end of Jesus' ministry as he enters Jerusalem before the crucifixion. Why does John do this? The answer becomes clear when we understand the allegorical significance of these accounts. Through the book of signs we are being introduced to the new spiritual order, an order that begins with the waters of baptism replacing the rituals of Judaism. The effect of these waters is one of cleansing. Through the waters of baptism the Christian dies to his old self; he dies with Jesus only to rise from the waters with the resurrected Christ. This cleansing, this death to the old self, is symbolized by the cleansing of the temple. The rising is made clear through Jesus' words to the Jews. The destruction of the "temple" will lead to the resurrection, the new spiritual order. John places the cleansing of the temple next to the wedding of Cana because, on the allegorical level, the cleansing belongs right at the beginning of the spiritual journey, immediately after the waters of baptism.

In addition to using the dialogues between Jesus and the Jews to enable his reader to penetrate the allegorical significance of his signs, John uses the dialogue between Jesus and Nicodemus. Again, Jesus uses the material world to say something about the spiritual world. Nicodemus misunderstands. His misunderstanding gives Jesus the opportunity to make his deeper meaning clear.

> "I tell you most solemnly, unless a man is born from above, he cannot see the kingdom of God." Nicodemus said, "How can a grown man be born? Can he go back into his mother's womb and be born again?" Jesus replied: "I tell you most solemnly, unless a man is born through water and the spirit, he cannot enter the kingdom of God. What is born of the flesh is flesh; what is born of the Spirit is spirit" (Jn 3:3–6).

In this dialogue Jesus is telling Nicodemus exactly what John has just finished teaching his readers through the allegorical level of his story of the wedding feast of Cana. In order to enter the kingdom one must be born again of water and the spirit; one must be baptized.

John then has Jesus elaborate on the significance of union with Christ. Everyone who believes in him will have eternal life. Notice that Nicodemus disappears. The scene turns from a dialogue to a monologue. The misunderstanding is the occasion for Jesus to give a theological discourse. This pattern which is established with Nicodemus will be seen many times in John's Gospel. The dialogues, interwoven with the signs, elaborate on the theological significance of the allegorical level of the signs. Through allegory and dialogue, John tries to share his deep spiritual insights with his readers.

Many who read John's Gospel do not think to look for an allegorical significance to the signs and so they miss John's point completely.

Such a person was once being considered for jury duty in a trial in which a man was accused of bootlegging. The defense attorney was hoping to soften up a staunchly religious teetotaling woman by asking her to reflect on Jesus' actions at the wedding feast at Cana. The conversation went like this:

Lawyer: "Do you drink alcoholic beverages?"

Woman: "No drop of alcohol has ever touched my lips."

Lawyer: "Do you think drinking alcoholic beverages is wrong?"

Woman: "Alcohol is a tool of the devil."

Lawyer: "Have you read what Jesus did at the wedding feast at Cana?"

Woman: "Yes, I have."

Lawyer: "And what do you think about Jesus' having provided more wine?"

Woman: "I'd think a whole lot more of him if he hadn't done it."

Neither the lawyer nor the woman understood what John's Gospel is about. If we apply the account of the wedding at Cana to ourselves our conversation should not be about our drinking habits but about the transformation we have experienced because of our new birth in the risen Christ. The meaning in John's signs comes from their allegorical significance.

An Allegory about Faith

The second sign in John's Gospel is the cure of the nobleman's son.

> He went again to Cana in Galilee, where he had changed the water into wine. Now there was a court official there whose son was ill at Capernaum and, hearing that Jesus had arrived in Galilee from Judea, he went and asked him to come and cure his son as he was at the point of death. Jesus said, "So you will not believe unless you see signs and portents!" "Sir," answered the official, "come down before my child dies." "Go home," said Jesus. "Your son will live." The man believed what Jesus had said and started on his way; and while he was still on the journey back his servants met him with the news that his boy was alive. He asked them when the boy had begun to recover. "The fever left him yesterday," they said, "at the seventh hour." The father realized that this was exactly the time

> when Jesus had said, "Your son will live"; and he and all his household believed.
>
> This was the second sign given by Jesus, on his return from Judea to Galilee (Jn 4:46–54).

After reading this account students often ask, "Why did Jesus speak so rudely to the poor man whose child was dying? The man had faith, or he wouldn't have asked for Jesus' help in the first place."

As was true in the account of the wedding feast at Cana, a detail which seems puzzling or incongruous may well be the key to the allegorical significance of the account. Instead of thinking of Jesus addressing his comment to the man, let us think of the risen Christ addressing these words to John's contemporaries. "So you will not believe unless you see signs and portents." Many Christians who lived after Jesus may have felt that the previous generation who saw Jesus in the flesh and witnessed his mighty signs with their own eyes had an advantage over them. John would not agree with such an opinion. John realizes that Jesus is just as present and powerful in the Church and in the sacraments as he was when he was physically present during his life on earth. This second sign is emphasizing the faith which is necessary to experience the power of Christ. His power to heal does not depend on his physical presence but on the faith of the person who believes in his presence and power despite his physical absence.

To emphasize this necessary faith John tells a story in which Jesus cures without actually being physically present to the sick person. "Go home," said Jesus. "Your son will live." The man believed what Jesus had said and started on his way.

The allegorical intent is not merely to recount an historical incident but to teach a present reality—the risen Christ is present and powerful to those who have faith.

Dialogue Clarifies the Allegory

Again this truth is taught not only allegorically through the account of a mighty sign, but also through a dialogue in

ALLEGORICAL SIGNIFICANCE OF THE SEVEN SIGNS IN JOHN'S GOSPEL

Sign—material world	Significance—spiritual world
1. Water changed to wine at Cana	At baptism we become a new creation
2. Cure of nobleman's son	We must have faith to grow in Christ.
3. Cure of man at pool in Bethzatha	The risen Christ, through his Church, still has power to forgive sins.
4. Miracle of the loaves	The Eucharist, Jesus' body and blood, gives spiritual nourishment.
5. Jesus walks on water	The risen Christ is always with us.
6. Cure of the man born blind	Christ is our light—he reveals the truth and shows us the way to the Father.
7. Raising of Lazarus	Our rebirth in baptism and life in Christ lead to eternal life.

which Jesus urges a woman to think allegorically and she brings others to faith in Christ. Before this second sign Jesus has a conversation with a Samaritan woman. This conversation follows the same pattern as did the conversation with Nicodemus. Jesus uses the material world to teach something about the spiritual world. Again the image used is water.

> Whoever drinks this water will get thirsty again, but anyone who drinks the water that I shall give will never be thirsty again: The water that I shall give will turn into a spring inside him, welling up to eternal life (Jn 4:14).

The woman has no idea in the world that Jesus is speaking not of well water but of baptism. Like Nicodemus, she understands the words on the material level and responds: "Sir, give me some water" (Jn 4:15). The misunderstanding gives Jesus the opportunity to prolong the conversation.

As the conversation continues, the woman begins to understand that the man to whom she is speaking is the Christ. As she goes back to town to spread the good news the disciples return to Jesus. The same pattern of misunderstanding continues. The disciples urge him:

> "Rabbi, do have something to eat"; but he said, "I have food to eat that you do not know about." So the disciples asked one another, "Has someone been bringing him food?" But Jesus said, "My food is to do the will of the one who sent me and to complete his work" (Jn 4:31–34).

Once more Jesus' words are taken literally. Through dialogue we realize that they are to be understood metaphorically.

John brings his story to a close by emphasizing the fact that the Samaritans came to believe, not from what others said but from their own experience.

> They said to the woman, "Now we no longer believe because of what you told us. We have heard him ourselves and we know that he really is the Savior of the world" (Jn 4:42).

John wants his audience to be like those Samaritans. Through the power of Christ's presence in water and bread, he wants them to experience the reality of the risen Christ. Their belief should not rest on the reported experience of others but on their own present experience of the risen Christ's presence among them. They must have faith to experience Christ's power as did the nobleman whose son was healed.

An Allegory about Forgiveness

The third mighty sign in John's Gospel is the cure of the sick man at the pool of Bethzatha.

> Some time after this there was a Jewish festival, and Jesus went up to Jerusalem. Now at the Sheep Pool in Jerusalem there is a building, called Bethzatha in Hebrew, consisting of five porticos; and under these were crowds of sick people—blind, lame, paralyzed—waiting for the water to move; for at intervals the angel of the Lord came down into the pool, and the water was disturbed, and the first person to enter the water after this disturbance was cured of any ailment he suffered from. One man there had an illness which had lasted thirty-eight years, and when Jesus saw him lying there and knew he had been in this condition for a long time, he said, "Do you want to be well again?" "Sir," replied the sick man, "I have no one to put me into the pool when the water is disturbed; and while I am still on the way, someone else gets there before me." Jesus said, "Get up, pick up your sleeping-mat and walk." The man was cured at once, and he picked up his mat and walked away (Jn 5:1–10).

Now that we are getting more accustomed to John's allegorical methods, some of his meaning will probably be more evident. Once again we have a Jewish feast day. Once again we have waters of Judaism which are inadequate. Once again we have Jesus' powerful actions accomplishing what the customs of Judaism are unable to accomplish. There is an additional allegorical meaning here which would have been evident to John's audience but which may have to be explained to a twentieth century American. John's audience would understand that the man's physical illness represented sin. Jesus' relieving the man of the effect of sin represents Jesus' power to forgive sin.

In previous chapters of this book we have traced the Israelites' understanding of the mystery of human suffering. In the story of the man and woman in the garden, the connection between suffering and sin is clearly illustrated. The Jews came to believe not only that sin inevitably caused suffering, but also that all suffering was due to sin. The connection between sin and suffering was very firm in their minds, as we can tell from a question which John pictures the disciples asking Jesus later in this same Gospel.

> Rabbi, who sinned, this man or his parents, for him to have been born blind? (Jn 9:2).

This belief made physical illness an obvious symbol for sin in the minds of John's audience.

While physical illness works as a symbol for sin for John's audience, possession by the devil does not. The reason for this is that possession was not seen as the fault of the one possessed. Demons were understood to be more powerful than humans and able to possess them without the cooperation of the one possessed. In other words, if a person were suffering physically from an illness, that person must have been a sinner because suffering is a punishment for sin. If a person were possessed, that person may well have been innocent. This may be the reason why there are no instances of possession in John's Gospel. Possession does not work as a symbol. It has no natural allegorical significance.

Dialogue Clarifies the Allegory

Once again, the allegorical significance of the sign of the curing of the man at the sheep pool is made explicit in dialogue. The Jews objected to Jesus' having cured the man on the sabbath. Jesus tells them:

> The Father judges no one; he has entrusted all judgment to the Son, so that all may honor the Son as they honor the Father (Jn 5:23).

John is teaching his audience that the risen Christ, present sacramentally in the Church, has power to forgive sin just as surely as did the historical Jesus. There is no reason to envy those who were Jesus' historical contemporaries. Christ is in authority in the present and has the power to free man from sin.

An Allegory about the Eucharist

The fourth sign in John's Gospel is the feeding of the multitude with the barley loaves and fishes.

> Some time after this, Jesus went off to the other side of the Sea of Galilee—or of Tiberias—and a large crowd followed him, impressed by the signs he gave by curing the sick. Jesus climbed the hillside, and sat down there with his disciples. It was shortly before the Jewish feast of Passover.
>
> Looking up, Jesus saw the crowds approaching and said to Philip, "Where can we buy some bread for these people to eat?" He only said this to test Philip; he himself knew exactly what he was going to do. Philip answered, "Two hundred denarii would only buy enough to give them a small piece each." One of his disciples, Andrew, Simon Peter's brother, said, "There is a small boy here with five barley loaves and two fish; but what is that among so many?" Jesus said to them, "Make the people sit down." There was plenty of grass there, and as many as five thousand men sat down. Then Jesus took the loaves, gave thanks, and gave them out to all who were sitting ready; he then did the same with the fish, giving out as much as was wanted. When they had eaten enough he said to the disciples, "Pick up the pieces left over, so that nothing gets wasted." So they picked them up, and filled

> twelve hampers with scraps left over from the meal of five barley loaves. The people, seeing this sign that he had given, said, "This really is the prophet who is to come into the world." Jesus, who could see they were about to come and take him by force and make him king, escaped back to the hills by himself (Jn 6:1–15).

Again the allegorical significance of this sign is rather obvious. John tells us that the time is shortly before the feast of Passover. John's audience, well aware of the significance of the Jewish Passover, and also of the fact that Jesus had initiated a new covenant celebration at his last Passover meal with his disciples, would not miss the meaning of such a detail. Once more Jewish rituals are being replaced by Christian ritual. The unleavened bread of the Passover ritual has become the living bread, the presence of the risen Christ in the Eucharist. Through Christ's power, the limited gifts of his people (the boy's few loaves and fishes) are multiplied so that there is more than enough to feed the whole Church no matter how large it grows—twelve baskets are left over. The number twelve, of course, recalls the twelve tribes and the twelve disciples. It represents the whole Church. Through the Eucharist the Church is and will always be nourished.

Dialogue Clarifies the Allegory

The allegorical significance of the sign is once more made explicit through dialogue. John pictures the crowd whom Jesus fed as unable to pierce the significance of his action. Jesus says to them:

> I tell you most solemnly, you are not looking for me because you have seen the signs but because you had all the bread you wanted to eat. Do not work for food that cannot last, but work for food that endures to eternal life (Jn 6:26–27).

Like the woman at the well who thought Jesus meant "water" in the literal sense of the word, the crowd thinks Jesus means "bread" literally. They ask for a sign, similar to the sign of manna, the bread which fed their ancestors during the exodus. Jesus tells them that he himself is the sign, the bread from heaven.

> I am the bread of life. He who comes to me will never be hungry; he who believes in me will never thirst (Jn 6:35).

The Paschal Lamb

Since John's fourth sign is about the risen Christ's presence in the Eucharist, it might be wise to stop and mention a related question before going on to the fifth sign. Many students are amazed to find, when they read John's account of Jesus' Last Supper with his disciples, that no mention is made of the institution of the Eucharist (Jn 13:1–17:26). They ask, "If John's Gospel is really about Christ's sacramental presence in the Church, why did he omit the institution of one of the sacraments?" John certainly handles the Last Supper in a very different way than do Mark, Matthew and Luke. In the Synoptic Gospels the Last Supper is the Passover meal. In John's Gospel the whole passion is moved up twenty-four hours. In John's Gospel the Jews are preparing for the Passover on the day Jesus dies (Jn 19:31, 42). Why the change in timing?

I think the answer to both questions, the altered time as well as the omission of the institution of the Eucharist, relates to John's allegorical method. First, why is there no account of the institution of the Eucharist? John has already established Christ's presence in the Eucharist through his fourth sign and through the following dialogue in which he has Jesus emphasize the fact that his flesh is real food. He does not need the Last Supper to introduce the Eucharist. By moving the event of Jesus' passion forward by twenty-four hours John has Jesus slain at the same time that the lambs are being slain for the Passover celebration. Allegorically there is a powerful message in this change of time. Once again the ineffective Jewish rituals are being replaced by Christian rituals. Historically the blood of the slain Passover lambs gave physical life to the Israelites' first-born at the time of their flight from Egypt (Ex 12:11–14). The blood of the new slain lamb, Jesus, gives not just physical life but spiritual life, eternal life. It is this deep comprehension of the saving effects of Jesus' passion, death, and resurrection which is alluded to when John the Baptist first gives witness to Jesus with the words, "Look, there is the lamb of God" (Jn 1:35). By moving the events of the passion forward twenty-four hours John allegorically compares the Passover lambs, and the effectiveness of the blood of each. Through Jesus comes eternal life.

An Allegory about the God Who Is with Us

John's fifth sign is Jesus' walking on water.

> That evening the disciples went down to the shore of the lake and got into a boat to make for Capernaum on the other side of the lake. It was getting dark by now and Jesus had still not rejoined them. The wind was strong, and the sea was getting rough. They had rowed three or four miles when they saw Jesus walking on the lake and coming toward the boat. This frightened them, but he said, "It is I. Do not be afraid." They were for taking him into the boat, but in no time it reached the shore at the place they were making for (Jn 6:16–21).

Through this sign John reminds his audience that the risen Christ is always present. In this episode the apostles feel alone, separated from Jesus under circumstances in which it would seem impossible that he might join them; they are in a boat in rough water. Jesus, however, is with them. Just as the apostles felt alone when they were not, so might John's audience sometimes feel alone. However, they too need not fear, for the risen Christ is present.

Dialogue Clarifies the Allegory

The same promise of Jesus' continued presence is made later in John's Gospel in dialogue. At the Last Supper Jesus says to his apostles:

> I will not leave you orphans;
> I will come back to you.
> In a short time the world will no longer see me;
> but you will see me,
> because I live and you will live.
> On that day
> you will understand that I am in my Father
> and you in me and I in you (Jn 14:18–20).

An Allegory about Spiritual Insight

The sixth sign in John's Gospel is the curing of the man born blind.

> As he went along, he saw a man who had been blind from birth. His disciples asked him, "Rabbi, who sinned, this man or his parents, for him to have been born blind?" "Neither he nor his parents sinned," Jesus answered. "He was born blind so that the works of God might be displayed in him.
>
> "As long as the day lasts
> I must carry out the work of the one who sent me;
> the night will soon be here when no one can work.
> As long as I am in the world
> I am the light of the world."
>
> Having said this, he spat on the ground, made a paste with the spittle, put this over the eyes of the blind man, and said to him, "Go and wash in the Pool of Siloam (a name that means 'sent')." So the blind man went off and washed himself, and came away with his sight restored (Jn 9:1–7).

Dialogue Clarifies the Allegory

In this sign John has Jesus explain the allegorical significance of the sign as he performs it. Just as Jesus gave physical sight to the blind man, so he gives spiritual sight to his people, the Church. Jesus is "the light of the world" (Jn 9:5).

The dialogue which follows the sign emphasizes the allegorical significance of the sign by dealing with blindness as both a physical condition and a spiritual condition. The man who is given both physical and spiritual light through Jesus' power and presence grows in faith. He begins by not knowing who Jesus is. Then he moves to the insight that Jesus must be a prophet. Next he realizes that Jesus must be from God or the power of God would not be manifested through him. Finally the once blind man sees the light clearly. He recognizes Jesus' divinity. "The man said, 'Lord, I believe,' and worshiped him" (Jn 9:38).

The Pharisees, on the other hand, become progressively blinder as they turn from the light of Christ. In the beginning, some of them appear willing to learn from Jesus as they debate the significance of Jesus' having given sight to the blind man.

> Then some of the Pharisees said, "This man cannot be from God; he does not keep the sabbath." Others said, "How could a sinner produce signs like this?" And there was disagreement between them (Jn 9:16).

However, they turned from the light and chose darkness instead. They refused to believe the evidence of their own senses and began to doubt that the man had ever been blind in the first place (Jn 9:18). They then became locked into their old misperceptions, ideas which they had developed as disciples of Moses. Because they believed that only sin could cause suffering, they could not see that the once blind man was a good and honest person. Because they believed that it was wrong to do any kind of work on the sabbath, they could not believe that Jesus, who healed on the sabbath, could be from God. Their old misperceptions blinded them to the light. Once again, John is making it evident that Jewish laws and rituals are inadequate. Light is not found in the law of Moses but in the person of Christ. This whole dramatic dialogue re-emphasizes a theme first introduced in John's prologue and later allegorically presented through the sixth sign—Jesus is "the light of the world." Those who reject his light choose death. But those who live in his light choose life, eternal life in the Church and in the kingdom.

An Allegory about Eternal Life

The seventh allegorical sign in John's Gospel is the raising of Lazarus.

> There was a man named Lazarus who lived in the village of Bethany with his two sisters, Mary and Martha, and he was ill. It was the same Mary, the sister of the sick man Lazarus, who anointed the Lord with ointment and wiped his feet with her hair. The sisters sent this message to Jesus, "Lord, the man you love is ill." On receiving the message, Jesus said, "This sickness will end, not in death but in God's glory, and through it the Son of God will be glorified."
>
> Jesus loved Martha and her sister and Lazarus, yet when he heard that Lazarus was ill he stayed where he was for two more days before saying to the disciples, "Let us go to Judea." The disciples said, "Rabbi, it is not long since the Jews wanted to stone you; are you going back again?" Jesus replied:
>
> > "Are there not twelve hours in the day?
> > A man can walk in the daytime without stumbling
> > because he has the light of this world to see by;
> > but if he walks at night he stumbles,
> > because there is no light to guide him."
>
> He said that and then added, "Our friend Lazarus is resting. I am going to wake him." The disciples said to him, "Lord, if he is able to rest he is sure to get better." The phrase Jesus used referred to the death of Lazarus, but they thought that by "rest" he meant "sleep," so Jesus put

INTERWEAVING OF ALLEGORICAL SIGNS AND SOME RELATED DIALOGUES IN JOHN'S GOSPEL

2:1–12	First Sign—Wedding at Cana
3:1–21	Dialogue with Nicodemus about being "born" again
4:5–26	Dialogue with woman at the well about living "water"
4:27–38	Dialogue with disciples about Jesus' "food"
4:43–54	Second Sign—Cure of Nobleman's Son
5:1–9	Third Sign—Cure of Man at Pool of Bethzatha
5:19–47	Dialogue with Jews about Jesus as judge
6:1–15	Fourth Sign—Miracle of the Loaves
6:16–21	Fifth Sign—Jesus Walks on Water
6:26–40	Dialogue with crowd about Jesus as the "bread" of life
6:41–66	Dialogue with Jews about Jesus as the "bread" of life
7:12	Dialogue with people about Jesus as the "light" of the world
9:1–7	Sixth Sign—Cure of the Man Born Blind
9:4–5, 13–41	Dialogues about Jesus as "light" and spiritual "blindness"
11:1–44	Seventh Sign—Raising of Lazarus
11:21–27	Dialogue with Martha about eternal life

Preceded by a Liturgical Hymn (1:1–18)

Followed by an account of the preparation for the passion (12:1—17:26), the passion itself (18:1—19:42), and the resurrection (20:1—21:25) it plainly, "Lazarus is dead; and for your sake I am glad I was not there because now you will believe. But let us go to him." Then Thomas—known as the Twin—said to the other disciples, "Let us go too, and die with him."

On arriving, Jesus found that Lazarus had been in the tomb for four days already. Bethany is only about two miles from Jerusalem, and many Jews had come to Martha and Mary to sympathize with them over their brother. When Martha heard that Jesus had come she went to meet him. Mary remained sitting in the house. Martha said to Jesus, "If you had been here, my brother would not have died, but I know that, even now, whatever you ask of God, he will grant you." "Your brother," said Jesus to her, "will rise again." Martha said, "I know he will rise again at the resurrection on the last day." Jesus said,

"I am the resurrection.
If anyone believes in me,
even though he dies he will live
and whoever lives and believes in me
will never die.
Do you believe this?"

"Yes, Lord," she said, "I believe that you are the Christ, the Son of God, the one who was to come into this world."

When she had said this, she went and called her sister Mary, saying in a low voice, "The Master is here and wants to see you." Hearing this, Mary got up quickly and went to him. Jesus had not yet come into the village; he was still at the place where Martha had met him. When the Jews who were in the house sympathizing with Mary saw her get up so quickly and go out, they followed her, thinking that she was going to the tomb to weep there.

Mary went to Jesus, and as soon as she saw him she threw herself at his feet, saying, "Lord, if you had been here, my brother would not have died." At the sight of her tears, and those of the Jews who followed her, Jesus said in great distress, with a sigh that came straight from the heart, "Where have you put him?" They said, "Lord, come and see." Jesus wept; and the Jews said, "See how much he loved him!" But there were some who remarked, "He opened the eyes of the blind man; could he not have pre-

> vented this man's death?" Still sighing, Jesus reached the tomb: it was a cave with a stone to close the opening. Jesus said, "Take the stone away." Martha said to him, "Lord, by now he will smell; this is the fourth day." Jesus replied, "Have I not told you that if you believe you will see the glory of God?" So they took away the stone. Then Jesus lifted up his eyes and said:
>
> "Father, I thank you for hearing my prayer.
> I knew indeed that you always hear me,
> but I speak for the sake of all these who stand round me,
> so that they may believe it was you who sent me."
>
> When he had said this, he cried in a loud voice, "Lazarus, here! Come out!" The dead man came out, his feet and hands bound with bands of stuff and a cloth round his face. Jesus said to them, "Unbind him; let him go free" (Jn 11:1–44).

The story of the raising of Lazarus is not primarily about physical death and life restored on earth. We are to move beyond the literal level, the material world, and understand that the story is about spiritual life.

Dialogue Clarifies the Allegory

Once more John uses a literal misunderstanding to try to enable his readers to move from one level of meaning to another.

> "Our friend Lazarus is resting. I am going to waken him." The disciples said to him, "Lord if he is able to rest he is sure to get better." The phrase Jesus used referred to the death of Lazarus, but they thought that by "rest" he meant "sleep," so Jesus put it plainly: "Lazarus is dead; and for your sake I am glad I was not there because now you will believe" (Jn 11:11–15).

By the time John is writing this Gospel many of the Christians who hoped to be alive for the second coming had died. The survivors found this very distressing. Would these people be saved too? Had they missed Christ by dying before he came again? Through this conversation before the raising of Lazarus John is teaching his audience that physical death is to the spiritual life no more than sleep is to life on earth. Sleep doesn't interrupt life on earth despite its appearance. Physical death does not interrupt eternal life despite its appearance. It is the present reality of eternal life which John is emphasizing in this account. Eternal life is entered into at baptism. It has already begun. It is now. It is not just something to look forward to in the future. To emphasize this truth John pictures Martha saying to Jesus:

> I know he will rise again at the resurrection on the last day (Jn 11:25).

Martha is looking forward in faith to something in the future. Jesus wants her to realize that the resurrection is now. He tells her this both in word and action. Jesus says:

> I am the resurrection.
> If anyone believes in me,
> even though he dies he will live,
> and whoever lives and believes in me will never die (Jn 11:26).

For the one who has faith in Christ, death is not death. Just as Lazarus regains physical life, so too does the Christian regain spiritual life through the presence of the risen Christ in his Church. Just as Jesus says to those present at the raising of Lazarus, "Unbind him; let him go free," so does John say the same words to the Church. Each believer is unbound and free, free from sin and death, by the power of the risen Christ. Eternal life has already begun.

Through his seven allegorical signs, then, John has been teaching his audience who Christ is and what significance Christ's life, death and resurrection have for the contemporary Church. Christ's followers are reborn in Christ through bap-

THE EFFECT OF JOHN'S ALLEGORICAL METHOD

I. The material world becomes a sign of Christ's presence.

water bread light wine health (absence of sickness) life food	All symbolize Christ's presence

"All that came to be had life in him" (Jn 1:1).

II. Everyday experiences become signs of Christ's presence.

Thirst symbolizes longing for Christ.
Hunger symbolizes longing for Christ.
Love reflects the presence of Christ.
Words remind one of the Christ who reveals the Father.
Freedom reminds one of the effects of Christ's passion.
Safety reminds one of Jesus' care.
Fruitfulness reflects union with Christ.

III. Conclusion: Don't look just to history to find Christ. Look to your present experience.

"Now we no longer believe because of what you told us; we have heard him ourselves and we know that he really is the Savior of the world" (Jn 4:42).

tism (first sign). They are cleansed and become part of the new temple, his body. They must have faith in his presence even when they cannot see him (second sign), believe in his power to forgive sin (third sign), derive spiritual nourishment from his presence in the Eucharist (fourth sign), rest secure in the fact that he is always with them (fifth sign), and live in his light (sixth sign) in order to receive eternal life (seventh sign).

Jesus Is "Raised Up"

John's Gospel, like the Synoptics, ends with an account of the passion, death and resurrection. While I would not want to describe this account as an allegory, it is true to say that the account is as much about the risen, triumphant Christ as it is about the suffering, historical Jesus. In John's Gospel, Jesus' defeat becomes his victory; his being raised up on the cross never obscures his being raised up to the Father in victory. The power and glory of the risen Christ shine through the passion account. John emphasizes the birth of the Church in Christ's death when he says:

> When they came to Jesus, they found he was already dead, and so instead of breaking his legs, one of the soldiers pierced his side with a lance; and immediately there came out blood and water (Jn 19:33–34).

Once more we see the paschal lamb who gives life. Once again we see, born from Jesus' suffering and death, the Church and the sacraments of baptism and the Eucharist. John closes his Gospel with a statement not about the past but about the present, not simply about the historical Jesus but about the risen Christ.

> There were many other signs that Jesus worked and the disciples saw, but they are not recorded in this book. These are recorded so that you may believe that Jesus is the Christ, the Son of God, and that believing this you may have life through his name (Jn 20:30–31).

An understanding of John's allegorical method is an indispensable tool for those who wish to understand the signs which John has given his readers to enable them to come to knowledge and faith in Christ.

Review Questions

1. What is an allegory?
2. What is the allegorical significance of the sign performed at the wedding feast of Cana?
3. What is the allegorical significance of the cleansing of the temple?
4. How do the dialogues between Jesus and the Jews, and between Jesus and Nicodemus, cast light on the allegorical signs?
5. What is the allegorical significance of the curing of the nobleman's son?
6. How does the incident between Jesus, the woman at the well, and her townspeople cast light on the allegorical sign?
7. What is the allegorical significance of the curing of the man at the Sheep Pool?
8. How does the dialogue between Jesus and the Jews cast light on the allegorical sign?
9. What is the allegorical significance of the multiplication of the loaves?
10. How does the dialogue between Jesus and the crowd cast light on the allegorical sign?
11. Why might John have omitted the institution of the Eucharist at the Last Supper and changed the timing of that meal in his Gospel?
12. What is the allegorical significance of Jesus' walking on water?
13. How do Jesus' words to his apostles at the Last Supper cast light on this sign?
14. What is the allegorical significance of the curing of the man born blind?

15. How does the dialogue which follows cast light on the allegorical significance of the sign?

16. What is the allegorical significance of the raising of Lazarus?

17. How does Jesus' dialogue with Martha cast light on this sign?

18. What is the significance of blood and water flowing from Christ's body after the crucifixion?

Discussion Questions

1. Have you read or studied allegories in the past? Name some.
2. Why might an author choose to write allegorically? Why is allegory uniquely suited to religious topics?
3. How does John invite his readers to look for an allegorical level to his material signs?
4. Is the message contained in the allegorical level of John's Gospel as applicable to us as it was to John's contemporaries? Explain.
5. In our culture do people still tend to look on sickness as a punishment of some sort? Why do you think human beings tend to connect suffering with punishment?
6. Do you ever find yourself envying Jesus' contemporaries? Why or why not?
7. Have you ever had the experience of feeling deserted by God and then realized in a powerful way that he is present after all? How did you recognize his presence?
8. John pictures the Pharisees as willfully blind. Are we sometimes willfully blind?
9. John pictures the blind man coming to faith and understanding slowly, as part of a process. Has your coming to faith been a process? Explain.
10. The Pharisees held on to old ideas which blinded them to new understandings. Do we ever do this? Can you give some examples?
11. Do you think we Christians act as though we believe in life after death? Why or why not?

12. When do you think eternal life begins? Why?
13. From what are we "unbound" by a belief in life after death? Does this belief make any real difference in your life?
14. Has reading John's Gospel enabled you to see the created world as a sign of Christ's presence in our midst? Explain.

9

Letters

What is a letter? Many students feel on much firmer ground when we move from John's Gospel to Paul's epistles. The literary form of a letter is familiar to all. When we think about letters, though, we realize that we are familiar with more than one kind of letter.

Sometimes a letter is simply a means of communication between two people who are not physically present to each other. This kind of letter is one side of a personal conversation and contains information which could have been said rather than written had the two people not been separated by distance.

Another kind of letter is a "pastoral" letter. The bishops of the United States sometimes address not only the Catholic community but the world community on matters of concern to all. The bishops write such letters as part of their teaching ministry. In no way are pastoral letters part of a casual conversation. Rather, the letters are to be regarded as having some authority. Exactly what authority such a letter has is a matter for discussion. The bishops themselves discussed the authority of their pastoral letter, "The Challenge of Peace: God's Promise and Our Response," by pointing out that not all statements in the letter have the same moral authority. Some statements are universally binding moral truths found in the teaching of the Church while others are applications or recommendations with which we might disagree. A letter written to a group of people as part of the teaching ministry of a person in authority is not the same kind of writing as a personal letter.

Still a third kind of letter with which we are familiar is the letter used as a literary device. Sometimes a novelist or an essayist will choose the form of a letter to reveal character or develop ideas. It is not unusual to have a whole novel consist of nothing but letters supposedly written over a period of years. By reading the letters in order one is able to see the character grow and change in response to varying circumstances.

Sometimes an editor or a biographer will collect, arrange, and publish the letters of an historical person. By reading such a collection of letters we are able to grow in our understanding of the life and times of the letter writer, as well as of his or her personality. We can also see how the writer grew and changed over time.

When we use the word "letter" or "epistle" in reference to the letters in the New Testament, to which of these kinds of letters are we referring? The question is not simply answered. As we shall see, some aspects of both the personal and pastoral letters are evident in the New Testament epistles. In addition, because we have a number of Paul's letters written over a period of some years, it is possible to see a growth in understanding in his letters.

Paul's Letters

Of the twenty-one epistles in the New Testament, thirteen are attributed to Paul. Of these thirteen, seven are considered to be Paul's without any doubt or debate while the authorship of the others is disputed. In this chapter, as we grow in our understanding of the literary form "letter," we will not enter the debate regarding the disputed letters but will accept those usually attributed to Paul as his.

The order in which the letters appear in the New Testament is not the order in which they were written. The compilers of the New Testament have arranged the letters from the longest to the shortest. If we want to be able to see Paul's growth in understanding we will have to look at the letters in the order in which they were written rather than in the order in which they now appear in the New Testament.

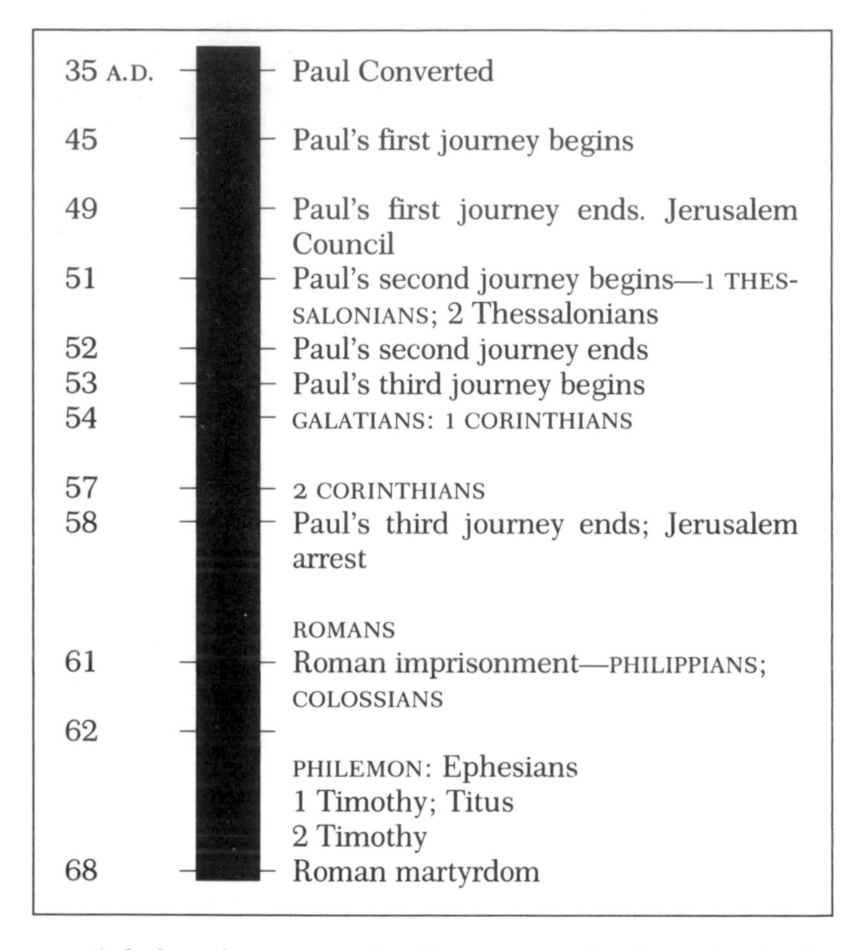

Scholars do not completely agree on the dates for Paul's letters because the two sources in Scripture for dating Paul's activities, Acts 9:1–30 and Galatians 1:11—2:3, are not entirely consistent. However, our inability to know exact dates is unimportant. We do not need to know the dates for each letter and each event. It is far more important to know the probable order of the events and letters because this allows us to see the growth process, the coming to knowledge which is, in addition to literary form, one of the important contexts within which we must understand what we are reading.

The accompanying time line will give us the approximate dates and the probable order of Paul's letters. Those in capitals are undoubtedly Paul's. The others are disputed. These dates would be generally accepted by most scholars with the exception of the date for Philippians. Some suggest that Paul may have been imprisoned earlier, in 54 A.D., and that Philippians dates to that earlier imprisonment.

So far we have looked carefully at the genre "letter," and have distinguished several kinds of letters with which we are familiar. We have also put Paul's letters in order. It remains now to compare Paul's letters to personal and pastoral letters, and to see Paul's growth. We will then come to understand how a knowledge of genre and of historical context helps us to understand the revelation which comes to us in the form of letters.

Personal Elements

Paul's letters could never be described as merely personal letters, parts of conversations which have no universal significance for the Church at all. While this is true, there are elements of Paul's letters which are personal and which affect his message. We will look at three characteristics of the letters which reflect their personal nature: personal messages, personal emotional characteristics or moods, and personal mental characteristics or ways of thinking. Recognizing these personal elements in Paul's letters will help us learn to separate the purely personal from the core of the revelation contained in the letters.

Personal Messages

Paul's letters usually begin with a salutation and a hymn of thanksgiving and end with a conclusion. The conclusion often includes personal messages. An example is Paul's conclusion to 1 Corinthians.

> I shall be coming to you after I have passed through Macedonia—and I am doing no more than pass through Ma-

FORM OF GRAECO-ROMAN AND JEWISH LETTERS

I.	*Opening formula*—	Paul includes the sender, the receiver and a blessing.
II.	*Thanksgiving*—	This section introduces the theme of the letter.
III.	*Body*—	This is the message of the letter. Paul expands the body to include doctrinal and ethical matters.
IV.	*Closing*—	This section includes personal greetings, doxologies, and benedictions.

cedonia—and I may be staying with you, perhaps even passing the winter, to make sure that it is you who send me on my way wherever my travels take me. As you see, I do not want to make it only a passing visit to you and I hope to spend some time with you, the Lord permitting. In any case I shall be staying at Ephesus until Pentecost because a big and important door has opened for my work and there is a great deal of opposition.

If Timothy comes, show him that he has nothing to be afraid of in you: like me, he is doing the Lord's work, and nobody is to be scornful of him. Send him happily on his way to come back to me; the brothers and I are waiting for him. As for our brother Apollos, I begged him to come to you with the brothers but he was quite firm that he did not want to go yet and he will come as soon as he can.

Be awake to all the dangers; stay firm in the faith; be brave and be strong. Let everything you do be done in love.

There is something else to ask you, brothers. You know how the Stephanas family, who were the first-fruits of Achaia, have really worked hard to help the saints. Well, I want you in your turn to put yourselves at the service of people like this, and anyone who helps and works with

> them. I am delighted that Stephanas, Fortunatus and Achaicus have arrived; they make up for your absence. They have settled my mind, and yours too; I hope you appreciate men like this.
>
> All the churches of Asia send you greeting. Aquila and Prisca, with the church that meets at their house, send you their warmest wishes, in the Lord. All the brothers send you their greetings. Greet one another with a holy kiss (1 Cor 16:5–19).

No one has difficulty understanding that this part of Paul's letter is just like a personal letter which any of us might write. Such personal greetings are so common in Paul's letters that scholars wonder if a letter which omits them is actually Paul's. One reason that the authorship of Ephesians is disputed is that it contains no personal greetings even though Paul had been to Ephesus.

Personal Emotional Characteristics

In addition to including personal messages, Paul's letters reveal his personality. Paul is a very complex person. We know that before his conversion he was a legalist, totally devoted to doing what was right as he understood it, and perfectly willing to use force, imprisonment, even murder as a means of putting things "right." Paul's conversion experience totally changed his understanding of what God wanted him to do, but it did not change his personality. Luke tells us that Paul and Barnabas had such a violent argument over Mark that they parted ways (Acts 15:36–40).

This angry side of Paul is evident in many of his letters but none more so than his letter to the Galatians. Paul interrupts his usual friendly greeting and immediately begins to defend himself against the charges which have been made against him.

> From Paul to the churches of Galatia, and from all the brothers who are here with me, an apostle who does not owe his authority to men or his appointment to any human

> being but who has been appointed by Jesus Christ and by God the Father who raised Jesus from the dead (Gal 1:12).

As Paul continues to re-explain to the Galatians that they are saved not by obedience to the law but by the grace of Christ he sounds very angry and aggressive.

> Are you people in Galatia mad? Has someone put a spell on you, in spite of the plain explanation you have had of the crucifixion of Jesus Christ? Let me ask you one question; was it because you practiced the law that you received the Spirit, or because you believed what was preached to you? Are you fools enough to end in outward observances what you began in the Spirit? Have all the favors you received been wasted? (Gal 3:1–3).

It is amusing that, while Paul reams out the Galatians, insulting them personally as well as correcting their misunderstanding, he gives them some advice on what tone to use when it becomes necessary to correct someone.

> Brothers, if one of you misbehaves, the more spiritual of you who set him right should do so in a spirit of gentleness, not forgetting that you may be tempted yourselves (Gal 6:1).

While Paul did not always succeed in correcting with a spirit of gentleness, he did realize that he could well be tempted himself. Paul expresses his own personal sense of sinfulness in his letter to the Romans.

> The law, of course, as we all know, is spiritual; but I am unspiritual; I have been sold as a slave to sin. I cannot understand my own behavior. I fail to carry out the things I want to do, and I find myself doing the very things I hate. When I act against my own will, that means I have a self that acknowledges that the law is good, and so the thing behaving in that way is not my self but sin living in me. The fact is, I know of nothing good living in me—living, that is, in my unspiritual self—for though the will to do what is good is in me, the performance is not, with the re-

sult that instead of doing the good things I want to do, I carry out the sinful things I do not want. When I act against my will, it is not my true self doing it, but sin which lives in me.

In fact, this seems to be the rule, that every single time I want to do good it is something evil that comes to hand. In my inmost self I dearly love God's law, but I can see that my body follows a different law that battles against the law which my reason dictates. This is what makes me a prisoner of that law of sin which lives inside my body.

What a wretched man I am! Who will rescue me from this body doomed to death? Thanks be to God through Jesus Christ our Lord!

In short, it is I who with my reason serve the law of God, and no less I who serve in my unspiritual self the law of sin (Rom 7:14–25).

In addition to revealing his sense of sinfulness to his readers, Paul is willing to admit when he has been hurt. Evidently, something happened between the Corinthians and Paul which hurt both of them very deeply. Paul refers to the pain and misunderstanding in his second letter to the Corinthians.

Well then, I made up my mind not to pay you a second distressing visit. I may have hurt you, but if so I have hurt the only people who could give me any pleasure. I wrote as I did to make sure that when I came, I should not be distressed by the very people who should have made me happy. I am sure you all know that I could never be happy unless you were. When I wrote to you, in deep distress and anguish of mind, and in tears, it was not to make you feel hurt but to let you know how much love I have for you (2 Cor 2:1–4).

Paul continues in his effort to reach reconciliation with the Corinthians by asking them to forgive the person who caused the pain and misunderstanding in the first place.

Someone has been the cause of pain, and the cause of pain not to me, but to some degree—not to overstate it—to all of you. The punishment already imposed by the majority

> on the man in question is enough; and the best thing now is to give him your forgiveness and encouragement, or he might break from so much misery. So I am asking you to give some definite proof of your love for him. What I really wrote for, after all, was to test you and see whether you are completely obedient. Anybody that you forgive, I forgive; and as for my forgiving anything, if there has been anything to be forgiven, I have forgiven it for your sake in the presence of Christ. And so we will not be outwitted by Satan—we know well enough what his intentions are (2 Cor 2:3–11).

Indeed, Paul is just as capable of expressing joy and love as he is capable of expressing anger. Paul's letter to the Philippians is filled with exuberance and good will. He expresses his deep love for them as he says:

> I thank my God whenever I think of you; and every time I pray for all of you, I pray with joy, remembering how you have helped to spread the good news from the day you first heard it right up to the present. I am quite certain that the One who began this good work in you will see that it is finished when the Day of Christ Jesus comes. It is only natural that I should feel like this toward you all, since you have shared the privileges which have been mine: both my chains and my work defending and establishing the Gospel. You have a permanent place in my heart, and God knows how much I miss you all, loving you as Christ Jesus loves you (Phil 1:3–8).

His wish for them is that they be full of joy.

> I want you to be happy, always happy in the Lord. I repeat, what I want is your happiness (Phil 4:4).

Paul's capacity to feel intense joy is a reflection of his wholeheartedness. Paul was a wholehearted Pharisee, and when he came to know Jesus he became a wholehearted apostle. Paul reveals his total gift of self to Jesus in his letter to the Philippians.

> My one hope and trust is that I shall never have to admit defeat, but that now as always I shall have the courage for Christ to be glorified in my body, whether by my life or by my death. Life to me, of course, is Christ, but then death would bring me something more; but then again, if living in this body means doing work which is having good results, I do not know what I should choose. I am caught in this dilemma: I want to be gone and be with Christ, which would be very much the better, but for me to stay alive in this body is a more urgent need for your sake. This weighs with me so much that I feel sure I shall survive and stay with you all, and help you to progress in the faith and even increase your joy in it; and so you will have another reason to give praise to Christ Jesus on my account when I am with you again (Phil 1:20–26).

Paul's sometimes angry and argumentative tone affects the clarity with which he develops his theological themes. This is evident when we compare his letter to the Galatians with his letter to the Ephesians or his letter to the Colossians with his letter to the Romans. In each comparison, the second letter explains more fully the ideas presented in the first, partially because Paul's personality to some extent overpowers his message in the angry and argumentative letter.

Personal Mental Characteristics

A third way in which Paul's letters can be compared to personal letters is that they reveal the way Paul personally thinks. Paul has a different way of explaining his conclusions than do many of us. We have been trained to argue logically, building one idea upon another. We try to explain how we reached a conclusion. We may find ourselves wanting Paul to explain how he reaches his conclusion. Paul disappoints us in this respect. Instead of explaining his method of arriving at a conclusion he elaborates on the conclusion itself, by analogy. Several examples will make this clear.

In Paul's letter to the Romans, he is explaining the fact that we are saved not through observance of the law but through faith. In order to explain this concept Paul turns to Abraham as an example.

> Is this happiness meant only for the circumcised, or is it meant for others as well? Think of Abraham again: *his faith,* we say, *was considered as justifying him,* but when was this done? When he was already circumcised or before he had been circumcised? It was before he had been circumcised, not after; and when he was *circumcised* later it was only *as a sign* and guarantee that the faith he had before his circumcision justified him. In this way Abraham became the ancestor of all uncircumcised believers so that they too might be considered righteous; an ancestor, also, of those who though circumcised do not rely on that fact alone, but follow our ancestor Abraham along the path of faith he trod before he had been circumcised (Rom 4:9–13).

Paul's train of thought confuses many students. After all, Paul is teaching something which is a radical change from the 1,250 years of tradition which preceded him. The Israelites understood the law to be an extension of the covenant. Their obedience to the law was their social expression of fidelity to the covenant. To say that fidelity to the law was unnecessary was a radical statement indeed. To appear to base this new teaching on an Old Testament passage about Abraham seems illogical. Surely Paul is drawing a lesson from the passage which has nothing to do with the intent of the authors. They were not teaching that fidelity to the law was unnecessary even if they did report Abraham's experience in such a way that they described him as justified by faith before they pictured him ritualizing the covenant relationship through circumcision.

Paul would probably agree with this objection. By using Abraham as an example he is not claiming that the text intended to say what he is using the text to illustrate. Paul is using the text from Genesis as an analogy. Abraham did not earn justification. It was a gift, not a reward for good behavior. While 1,250 years of tradition sets an example of fidelity to the law, Abraham can be seen in a position analogous to present-day Gentiles. Neither earned the privilege of being chosen. Both are saved by faith. If one understands Paul's use of the Old Testament as an analogy rather than as a claim that the text is saying what he is using it to illustrate, his point becomes much clearer.

Another example of Paul's use of the Old Testament is in his letter to the Romans.

> Well then, sin *entered the world* through one man, and through sin death, and thus death has spread through the whole human race because everyone has sinned. Sin existed in the world long before the law was given. There was no law and so no one could be accused of the sin of "law-breaking," yet death reigned over all from Adam to Moses, even though their sin, unlike that of Adam, was not a matter of breaking a law.
>
> Adam prefigured the One to come, but the gift itself considerably outweighed the fall. If it is certain that through one man's fall so many died, it is even more certain that divine grace, coming through the one man, Jesus Christ, came to so many as an abundant free gift. The results of the gift also outweigh the results of one man's sin: for after one single fall came judgment with a verdict of condemnation; now after many falls comes grace with its verdict of acquittal. If it is certain that death reigned over everyone as the consequence of one man's fall, it is even more certain that one man, Jesus Christ, will cause everyone to reign in life who receives the free gift that he does not deserve, of being made righteous. Again, as one man's fall brought condemnation on everyone, so the good act of one man brings life to all and makes them justified. As by one man's disobedience many were made sinners, so by one man's obedience many will be made righteous (Rom 5:12–20).

For a person who reads Genesis 2:4–3:24 as history this passage causes no difficulty. An historic Adam is responsible for man's state of sin and an historic Jesus is responsible for man's redemption. However, if one reads Genesis 2:4–3:24 not as history but as a symbol story dealing with the problem of suffering, the present passage causes some consternation.

Doesn't Paul insist on the fact that sin entered the world through one man?

Let us approach the question from another angle. At this point in time, the 1980's, we do not know positively whether the human race descended from one couple (monogenesis) or from more than one couple (polygenesis). If science were to prove beyond any doubt that we did not all descend from one couple, would we have to either reject the conclusion of science or reject the teaching in Paul's letter? Would Paul's letter be nullified?

In order to answer this question we must state clearly just what it is Paul is teaching. In this passage Paul is teaching the pervasiveness of grace. All are saved through Jesus. In order to explain this teaching, Paul uses the Old Testament as an analogy, as he did in our previous examples. He is comparing the first Adam to the second Adam in order to emphasize the totally contradictory effects of their roles. Just as the whole world had been in sin, now the whole world is justified. Paul's teaching about Christ is true whether or not his statement that all sin entered the world through one man's fall is accurate.

Teachings vs. Presuppositions

At this point it is not unusual in a class discussion to have both fundamentalists and contextualists confused, perhaps even angry. "Are you saying that Paul is wrong?" is a question which is often asked.

In response we must ask, "Wrong about what?" Paul is a human being with faults and misperceptions even as he is a chosen instrument of God's revelation. Paul is sometimes wrong in his presumptions. For instance, Paul was wrong in his presumption that the second coming would be imminent. This misunderstanding is at the base of his advice against marriage and is clearly stated in his first letter to the Corinthians.

> Brothers, this is what I mean: our time is growing short. Those who have wives should live as though they had

> none, and those who mourn should live as though they had nothing to mourn for; those who are enjoying life should live as though there were nothing to laugh about; those whose life is buying things should live as though they had nothing of their own; and those who have to deal with the world should not become engrossed in it. I say this because the world as we know it is passing away (1 Cor 7:29–31).

Paul was wrong about the timing of the end of the world. But he was not wrong in what he was teaching—we should always live so as to be ready. The presumption behind the teaching is wrong, but the teaching is not.

To go back to Paul's teaching on the pervasiveness of grace in Romans 15:12–30, Paul's presumption behind the teaching that all sin entered the world through one man may be inaccurate, but his teaching that all men are redeemed through Christ is not wrong.

This distinction between what is presumed and what is taught is very important in understanding the revelation in Scripture. In the creation story in the Book of Genesis, the presumption is that the world is flat. This presumption turned out to be inaccurate. However, the teaching that God created the world, no matter what shape it is, is right. Even men who are inspired when it comes to spiritual truths are limited to the knowledge of their contemporary generation when it comes to scientific truth, and they are also sometimes limited when it comes to the social ramifications of the particular spiritual truths which they are teaching.

We see Paul struggling with the social ramifications of the Gospel in his attitude toward wives and slaves. In a burst of spiritual insight Paul tells the Galatians:

> You are, all of you, sons of God through faith in Christ Jesus. All baptized in Christ, you have all clothed yourselves in Christ, and there are no more distinctions between Jew and Greek, slave and free, male and female, but all of you are one in Christ Jesus (Gal 3:26–29).

ELEMENTS IN PAUL'S LETTERS

In common with PERSONAL LETTERS	Paul's letters include • personal messages. • personal emotional characteristics—moods. • personal mental characteristics—ways of thinking.
In common with PASTORAL LETTERS	Paul teaches spiritual truths with authority as he reflects social and "scientific" presumptions of his time.
In common with EDITED, SEQUENTIAL LETTERS	The letters reflect a growth in understanding as years pass. • In understanding of Church. • In understanding the effects of Jesus' saving acts. • In understanding the social ramifications of the Gospel message.

Yet, in his letters to the Colossians and to the Ephesians Paul presumes that women and slaves are in a subservient position to men, as indeed they were in his society.

> Wives, give way to your husbands, as you should in the Lord . . . . Slaves, be obedient to the men who are called your masters in this world (Col 3:18, 22).

> Wives should regard their husbands as they regard the Lord . . . . Slaves, be obedient to the men who are called

> your masters in this world, with deep respect and sincere loyalty, as you are obedient to Christ (Eph 5:21; 6:5).

Such passages do not mean that Paul is teaching the proper order of society—slavery should be allowed and wives should be owned by their husbands. Paul is not commenting on the order of society; he is simply accepting the way things were. Given that order, Paul is telling his readers how to behave so as to grow in holiness. Were Paul alive today and writing to twentieth century Americans, he would be able to write of marriage in an even more inspiring way than he did in the first century. Paul's insight that marriage is a sign of Christ's love for his Church (Eph 5:21–33) would be all the more true if he had lived in an age when wives, far from being merely property, were treated with the dignity due each human being. Then, instead of saying that men should "love" their wives (Eph 5:25) but women should "respect" their husbands (Eph 5:33), Paul might have said that women, too, should love their husbands. Only where there is freedom can there be love.

In one instance, at least, Paul did see the ramifications of his statement in Galatians that there would be no distinction between slaves and free. Paul's letter to Philemon is written for the expressed purpose of asking Philemon to welcome back his runaway slave, Onesimus, as a brother.

> I know you have been deprived of Onesimus for a time, but it was only so that you could have him back for ever, not as a slave any more, but something much better than a slave, a dear brother; especially dear to me, but now much more to you, as a blood-brother as well as a brother in the Lord. So if all that we have in common means anything to you, welcome him as you would me; but if he has wronged you in any way or owes you anything, then let me pay for it. I am writing this in my own handwriting; I, Paul, shall pay it back—I will not add any mention of your own debt to me, which is yourself (Phlm 15–17).

The fact that Paul's letters reflect some presumptions which we no longer accept in no instance invalidates the spiritual truth which Paul is teaching. The pervasiveness of grace, the necessity to be always ready for the coming of the Lord, the advice to treat each other with the love and respect with which we would treat Christ are all profoundly true spiritual insights. The fact that these teachings are accompanied by presumptions which science or a growth in social consciousness would now question in no way lessens the value of the revelation which we receive through Paul's letters.

Just as we can trace a growth in Paul's thinking when it comes to the question of slavery, so can we see a growth in his understanding in those areas in which Paul made his most important contribution to Christian revelation, Paul's soteriology and his understanding of Church.

Paul's Soteriology Grows

Soteriology is the word theologians use when they talk about theology which deals with salvation as it was affected by Jesus Christ. In Paul's early letters his soteriology is not fully developed. For instance, in Paul's first letter to the Thessalonians he speaks of Jesus' death and resurrection as events which had some connection to the resurrection of those who have died in Christ.

> We want you to be quite certain, brothers, about those who have died, to make sure that you do not grieve about them, like the other people who have no hope. We believe that Jesus died and rose again, and that it will be the same for those who have died in Jesus: God will bring them with him. We can tell you this from the Lord's own teaching, that any of us who are left alive until the Lord's coming will not have any advantage over those who have died. At the trumpet of God, the voice of the archangel will call out the command and the Lord himself will come down from heaven; those who have died in Christ will be the first to rise, and then those of us who are still alive will be taken up in the clouds, together with them, to meet the Lord in the air. So we shall stay with the Lord for ever. With such thoughts as these you should comfort one another (1 Thes 4:13–18).

Those words were written to comfort those who were worried because their loved ones had died before Jesus' return. Paul wants to assure the Thessalonians that the dead have not missed out on salvation because they died before Jesus' return. The dead as well as the living would rise, just as Jesus himself had.

In later letters Paul's teaching about the effects of Jesus' death and resurrection are expanded as his and the Church's depth of understanding increased. A much fuller development of soteriology is found in the letter to the Ephesians.

> Blessed be God the Father of our Lord Jesus Christ,
> who has blessed us with all the spiritual blessings of heaven
> in Christ.
> Before the world was made, he chose us, chose us in Christ,
> to be holy and spotless, and to live through love in his
> presence,
> determining that we should become his adopted sons,
> through Jesus Christ
> for his own kind purposes,
> to make us praise the glory of his grace,
> his free gift to us in the Beloved,
> in whom, through his blood, we gain our freedom, the
> forgiveness of our sins.
> Such is the richness of the grace
> which he has showered on us
> in all wisdom and insight.
> He has let us know the mystery of his purpose,
> the hidden plan he so kindly made in Christ from the
> beginning
> to act upon when the times had run their course to the end:
> that he would bring everything together under Christ, as
> head,
> everything in the heavens and everything on earth.
> And it is in him that we were claimed as God's own,
> chosen from the beginning,
> under the predetermined plan of the one who guides all
> things
> as he decides by his own will;
> chosen to be,
> for his greater glory,

> the people who would put their hopes in Christ before he came.
> Now you too, in him,
> have heard the message of the truth and the good news of your salvation,
> and have believed it;
> and you too have been stamped with the seal of the Holy Spirit of the Promise,
> the pledge of our inheritance
> which brings freedom for those whom God has taken for his own,
> to make his glory praised (Eph 1:3–14).

In this hymn we see the events of Jesus' death and resurrection in the context of a universal, cosmological plan which affects our redemption. First, through Jesus' saving actions the human race is reconciled with the Father. We are at peace with God, in his favor, and involved in an intimate relationship with him.

> And it is in him that we were claimed as God's own (Eph 1:11).

Second, Jesus has made expiation for our sins. Expiation is not to be understood as a kind of appeasement of an angry God. Rather, expiation refers to the fact that in Christ our sins are "covered over" or "wiped out."

> He chose us, chose us in Christ,
> to be holy and spotless and live through love in his presence (Eph 1:4).

Third, through Jesus' saving acts we are liberated from death, from sin, and from the law.

> Through his blood, we gain our freedom, the forgiveness of our sins (Eph 1:7).

Finally, because our sins are forgiven, we are justified; we have been made whole.

> Now you too, in him
> have heard the message of the truth and the good news of your salvation,
> and have believed it;
> and you have been stamped with the seal of the Holy Spirit of the Promise,
> the pledge of our inheritance
> which brings freedom for those whom God has taken for his own,
> to make his glory praised (Eph 1:13–14).

Paul's Ecclesiology Grows

As Paul's understanding of the effects of Jesus' death and resurrection grows, so does his understanding of Church. In his early letters Paul uses the word "church" to refer to a local church:

> From Paul, Silvanus and Timothy, to the church of Thessalonica (1 Thes 1:1),

or to refer to Judean churches:

> For you, my brothers, have been like the churches of God in Christ Jesus which are in Judea (1 Thes 2:14).

In Paul's later letters his idea of Church has become universal and has become identified with the body of Christ. This hymn in the letter to the Colossians beautifully expresses the depth of Paul's understanding of Jesus' cosmological role and of the Church as Christ's body.

> He is the image of the unseen God
> and the first-born of all creation,
> for in him were created
> all things in heaven and on earth:
> everything visible and everything invisible,
> Thrones, Dominations, Sovereignties, Powers—
> all things were created through him and for him.

PAUL'S GROWTH IN UNDERSTANDING

The effects of Jesus' saving actions	**Early** Jesus rose and so will we. **Later** Jesus brought about • our reconciliation with the Father. • expiation for our sins. • our liberation from death, sin, and the law. • our justification.
The Church	**Early** A local group of believers. **Later** A universal concept—we are all part of Christ's body and he is our head.

Before anything was created, he existed,
and he holds all things in unity.
Now the Church is his body,
he is its head.

As he is the Beginning,
he was first to be born from the dead,
so that he should be first in every way;
because God wanted all perfection
to be found in him
and all things to be reconciled through him and for him.
everything in heaven and everything on earth,
when he made peace
by his death on the cross (Col 1:15–20).

Many scholars believe that this is a Christian liturgical hymn which grew up in the worshiping community and was appropriated by Paul. Both the letter to the Ephesians and the letter to the Colossians predate Mark's Gospel by several years. The Christian community had come to this profound understanding of Christ's identity and role in salvation history as well as their own intimate union with him as members of his body, as Church, by the early 60's.

The letter to the Colossians also reflects the fact that Paul expected his letters to be read in the churches.

> After this letter has been read among you, send it on to be read in the church of the Laodiceans; and get the letter from Laodicea for you to read yourselves (Col 4:16).

Paul's words carried great authority in the early Church just as a pastoral letter or an encyclical does in today's Church. Paul's letters were an extension of his teaching ministry. They contain profound insights about Christ and his Church, insights which have been recognized as inspired by the worshiping community for many centuries. However, in reading Paul's letters we must not let the fact that Paul was inspired blind us to the fact that Paul wrote in a literary form which allowed room for his personal greetings, his personal feelings, and his personal ways of explaining his inspired insights. Only when we read Paul's words in the context of their literary form and their historic circumstances will we be able to understand the revelation which they contain.

Review Questions

1. Can we date Paul's activities precisely? How crucial are exact dates to our understanding of Paul's epistles?
2. Why is it important to know the order in which the letters were written?
3. In what three ways are Paul's epistles comparable to personal letters?

4. Describe Paul's personality.
5. Describe Paul's method of argument.
6. What is Paul's point when he uses Abraham to illustrate his teaching about grace and the law?
7. What is Paul teaching when he compares the first Adam and the second Adam in Romans 15:12–30? How can this passage be compatible with an understanding of Genesis 2:4–3:24 as a symbol story rather than an historic account?
8. Does Paul teach that racism and sexism are part of God's created order? Explain. What is Paul's spiritual insight in Colossians 3:18 and Ephesians 5:21?
9. In what two main areas did Paul make a profound contribution to Christian revelation?
10. What did Paul come to understand as the effect of Jesus' redemptive actions?
11. In what way did Paul's understanding of Church grow?
12. What is the difference between these two statements: "Christ has a redemptive role" and "Christ has a cosmological role"?

Discussion Questions

1. What are the varieties of letters with which you have personal experience? How do these various kinds of letters compare to the epistles in the New Testament?
2. Do you think you would like Paul if you met him? Why or why not?
3. Is it your observation that a conversion experience does or does not change a person's personality? Explain. Do you think it should?
4. How do you react to Paul's open admission of his own sinfulness? Do you expect more from him? Are you grateful that he revealed his weakness? Would you appreciate or resent this kind of behavior in today's religious leaders?
5. What is the difference between an argument based on logic and one based on analogy? Which do you find more satisfying?

6. Do you think it is all right for Paul to use Old Testament passages to cast light on problems which the passages did not originally address? Can you see any relationship between Paul's doing this and the way in which Scripture took form in the first place?
7. What is the distinction between what is presumed and what is taught in revelation? What mistakes have we made in the past by neglecting this distinction? If this distinction were remembered would there be any contradiction between revelation and scientific truth? Explain.
8. Do you think Paul would support racism today? Would he support sexism? Explain.
9. Are there things about the order of our society which we don't question—which we presume are just the order God ordained when actually the order is a reflection of a state of sin? What about the distribution of wealth in today's world?
10. How do you experience the effect of Jesus' saving acts in your everyday life? What difference does it actually make?
11. Paul teaches that all are created through Christ and that the Church is Christ's body. What ramification does this have socially? Economically?
12. If man had not sinned would Christ still be involved with us? Explain.

10

Revelation

When Paul refers to his own writing as a letter (Col 3:16), an American reader knows to what literary form he is referring. The same is not true when the author of the Book of Revelation names his genre. "This is the revelation given by God to Jesus Christ so that he could tell his servants about the things which are now to take place very soon; he sent his angel to make it known to his servant John, and John has written down everything he saw and swears it is the word of God guaranteed by Jesus Christ" (Rev 1:1–2).

In this introduction the author of the Book of Revelation has not only identified the form in which he is writing but he has utilized several of the conventions of the form we call "revelation" or "apocalyptic" writing.

Few books in the Bible are misinterpreted and abused as much as the Book of Revelation. Those who are unfamiliar with the literary form "revelation" misinterpret everything about this book: its subject matter, its tone, and its purpose. They read it as though the intent of the author were to describe what it will be like at the end of the world. They misrepresent the book by quoting it in a way that instills fear in people. Some even use this book to plant the seeds of hopelessness: they misinterpret the numbers in the book and assume that only 144,000 people of all those who ever lived on the face of the earth will be saved. All of these misunderstandings disappear when one interprets the book in the context of its literary form.

In the Bible we have two examples of apocalyptic writing

or revelation: the Book of Daniel in the Old Testament and the Book of Revelation in the New Testament. These works were written in a four hundred year period and under similar circumstances. Apocalyptic literature is written to people who are suffering from persecution. The intent of the author is to assure his audience that the God of history is in control of the present situation so that one need not fear: the persecution will end and good will triumph over evil.

Function of Apocalyptic Writing

The function of apocalyptic literature might be compared to the function of a prophet. A prophet is not a fortune-teller. His role is not to see into the future but to speak for God in the contemporary situation. The prophet's message often concerns the future because he warns the people of the future ramifications of their present behavior: infidelity to the covenant brings suffering while fidelity to the covenant brings joy. But the prophet's primary intent is to speak to his contemporaries about their present situation.

The author of apocalyptic writing is also speaking to his contemporaries about their present situation. Far from trying to frighten his audience about the end of the world, the author is trying to fill his audience with hope about the end of their present severe suffering. Apocalyptic writing is about the present suffering and the immediate future when the persecution will end. It is not about the far distant future. It is not about "the end of the world" as we use that phrase now.

Conventions of Apocalyptic Writing

The social situation in which apocalyptic writing takes place accounts for some of its conventions. The word "convention" is used when talking about literature to refer to some characteristic of the writing, be it in form or style or content, which has become an accepted element of that kind of writing. For instance, in writing a letter, it has become a convention to begin with the word "Dear" whether or not the person to whom you are writing is dear to you. "Dear" is a convention in the form "letter" and does not reflect the personal feelings of the letter writer. When writing an epic it is a convention to call upon various gods for inspiration. If a Christian writer were to call on the god of history and the god of music to inspire him as he writes his epic, he is merely employing a convention of the form "epic." He is not revealing to his audience that he actually believes in many gods rather than in one God.

In order to understand apocalyptic writing one must understand the conventions which it employs. Otherwise one may mistake a convention of the form for a statement of fact or belief and thus misunderstand the intent of the author.

Visions

One convention of apocalyptic writing is that it presents itself as a hidden revelation which was known only to God but which was given by God or by an angel to a person who is now receiving the revelation. The first sentence of the Book of Revelation says exactly this. God gave this revelation to Jesus Christ who gave it to an angel who gave it to John.

This same convention is used by the author of the book of Daniel. Daniel has a series of visions which he is unable to understand. The angel Gabriel is told to interpret the visions for Daniel.

> As I, Daniel, gazed at the vision and tried to understand it, I saw someone standing before me who looked like a man. I heard a man's voice cry over the Ulai, "Gabriel, tell him the meaning of the vision!" He approached the place where I was standing; as he approached I was seized with terror, and fell prostrate. "Son of man," he said to me, "understand this: the vision shows the time of the end" (Dan 8:15–17).

Sealed Revelation

The revelation which is given has been in a sealed book and will only be opened at the end time.

> Then I said, "My lord, what is to be the outcome?" "Daniel," he said, "go away: these words are to remain secret and sealed until the time of the end. Many will be cleansed, made white and purged; the wicked will go on doing wrong; the wicked will never understand; the learned will understand. From the moment that the perpetual sacrifice is abolished and the disastrous abomination erected: one thousand two hundred and ninety days. Blessed is he who stands firm and attains a thousand three hundred and thirty-five days. But you, go away and rest; and you will rise for your share at the end of time" (Dan 12:8–13).

Since the revelation is only to be read at the end times, and the contemporary audience is reading it, then the author is saying that the present times are the end times. The present times are the times of devastation. But in just a short time the persecutions will end, so the audience should stay firm and full of hope.

In the Book of Revelation, too, the convention of the sealed revelation is used.

> I saw that in the right hand of the One sitting on the throne there was *a scroll that had writing on back and front* and was sealed with seven seals. Then I saw a powerful angel who called with a loud voice, "Is there anyone worthy to open the scroll and break the seals of it?" But there was no one, in heaven or on earth or under the earth, who was able to open the scroll and read it. I wept bitterly because there was nobody fit to open the scroll and read it, but one of the elders said to me, "There is no need to cry: *the Lion* of the tribe *of Judah, the Root* of David, has triumphed, and he will open the scroll and the seven seals of it" (Rev 5:1–5).

It is important to understand that the visions in apocalyptic writing are a convention of the form. The author is not claiming to have historically and realistically seen these visions. Rather, he is using an accepted literary form to send a message of hope to a people in distress.

It takes time for students to understand that when we speak of one literary form, we are not speaking of the whole New Testament or of the whole Bible. Each book must be interpreted in the context of its own literary form. It is not unusual at this point for a student to remember other visions, for instance the vision that Paul had on the road to Damascus (Acts 9:3–9) or the vision that Peter had which led him to understand that Gentiles were to be included in the covenant (Acts 10:9–16). A student may well ask, "Are you saying that these other visions are literary conventions?" Obviously, the answer to that question is "No." The Acts of the Apostles is the same literary form as Luke's Gospel. It is a compilation of inherited materials of a variety of literary forms. The stories in Acts of Paul's and Peter's experiences are in no way comparable to the Book of Revelation. The author of the Book of Revelation is not recounting an experience but is using an accepted literary form to encourage an audience in terrible distress.

The writer of an apocalypse may or may not be inspired, just as the writer of a letter may or may not be inspired. Whether or not the author is inspired cannot be determined by the "claim" of a vision since that is a convention of the form. We will talk about why the Book of Revelation is considered revelation, while much apocalyptic writing is not, later in this chapter.

Symbolic Language

"Why," students ask, "did the author of apocalyptic literature choose to write in a form which is so difficult to understand? You'd think if his message was to encourage people, he would write in a form which was easier to understand."

Once again, the social situation in which apocalyptic literature was written accounts for its convention of speaking through symbols. The symbolic language is a kind of "in group" language, a code which is understandable to the persecuted audience to whom it is addressed but not understandable to the persecutors, the powerful leaders of society who would kill the author if they knew who he was and would kill the readers if the persecutors understood what they were reading.

The Book of Daniel was written during the persecution under Antiochus Epiphanes, very probably between 167 and 164 B.C. At this time the Jews were suffering through one of the worst periods of their entire history. Antiochus Epiphanes wanted to Hellenize Jewish life, and so he issued an order outlawing the Jewish religion. He made it a capital offense to circumcise children, to possess a copy of the Torah or to observe the sabbath. His troops desecrated the temple by erecting an altar to Zeus, "the abomination of desolation," and sacrificing swine on it. Jews were forced to honor Zeus and to eat swine. If they refused, they had to hide or die. The author of the Book of Daniel is encouraging these persecuted Jews in code language.

The Book of Revelation was also written at a time of persecution. Domitian, who ruled from 81–96 A.D., made it illegal not to take part in religious ceremonies honoring state gods. Christians who refused were subject to criminal charges. Those who would not address Domitian himself as "Lord and God" were to be killed. The author of the Book of Revelation uses the same literary form as did the author of the Book of Daniel, and for the same reason. He wanted his audience, but not their persecutors, to understand his message.

Some of the symbolic language used in apocalyptic literature is familiar to us but most of it is not. In the passage which we recently quoted from the fifth chapter of the Book of Revelation Gabriel speaks of "the Lion of the tribe of Judah, the Root of David" who has triumphed. Most modern Christians recognize these words as a reference to Christ. In this one example we can illustrate several important facts about the symbols in apocalyptic literature. The first is that the meaning comes through translating the symbols into ideas, not in trying to picture them visually in our minds. Second, the meaning can only be understood if we are familiar with the literary allusions upon which they depend. It is impossible to understand the Book of Revelation if one is unfamiliar with the Book of Daniel. It is impossible to understand the Book of Daniel unless one is familiar with the imagery in Ezekiel.

Perhaps the interdependence of the symbolic language in these books can best be understood by giving a specific example. In the Book of Revelation we read of John's vision.

> I turned round to see who had spoken to me, and when I turned I saw seven golden lamp-stands and, surrounded by them, a figure *like a Son of man,* dressed in a long robe tied at the waist with a *golden girdle. His head* and *his hair* were *white as wool* or as snow, *his eyes* like a *burning flame, his feet like burnished bronze* when it has been refined in a furnace, and *his voice like the sound of the ocean.* In his right hand he was holding seven stars, out of his mouth came a sharp sword, doubled-edged, and his face was like the sun shining with all its force (Rev 1:12–16).

The real significance of this description can only be understood if one recognizes in it an allusion to the Book of Daniel.

> Thrones were set in place
> and one of great age took his seat.
> His robe was white as snow,
> the hair of his head as pure as wool.
> His throne was a blaze of flames,
> its wheels were a burning fire.
> A stream of fire poured out,
> issuing from his presence.
> A thousand thousand waited on him,
> ten thousand times ten thousand stood before him.
> A court was held
> and the books were opened. . . .
> I gazed into the visions of the night.
> And I saw, coming on the clouds of heaven,
> one like a son of man.
> He came to the one of great age
> and was led into his presence.

> On him was conferred sovereignty,
> glory and kingship,
> and men of all peoples, nations and languages became his
> servants (Dan 7:10, 13–14).

In this vision Daniel is seeing the heavenly court. One familiar with the Book of Ezekiel would recognize the setting (Ez 1:4–28). "Thrones set in place" symbolize the fact that the time of judgment has arrived. The one of great age who took his seat is God. He is dressed in white, a symbol of purity, of victory over evil. His hair is pure as wool, a symbol of wisdom. His throne is a blaze of flame. Fire is often a symbol of God's presence, from the burning bush to the tongues of fire at Pentecost. Fire symbolizes power and majesty. The thousand who wait on him symbolize a great number; ten thousand times ten thousand symbolizes an infinite number. The "book" is opened. God has power over the course of events. He will reveal what is to come. He will overcome the evil forces of persecution.

The vision from the Book of Daniel continues. "One like a son of man" comes on the clouds of heaven. This "son of man" is a contrast to the beasts (evil forces) who came from the depths of the sea. To him is given dominion. He is a messianic figure.

Christians who read the Book of Daniel consider this a reference to Christ. In the Book of Daniel itself, however, the angel interprets the "one like a son of man" to be "the saints of the most high" (Dan 7:27), the holy people of Israel. Power will be taken away from the beast (Antiochus Ephiphanes) and given to "one like a son of man" (God's chosen people). The God of history will once again save his people.

When we are familiar with this vision from the Book of Daniel, the meaning of the vision in the Book of Revelation becomes much clearer. A figure "like a son of man" is dressed in a long robe. His head and his hair are "white as white wool or as snow." Here the author of the Book of Revelation is combining two figures from Daniel's vision: the one "like a son of man," is identical to the one in a long robe with hair as white as wool. In other words, the author is combining what had come to be understood as a reference to the Messiah, the "Son of Man," Jesus, with the figure of God himself. This is a highly developed Christological statement: Jesus is God. All of the other symbols show the majesty, strength, power, and stability of God: fire, feet like burnished bronze, a voice like the sound of the ocean, a sharp, double-edged sword coming from his mouth and his face like the sun. This figure has sovereignty over all of God's people. He holds the seven stars, the seven churches, in his hands. Seven is not a literal but a symbolic number symbolizing completeness. The Messiah, the risen Christ, God, has sovereignty over the whole world.

In this single example we can learn a great deal about the conventional use of symbols in apocalyptic literature. We can see how the meaning comes from translating the symbols into ideas and from understanding the symbols in the context of the Jewish literature which was extremely familiar to the original audience, but not to their persecutors.

Symbolic Numbers

Seven is not the only number used in a symbolic way in the Book of Revelation. Numbers are constantly being used to symbolize wholeness or to symbolize lack of wholeness. Numbers which symbolize wholeness are three (indivisible; the Trinity), four (four corners of the earth), seven (indivisible), ten, twelve (twelve tribes, twelve apostles), and one thousand. Multiples of these numbers also signify wholeness or completeness. One of the numbers which fit into this group is the number 144,000 (12 × 12 × 1,000).

> Next I saw four angels, standing at *the four corners of the earth,* holding the four winds of the world back to keep them from blowing over the land or the sea or in the trees. Then I saw another angel rising where the sun rises, carrying the seal of the living God; he called in a powerful voice to the four angels whose duty was to devastate land and sea, "Wait before you do any damage on land or at sea or to the trees, until we have put the *seal on the foreheads*

SOME SYMBOLS IN THE BOOK OF REVELATION

On the side of Good

Angel—God's messenger
4—the whole world; a complete number
4 animals in heavenly court (see Ezekiel 1:5–21)—all that is best in the created world
7—Completeness
12—Completeness
24 elders in heavenly court—the whole Church (12 tribes plus 12 apostles)
Lamb—Christ
Bride—God's people, the Church
Woman—Israel giving birth to the Messiah (also Mary and the Church)
Virgins—Those who have been faithful; single-hearted
White—Purity
White robe washed in blood—Apparel of those saved by Christ
Eyes—Wisdom
Horns—Authority (because powerful)
Long robe—Priesthood
Thrones—Heavenly court; place where judgment takes place
New Jerusalem—God's redeemed people

On the side of Evil

3½ years, 42 months, 1,260 days—a short, limited period
666—The evilest one (Nero Caesar)
Dragon—Satan, evil forces
Babylon—Not God's people (Rome)
Beast—Those who work for evil; Roman officials
Black—death
Scarlet—harlotry, luxury
Sea—Opposite of heaven; evil comes from the sea

> of the servants of our God: Then I heard how many were sealed: a hundred and forty-four thousand, out of all the tribes of Israel" (Rev 7:1–4).

Far from finding this account discouraging, those who read these words were filled with hope. Persecution did not mean that God had lost control of the course of history, nor did it mean that those faithful to God were in danger of being overcome or lost. A number too large to name, the whole Church, would be saved. The number 144,000 is not to be read as finite but as infinite. All of God's servants were already saved.

Numbers which symbolize incompleteness are any fraction, six (one less than seven and 1/2 of twelve so very imperfect), or numbers which are fractions of days or years (3 1/2 days, 43 months or 1,260 days because they represent 3 1/2 years). So when one reads:

> They will trample the holy city for forty-two months. But I will send my two witnesses to prophesy for those twelve hundred and sixty days, wearing sackcloth (Rev 11:3–4),

one does not become discouraged because the persecution will be so long. Rather one becomes hopeful because the persecution, far from being interminable, is limited in duration and will end.

The number 666 is another symbolic number. The Book of Revelation describes the persecutions which the people have experienced in these words:

> Through the miracles which it was allowed to do on behalf of the first beast, it was able to win over the people of the world and persuade them to put up a statue in honor of the beast that had been wounded by the sword and still lived. It was allowed to breathe life into this statue, so that the statue of the beast was able to speak, and to have *anyone who refused to worship the statue of the beast* put to death. He compelled everyone—small and great, rich and poor, slave and citizen—to be branded on the right hand or on the forehead, and made it illegal for anyone to buy or sell anything unless he had been branded with the name of the beast or with the number of its name.

> There is need for shrewdness here: if anyone is clever enough he may interpret the number of the beast: it is the number of a man, the number 666 (Rev 13:14–18).

The number 666, or 616 as it sometimes appears, is interpreted by many commentators to be Caesar Nero or Caesar God. In Greek and Hebrew, letters were used for numbers. The numerical value of each letter was determined by its place in the alphabet. The number of a person's name could be obtained by adding up the numerical value of each of the letters in the name.

The number 666 could also be interpreted to mean the most evil of the evil. In a language which did not have comparative (add "er" to the root word) or superlative (add "est" to the root word) forms, to repeat the word three times was to express the superlative. Thus God is "Holy, Holy, Holy, Lord God of Hosts." The number 666 could thus be symbolic of the superlative evil.

In any event, the author is speaking about a persecution known to his audience. He is not speaking about possible future persecutions unknown to the audience. To read the number as though it were identifying a person living in the twentieth century is to misread it.

Departing from Convention

All the conventions of apocalyptic literature which we have noted so far, the use of visions, angels, a sealed book, symbolic numbers, etc., are found in both the Book of Daniel and the Book of Revelation. In some respects, however, the Book of Revelation does not adhere to the conventions of its form.

Most apocalyptic literature is attributed to a venerated figure of a past generation. The Book of Daniel was written during the persecution under Antiochus Epiphanes, probably between 167 and 164, but it is set several hundred years earlier in Babylon. It is a convention of apocalyptic literature to describe past events as though they were future events. An example of this is Daniel's vision of the four beasts.

CONVENTIONS OF APOCALYPTIC LITERATURE

1. The work contains a hidden revelation which was known only to God.
2. God or an angel gave the revelation to a person.
3. The person receives the revelation in a vision.
4. The revelation is in a sealed book.
5. The revelation is to be opened only at the end time.
6. The revelation is communicated through symbolic language and numbers.
7. The book is attributed to a venerated figure of a past generation.
8. The setting of the book is a past time so past historic events are presented as though they will be future events.

In the first year of Belshazzar king of Babylon, Daniel had a dream and visions that passed through his head as he lay in bed. He wrote the dream down, and this is how the narrative began: Daniel said, "I have been seeing visions in the night. I saw that the four winds of heaven were stirring up the great sea; four great beasts emerged from the sea, each different from the other. The first was like a lion with eagle's wings; and as I looked its wings were torn off, and it was lifted from the ground and set standing on its feet like a man; and it was given a human heart. The second beast I saw was different, like a bear, raised up on one of its sides, with three ribs in its mouth, between its teeth. 'Up!' came the command. 'Eat quantities of flesh!' After this I looked, and saw another beast, like a leopard, and

WAYS IN WHICH THE BOOK OF REVELATION DEPARTS FROM THE CONVENTIONS

1. The work is attributed to a (then) present day author rather than a venerated figure from the past.
2. The setting is the (then) present rather than the past.
3. The book is not sealed since the (then) present time is understood to be the end time.

> with four bird's wings on its flanks; it had four heads, and power was given to it. Next I saw another vision in the visions of the night: I saw a fourth beast, fearful, terrifying, very strong; it had great iron teeth, and it ate, crushed and trampled underfoot what remained. It was different from the previous beasts and had ten horns.
>
> "While I was looking at these horns, I saw another horn sprouting among them, a little one; three of the original horns were pulled out by the roots to make way for it; and in this horn I saw eyes like human eyes, and a mouth that was full of boasts" (Dan 7:1–9).

Since the setting is the first year of Belshazzar, king of Babylon, Daniel appears to be describing future events. This is a convention. Actually the book was written after the events took place. The four beasts symbolize the four political powers: the Babylonian empire, the empire of the Medes, the Persian empire, and the empire of Alexander, which ruled the world between the time of Daniel and the time of the author of the Book of Daniel. This convention would not have misled the contemporary audience. They would understand that the author was describing the historic past and that the culmination of history was described as their own time. The fourth beast, their present persecutors, will be destroyed and power will be restored to God's people.

> The fourth beast is to be a fourth kingdom on earth,
> different from all other kingdoms.
> It will devour the whole earth,
> trample it underfoot and crush it.
> As for the ten horns: from this kingdom
> will rise ten kings, and another after them;
> this one will be different from the previous ones
> and will bring down three kings;
> he is going to speak words against the Most High,
> and harass the saints of the Most High.
> He will consider changing seasons and the Law,
> and the saints will be put into his power
> for a time, two times, and half a time.
> But a court will be held and his power will be stripped from him,
> consumed, and utterly destroyed.
> And sovereignty and kingship,
> and the splendors of all the kingdom under heaven
> will be given to the people of the saints of the Most High.
> His sovereignty is an eternal sovereignty
> and every empire will serve and obey him (Dan 7:23–27).

The author of the Book of Revelation departs from this convention. Rather than setting his book in the past, he sets it in the present.

> My name is John, and through our union with Jesus I am your brother and share your sufferings, your kingdom, and all you endure. I was on the island of Patmos for having preached God's word and witnessed for Jesus (Rev 1:9).

The author is not attributing his work to a venerated ancestor but is claiming the work as his own. Scholars suggest that he departed from the convention of his form in order to claim the authority which would accompany the work if the author were known. He wanted his writing to be accepted as authoritative by the churches whom he is correcting and teaching.

Why Revelation?

What is the author of the Book of Revelation teaching the churches, and why has his work been accepted as revelation, as canonical, by succeeding generations?

The Book of Revelation is accepted as revelation because of the role which it assigns to Christ. The author understands and teaches the cosmic significance of Christ's role in history.

All through Scripture we encounter a God of history, a God who acts in and through events in a purposeful manner. In the Book of Revelation we see the role which Christ plays in the course of history.

The setting for the Book of Revelation is the heavenly court. All of the action proceeds from God's court. Jesus is consistently pictured as being in heaven beside the throne of God.

> Those who prove victorious I will allow to share my throne, just as I was victorious myself and took my place with my Father on his throne (Rev 3:21).

> They will never hunger or thirst again; neither the sun nor scorching wind will ever plague them, because the Lamb who is at the throne will be their shepherd and will lead them to springs of living water, and God will wipe away all tears from their eyes (Rev 7:17).

The lamb who is now in heaven beside the throne of God has, by his sacrifice, freed man from sin.

> . . . from Jesus Christ, *the faithful witness, the first-born* from the dead, *the ruler of the kings* of the earth. He loves us and has washed away our sins with his blood, and made us a *line of kings, priests to serve* his God and Father (Rev 1:5–6).

> You are worthy to take the scroll
> and break the seals of it,
> because you were sacrificed, and with your blood
> you bought men for God
> of every race, language, people and nation

BOOK OF REVELATION

Setting—Heavenly court.

Action, Events—The action and events proceed from the heavenly court.

Visions of the heavenly court:

1:9–20	The vision which begins here precipitates the sending of the seven letters.
4:1–11	The vision which begins here precipitates the opening of the seven seals.
8:2–5	The vision which begins here precipitates the blowing of the seven trumpets.
12:1–6	The vision which begins here precipitates the battle between the devil and the woman.
14:1—15:4	The vision which begins here precipitates the pouring out of the seven bowls.
19:1–10	In this vision the Word goes forth to fight the final battles.
21:1–8	This vision reveals the final victory of good over evil.

Conclusion: God has not lost control of events. Good will conquer evil.

and made them a line of kings and priests
to serve our God and to rule the world (Rev 5:9–10).

Because Jesus sacrificed himself to free men from sin, and triumphed over death by his resurrection, he will now direct the course of human history. Only he is worthy to open the seals and put into effect God's plan for history. The lamb will direct the course of history toward a goal that gives meaning to human life.

Each of the visions in the Book of Revelation begins in the heavenly court. As seven seals are opened, or seven trumpets are blown, or seven bowls are poured out, various sufferings visit the earth. All of these are of limited duration and none of them conquers God's people. At the end of time Jesus, the lamb, appears in judgment.

> And now I saw heaven open, and a white horse appear; its rider was called Faithful and True; he is *a judge with integrity,* a warrior for justice. His eyes were flames of fire, and his head was crowned with many coronets; the name written on him was known only to himself; *his cloak was soaked in blood.* He is known by the name, the Word of God (Rev 19:11–13).

Through the power of Christ all evil is finally conquered. After the defeat of evil, there is a new heaven, a new earth, and a new Jerusalem. In the new Jerusalem Jesus is with God, the source of light, happiness, and eternal life.

> I saw that there was no temple in the city since the Lord God Almighty and the Lamb were themselves the temple, and the city did not need the sun or the moon for light, since it was lit by the radiant glory of God and the Lamb was a lighted torch for it. *The pagan nations will live by its light* and the kings of the earth will bring it their treasures. *The gates of it will never be shut by day*—and there will be no night there (Rev 21:22–25).

As has been mentioned, it is a convention of apocalyptic literature that the visions are to be kept in a sealed book until the end time. This convention is followed in the Book of Daniel.

> "Daniel," he said, "go away. These words are to remain secret and sealed until the time of the End" (Dan 12:9).

In the Book of Daniel the setting, the time when the book was sealed, was during the Babylonian exile, and the end time, the time when the visions were revealed, was the time of the author, during Antiochus' persecutions.

The author of the Book of Revelation uses his own time as the setting and departs from the convention of sealing the visions.

> This, too, he said to me, "Do not keep the prophecies in this book a secret, because the Time is close. Meanwhile let the sinner go on sinning, and the unclean continue to be unclean; but those who do good go on doing good, and those who are holy continue to be holy. Very soon now, I shall be with you again, *bringing the reward to be given to every man according to what he deserves*. I am the Alpha and the Omega, *the First and the Last*, the Beginning and the End. Happy are those who will have washed their robes clean, so that they will have the right to feed on the tree of life and can come through the gates into the city (Rev 22:10–15).

In this passage the author makes it clear that he is speaking to his audience about their own time in history. The end time to which they look forward is the end of the persecutions which they are presently enduring.

Students are sometimes disappointed to learn that the Book of Revelation was not written to help Christians who lived two thousand years later to figure out if the end of the world is imminent. We, like the people of Jesus' generation, seem to want to concentrate on a question which is a waste of time and effort. Jesus continually waylaid questions which were directed at discovering *when* "all this would come to pass." Jesus is never talking about the end times in order to help people figure out "when" they will occur. Rather his interest is in teaching people "how" to be ready. He discourages conjectures about "when" by saying, "But as for that day or hour, nobody knows it, neither the angels of heaven, nor the Son, no one but the Father" (Mk 13:32).

Jesus' message about the end times is not "figure out when it is," but "be ready now." A concern about "when" is a useless diversion. If we follow Jesus' advice to be ready now we have no reason to be concerned about "when."

The author of the Book of Daniel understood his time to be the end time. Jesus told his listeners, "I tell you solemnly, before this generation has passed away all these things will have taken place" (Mk 13:31). We have already seen that Paul told his audience that the end was near. The author of the Book of Revelation considered his time the end time. The coming of the kingdom and the end time both seem to be both present and future realities. Our concentration is supposed to be on being ready in the present.

If the Book of Revelation is not telling twentieth century readers what to look for as signs of the end of the world, what is it telling us? What can a person of our time gain from reading the Book of Revelation?

The theme of the Book of Revelation holds just as true for every generation as it did for its original audience. We, too, need to hear and believe that we have no reason to fear because Jesus, the Lord of history, has already conquered evil. The process of Christ's coming is not complete, but the fact of his coming and the fact of his victory over evil are already established. We need not fear, we need only be faithful and be ready, for victory is ours in the risen Christ.

Review Questions

1. Under what circumstances is apocalyptic literature written?
2. What is its theme?
3. How is the function of apocalyptic literature comparable to the function of a prophet?
4. What is a literary convention?
5. What are some literary conventions of apocalpytic writing?
6. Why are so many symbols used in apocalyptic writing?
7. With what Old Testament books does the author of the Book of Revelation presume his audience is familiar?
8. How does the author of the Book of Revelation state his belief that Jesus is God in Revelation 1:12–16?
9. How are numbers used in the Book of Revelation?

What does 144,000 mean in Revelation 7:1–4? What does 666 mean in Revelation 13:18?

10. In what ways does the author of the Book of Revelation depart from the conventions of apocalyptic literature?

11. Why is the Book of Revelation accepted as inspired?

12. Did Jesus show an interest in telling his followers when the end would come? What was his concern? Explain.

13. In what way might the end time be seen as both a present and future reality?

14. If the Book of Revelation is not teaching us about the end of the world what value can it have for a twentieth century audience?

Discussion Questions

1. Is the idea that prophecy and apocalyptic literature are not comparable to "fortune-tellers" in the sense that they are not trying to see into the future new to you? Do you wish God had given us fortune-tellers in this sense? Why or why not?
2. Have you ever been frightened by the Book of Revelation? Why? Would the author be pleased with this reaction to his work? Why?
3. Why, in apocalyptic literature, is the claim to have had a vision not in itself a claim to be divinely inspired?
4. Does the imagery in the Book of Revelation seem less bizarre if you translate it into ideas rather than pictures? Give some examples.
5. Have you ever been told that only 144,000 people will be saved? How would you explain the meaning of this statement in the Book of Revelation to a person who misunderstood it?
6. Have you ever heard a person attribute the description 666 to a modern world figure? Why is such an interpretation an abuse of the Book of Revelation?
7. In what way might each generation be accurate in thinking of the end time as the present time? In what way might this idea be inaccurate?
8. Do you find the Book of Revelation comforting? Explain.

Conclusion

If a person who could not read received a love letter, how would you go about helping that person? You could read the letter for him. But wouldn't it be much better in the long run to teach that person the alphabet so that he could read the letter for himself? The person might feel impatient to be hearing the names and sounds of the letters rather than the living words of love. But the arduous task of learning the forms in which sounds have become letters will be well worth the effort. A whole world of meaning will open up.

Those who are motivated by a deep love for the Lord want to hear his word. Many read the Bible, having learned the forms of the letters, but not the forms of the books. As a result they are unable to understand what they are reading. This book may seem "off the subject" for those who long to hear God's word. However, if one takes the time to learn the literary forms which are contained in the library which we call the Bible, the living word becomes much more understandable.

It is my hope and prayer that this book will enable you to grow in your knowledge and love of the word: the written word which is literature, the living word which is Scripture, and the Word of God, Jesus the Christ, who sends his Spirit to dwell in our hearts as he leads us to the Father.

Now, are there any questions? I learn a great deal from your questions.

Selected and Annotated Bibliography of Bible Study Aids for the Beginner

Commentary: Single Volume

Jerome Biblical Commentary (Englewood Cliffs, N.J.: Prentice-Hall, 1968).

> This is the best single volume commentary available. The introductions to each book are scholarly, thoroughly, and clearly written. The commentaries address almost any question which would come to mind. The volume includes excellent articles on topics which the beginner often finds troublesome: Inspiration and Inerrancy, Canonicity, Aspects of Old and New Testament Thought, and much more. This is a very valuable resource to own and use over the years.

Concordance

A concordance is an alphabetical arrangement of the principal words contained in the Bible, with citations of the passages in which they occur. It has two principal uses, both essential for anyone seriously interested in the Bible.

1. A concordance enables you to locate a passage if you can remember any principal word in the passage. This means that you can look up a passage and read it in context in order to determine its meaning.

2. A concordance has gathered in one place all the examples of the use of a word. This enables you to flesh out the mean-

ing of the word or to trace the growth in a concept because you can read every instance in which the word appears.

An excellent concordance is:

Darton, Michael, *Modern Concordance to the New Testament* (Garden City, N.Y.: Doubleday and Co., Inc., 1976).

This concordance is both verbal and thematic and is designed to be used by readers of a variety of translations of the Bible.

Dictionaries

The beginning Bible student may not realize that a dictionary of the Bible does much more than simply define words. It traces concepts through history. For instance, I might want to know if the word "heaven" meant the same thing to Abraham, or to Paul, as it does to me. A dictionary of the Bible will explain the word in its various historical contexts.

Two excellent dictionaries are:

Hartman, Louis F., *Encyclopedic Dictionary of the Bible* (New York: McGraw-Hill Book Co. Inc., 1963).

McKenzie, John, *Dictionary of the Bible* (Milwaukee: Bruce, 1965).

Introductory Books for the Serious Student: Introductory Study Commentaries

Collegeville Bible Commentaries (Collegeville, Minn.: Liturgical Press, 1984).

These commentaries, first published in the 1960's and now updated, come in pamphlet form. Each pamphlet contains an excellent introduction to a particular book of the Bible, the biblical text itself, a scholarly but conversationally written commentary, and discussion questions. This is an excellent study guide for individual or group study.

Journey—a guided study program in the Catholic Faith by the Divine Word International Center of Religious Education (Mahwah, N.J.: Paulist Press, 1979).

These commentaries are in pamphlet form. Each pamphlet contains an introduction to the particular book being studied, lessons which do not include the biblical text but do include specific references to passages which should be read, commentary, practice questions, an answer key to the practice questions, and recommendations for a group meeting. This is an excellent guide for a beginner interested in serious study.

Introductory Textbooks: Old Testament

Anderson, B.W., *Understanding the Old Testament* (3rd revised edition; Englewood Cliffs, N.J.: Prentice-Hall, 1979).

Anderson gives the student all the background information needed to read the books of the Old Testament in their biblical and social contexts. An extended bibliography is included.

Boadt, Lawrence, *Reading the Old Testament: An Introduction* (Mahwah, N.J.: Paulist Press, 1984).

This is a solid, scholarly introduction to the Old Testament aimed at Christian readers but written with ecumenical sensitivity in an easy to comprehend style. Each chapter includes study questions aimed at reviewing the content of the chapters. Bibliography included.

New Testament

Kee, H.C., *Understanding the New Testament* (4th edition; Englewood Cliffs, New Jersey: Prentice-Hall, 1983).

In this fourth edition, there is a heavy emphasis on the sociology of knowledge and the sociology of religion. This is a good book for those deeply interested in the cultural situation within which Christianity was born.

Perkins, Pheme, *Reading the New Testament: An Introduction* (Mahwah, N.J.: Paulist Press, 1978).

This introduction is much lighter than Kee's book. Perkins writes in a conversational style, often as a teacher speaking directly to a student. She presumes no previous knowledge on the part of the reader and introduces the beginner to literary, historical and theological concepts in relation to the New Testament. In addition to study questions and a print bibliography, an extensive audio-visual bibliography is included.

Introductory Books for Study and Group Discussion

Burke, John, *Beginners' Guide to Bible Sharing, Vols. I, II* (Dubuque, Iowa: Wm C. Brown Co., 1984).

These two volumes contain a four phase program aimed at providing a basic approach to reading and praying, studying and sharing the Bible. Each of the four units provides for thirty small group meetings. The first phase explains great themes of the Bible, the second the Acts of the Apostles, the third the Gospel according to Luke, and the fourth the Letter to the Romans.

Farrell, Melvin, *Getting To Know the Bible* (Milwaukee: Hi Time Publishing Corp., 1984).

This book contains twenty-four excellent short articles which introduce the reader to necessary background information about the Bible, the Old Testament, and the New Testament. A discussion guide (printed separately) provides an opening prayer, key ideas, an activity, discussion questions and a closing prayer for each article.

Riley, William, *The Bible Study Group: An Owner's Manual* (Notre Dame, Indiana: Ave Maria Press, 1983).

This book starts off with six chapters on the mechanics of a Bible study group. It then gives study and discussion material for twenty-two meetings. The meetings address such topics as Covenant, God and Nationhood, and A First Look at Prophecy.

Wenig, Laurin J., *The Spring of Life: Your Introduction to Sacred Scripture* (Milwaukee: Hi Time Publishing Corp., 1981).

This book introduces the reader to the Bible through fourteen short chapters written in a simple, conversational style. A discussion leader's guide turns each chapter into an easily followed format for group reflection and discussion.

Daily Scripture Guides

Brett, Laurence, *Share the Word* (Washington, D.C.: Noll Printing Co., published bi-monthly).

Share the Word follows the Sunday lectionary readings. In addition to daily Bible readings, it has commentary on the Sunday readings and a group study and sharing guide for each week.

Martin, George, *God's Word Today* (Ann Arbor: God's Word Today, published monthly).

This is a practical guide to reading and understanding the Bible on a daily basis. For each day the guide gives a reading reference to the Bible, a commentary, a reflection, and a "prayer starter."